MONEY COACH GU

TOP FUNDS

A WINNING APPROACH TO MUTUAL FUNDS IN CANADA

1997

DUFF YOUNG

edited by RILEY MOYNES

Addison-Wesley Publishers

ASHLAR HOUSE INC.

Design and Art Direction: Kyle Gell, ArtPlus

Computer Illustration and Graphics: Kyle Gell, Kevin Ghiglione, Allan Moon, Valentino Sanna, Dave Murphy, Adele Webster

Cover Design: Dave Murphy/ArtPlus

Cover Photos: Ray Boudreau, Robert Cybulski

Printing and Binding: Metropole Litho Inc.

Although every effort has been made to ensure the accuracy and completeness of the information contained in this book, the author and the publisher assume no responsibility for errors, inaccuracies, omissions or any inconsistency herein. Readers should use their own judgement and/or consult a financial expert for specific applications to their individual situations. Any slights of people or organizations are unintentional.

Canadian Cataloguing in Publication Data

The National Library of Canada has catalogued this publication as follows:

Main entry under title:

Young, Duff, 1967–

Top Funds 1997

Annual.

1996–

Issues for 1996– by Duff Young with Riley Moynes

ISSN 1204-9654

ISBN 0-201-89295-2 (1997)

1. Mutual funds – Canada. I. Young, Duff, 1967–

II. Moynes, Riley E., 1944–

HG5154.5.M68 3 332.63′27 C96-300545-6

ISBN 0-201-89295-2

Printed and bound in Canada

1 2 3 4 5 – MET – 01 00 99 98 97

CONTENTS

ACKNOWLEDGEMENTS

Producing and updating a book of this calibre is a monumental task because of its level of detail, its design, and the ever-changing nature of the funds themselves. Of greatest assistance in this project has been Peter Loach, Midland Walwyn's senior fund analyst. Valuable production and editorial assistance was provided by Andy Yull, Jonathan Allison, Heather Rignanesi, Kelly Lancaster, Rudy Luukko, Deborah Read, Kim Love, Peter Matthews, and Jeff Miller. Special appreciation is extended to the executives and especially the Financial Advisors of Midland Walwyn (*http://www.midwal.ca*) for their commitment to sharing leading-edge research and their generosity in allowing the reproduction, for the first time, of major parts of their proprietary fund research database. Thanks are also extended to The Equion Group (*http://www.equion.com*) for its early support and for the use of the decision tree concept.

TOP FUNDS JUST KEEP ON COMING

Although some people buy mutual funds as "hands off" investments, many others like to stay informed about the funds and their managers. For those investors, a service is available free of charge to readers of *Top Funds 1997*.

Just fill out and return the response card in this book and you'll receive a *Top Funds* update containing important new developments for mutual fund investors. Typically, this update appears during the summer.

Then, each fall, a new edition of *Top Funds* will appear, with new reviews and insights. In each new edition, you'll find out when we were right and when we goofed.

INTRODUCTION

Mutual funds are without doubt the fastest growing and most popular type of investment available today. And over the past few years, this rising popularity has spawned a number of good books on the subject of mutual funds.

So why do you need *this* book?

There are several reasons. I'm constantly asked for advice on mutual funds and on how to pick the "top" funds. Every day, I meet people who want comparative information on funds and fund managers, based on data that is relevant, well researched, and up-to-date.

The problem I've found, however, is that the most common method of selecting funds today — that is, on the basis of published 1-, 3-, 5- and 10-year performance statistics — is not only inadequate, but can actually be misleading. So I've developed what I believe to be a better performance measurement system to identify the **real** Top Funds.

These funds are further qualified with other important information, including changes in fund management, management style and expense ratios. How often has a fund been outperformed by "risk free" investments like GICs — or lost money? These are simple questions that every investor should ask, and I try to provide the answers here. Finally, I've identified which management styles complement one another to create the best "package" of funds, so you can apply my analysis to make well-informed decisions.

Top Funds is based on innovative state-of-the-art research techniques and facilities which, to my knowledge, have never been used before in Canada. And while I start with research-proven data to reach my conclusions and recommendations, I've also added a good dose of common sense: I interviewed hundreds of managers and factored in my personal experience in research and in dealing with individual investors.

The *Top Funds* mix of quantitative and qualitative research is what makes this book unique. With over 1200 funds available today — I provide a way to cut through the hype and concentrate on only the best funds. The result: you save hours of your precious time!

Naturally, there were several good funds that almost made the *Top Funds* list, but didn't quite — at least, not this year. And many of last year's *Top Funds* were edged out by stronger competitors, which just goes to show that the *Top Funds* list isn't cast in stone. I'll be reviewing all the funds over the next year and adjusting the list according to my findings.

Finally, I felt it was important to present the material as interestingly and simply as possible. So I took the approach that proved so popular in Riley's earlier book, *The Money Coach*. The result, I think, combines rigorous research with an attractive format to provide clear and, ultimately, truly useful recommendations.

This introduction would not be complete without a grateful personal acknowledgement. I'd like to dedicate *Top Funds* to my wife Jennifer and our little girl Courtney.

Duff Young, CFA

In this the third edition of *Top Funds*, our respective roles continue to evolve. In the past it was very much a partnership, with Duff responsible for conducting the research and anecdotally commenting on each of the Top Funds, and me responsible for writing many of the other sections of the book and fine-tuning the fund essays. This year, Duff has taken virtually complete responsibility for the research and the essays, as well as several of the new components. My role has been more editorial, with a view to ensuring a visual and stylistic 'connection' with *The Money Coach*. We have consciously attempted to link the books closely as to style and look — areas where *The Money Coach* has received such critical and popular acclaim. I hope you'll enjoy the results and benefit from the strategies outlined here.

As always, I particularly want to acknowledge the ongoing support and eternal patience of my wife and partner Yvonne.

Riley Moynes

1 ON A ROLL:

MONEY MANAGEMENT IN THE '90s

What accounts for the extraordinary growth of mutual funds in the past decade? Much of it, I believe, can be attributed to an increasingly complex world which is changing so fast that individual investors are no longer able to function comfortably. The result has been a dramatic move in Canada and worldwide to "managed money."

For most people, this has been through mutual fund investments, although other managed-money vehicles have also emerged — including closed-end funds, wrap accounts, REITs (real estate investment trusts), "investment" life insurance, limited partnerships, and private money management.

The trend towards managed money — although certainly helped by low interest rates and generally positive market conditions — has been driven largely by the growing number of people who recognize that they are no longer restricted to the traditional choice of Guaranteed Investment

Certificates (GICs), Canada Savings Bonds (CSBs), Treasury bills, or term deposits on one hand, and direct stock market investment on the other. It's based as well on an understanding that an extra single-percentage-point return, when compounded over the long term, can yield significantly more accumulated wealth; and it's based on a belief that a full-time professional will almost always achieve better investment results than a part-time amateur.

All of these events have contributed to phenomenal growth in the mutual fund industry in Canada, as shown below:

FUND PHENOMENON

Actual and projected growth of the Canadian mutual fund industry

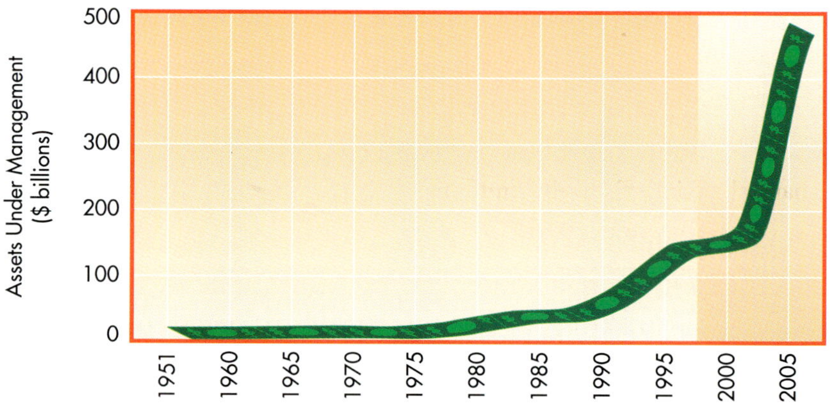

And the growth shows no sign of slowing down. In fact, a report prepared by Gordon Capital Corp. in September 1993 predicts that assets under management by the Canadian mutual fund industry will soar to $474 billion by the end of 2002. Today, that estimate looks conservative!

So welcome to the era of "managed money" — an era that promises to offer you more investment choices than ever. And that's where I come in. Because it's my job to to assist you in selecting the mutual fund or funds that best suit your needs.

If you're an experienced mutual fund investor, you may want to skip ahead to the next part of this book, where I provide the rationale for the recommended Top Funds. But if the whole business of mutual funds is relatively unfamiliar, let's take a moment to look at the basics.

WHAT IS A MUTUAL FUND?

A mutual fund is a "pool" of money to which thousands of people contribute. This pool of money is managed by professional money managers who invest the money in Treasury bills (T-bills), safe and secure government or corporate bonds, and in shares of generally proven Canadian and international corporations. They keep a watchful eye on the economy, on political, demographic and economic trends, and on international events in order to determine where and how the pool of money can be invested to produce the most solid, long-term growth.

THE BENEFITS OF MUTUAL FUNDS

Professional Money Management

Most people haven't got the time to oversee their financial affairs effectively. And they're not trained to be expert money managers. But with an investment in mutual funds, they benefit from the experience and skills of some of the world's best money managers.

One of the most successful mutual funds ever, the **Templeton Growth Fund**, which is managed by Sir John Templeton and his team, provides a good example. If you had invested $10,000 in this fund when it began in 1954, you would have seen your investment grow to be worth $3.7 million by 1996. That's an average annual compounded growth rate of over 15.5%!

Diversification

Most people aren't wealthy enough to be able to diversify properly on their own by buying stocks of various companies in a number of countries. Because of the size of the mutual fund "pool," often totalling millions or billions of dollars, investors can purchase a share of a vast array of securities, bonds, and other investments. This allows you to achieve the security that comes from "not putting all your eggs in one basket."

"Hands-Off" Investment

As mentioned earlier, most people don't have the time, the inclination, or the expertise to do the research necessary to make wise investment decisions. This is all looked after for investors by professional money managers for whom this is a full-time job.

Lots of Choice

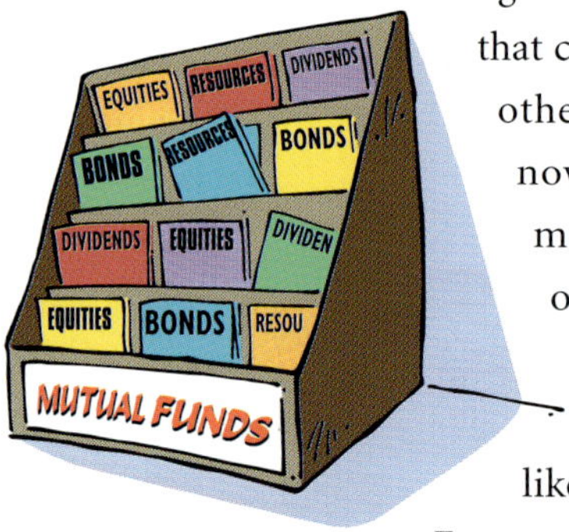

Regardless of your circumstances, there are mutual funds that can meet your needs. Some people want income now; others, who will require income later, opt for growth now. Some investors are aggressive while others are much more conservative. Some select equity funds, others prefer real estate funds, and still others like mortgage funds — or a mixture of each. Some wish to invest in specialty funds like gold; others like to invest in specific foreign regions like Japan or Europe. With so many funds available to choose, there is truly a fund to meet just about every need.

TYPES OF MUTUAL FUNDS

With over 1200 mutual funds now available in Canada, the job of finding the right ones can be very difficult. So I've outlined here the major types of funds and also given some sub-groupings under several of the major headings. For example, I've categorized Canadian equity funds by the typical size of companies held, and international funds by regional focus.

One perception that persists in the minds of many people is that a mutual fund is the same as a stock market investment. While this **may** be true (some funds do buy stocks) it is not **automatically** true. In fact, since there are mutual funds available to meet just about every investment preference (and for some people, that doesn't include stocks), many funds hold no stocks (or "equities") at all. These include funds that buy bonds, mortgages, Treasury bills, gold, real estate, and other assets.

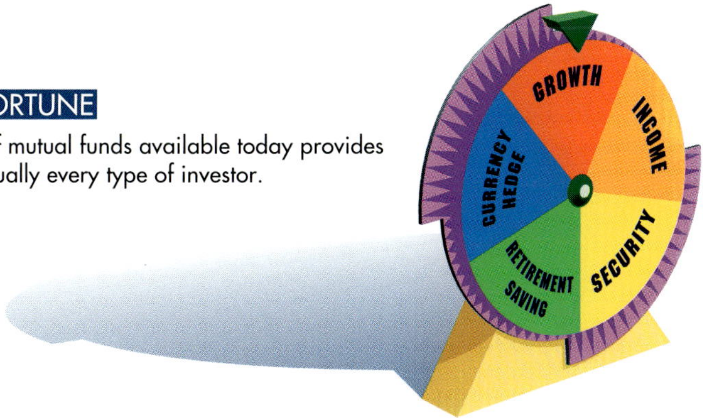

WHEEL OF FORTUNE

The wide range of mutual funds available today provides something for virtually every type of investor.

Money Market Funds

These funds generally hold short-term debt securities of the highest quality, and therefore offer the lowest level of risk. They invest in government Treasury bills or bank guaranteed deposits (GICs), and their purpose is to provide current income where necessary without taking any risks with the capital.

Not surprisingly, these funds are very popular when interest rates are high and less so when rates are lower. They are generally seen as temporary "parking spots" for money held by people seeking alternatives to savings accounts (which generally pay less than money market funds), and are usually not desirable as a long-term investment.

Money Market funds come in several varieties:

Canadian money market funds invest in a range of short-term vehicles. Among them are federal or provincial government guaranteed Treasury bills (T-bills) which are issued for terms up to one year. (T-bills are sold at a discount and the return to the investor is the difference between the lower purchase price and the full face value paid when the bill matures.)

The advantage of investing in T-bills through a mutual fund is that the fund can buy significantly larger quantities than you can (unless you have several million dollars in the bank), so the price is lower, and chances are you'll get a better return.

Money market funds also invest in GICs, short-term promissory notes issued by major corporations (called "corporate paper"), and "bankers' acceptances." (The latter are promissory notes issued by corporations and guaranteed by a bank that the amount of the note will be paid in full on the date specified.)

As with T-bills, all of these are short-term and highly liquid investments which are usually issued in amounts of several hundred thousand dollars, so most individual investors only have access to these vehicles through a mutual fund.

US money market funds are similar to their Canadian counterparts, although they now offer higher returns since US interest rates are higher than those in Canada. Nevertheless, these funds may be good for people who want to diversify into US dollars as a hedge against the fall of the Canadian dollar, or who require US currency on a frequent basis.

DOLLAR DEFENCE

How US$ Money Market Funds Can Pay Off When the C$ Falls

Money market funds provide the highest degree of security and safety and, over the long term, the lowest "real" rate of return (that is, after inflation).

Fixed-Income Funds

These funds generally hold assets that pay a fixed rate of return — such as bonds and mortgages — and may also hold preferred stocks which pay dividends. They are secure and provide a reliable source of income, so they are popular with conservative investors and with retirees or other people who require a steady income. While there may be a capital gain to the investor if long-term interest rates decline (see *Top Funds Close Up*), the major objective of these funds is generally to achieve maximum income while preserving invested capital and minimizing risk.

Because they are sensitive to interest rates, fixed-income funds will provide strong returns during times of declining rates and may actually lose value when rates rise. Because of this, these funds are riskier than money market funds. On the other hand, they have the potential to provide higher returns than money market funds generally do.

Bond Funds

These funds generally invest in Government of Canada, provincial, municipal, or corporate bonds, or any combination thereof. The focus is on maximizing income, and any capital gains are an incidental advantage.

Canadian bond funds rebounded over the past couple of years after a particularly bad year in 1994. 1994 had been the worst bond market in three decades. That drought ended with a rally in the first half of 1995, when a number of funds clocked gains of 20 percent plus.

International bond funds have diminished in popularity recently, but deserve attention now for diversification reasons, and as the trend towards international investing picks up momentum again. These funds are similar to Canadian bond funds in their investment objectives, but hold bonds denominated in foreign currencies, including the pound sterling, deutschemarks, US dollars, French francs, etc.

What type of international bond fund offers the best opportunities? Look for funds with exposure to

Top Funds Close Up

What happens to the value of your investments if interest rates rise?

Dan Richards, president of Marketing Solutions, surveyed over 5,000 people in 1994 with this question. Surprisingly, 30% said that the value of their investments would go up with rising interest rates. Sorry folks — guess again. Higher interest rates have a negative impact on all fixed-income investments except cash (that is, money market funds). That's because no one would be as interested in buying your 9% bond when new bonds are available at 10%. So your old 9% issue (or those held by your bond fund) must fall in price to remain attractive to buyers on the bond market.

Stocks, too, often fall in value when interest rates rise. That's because companies who are big borrowers will face higher interest charges (and less profits) when rates rise. GICs can also fall in value, but their prices are generally not listed daily, so you may not notice the change.

In fact, there would be little point in tracking the value of a GIC, since you probably couldn't sell it anyway. Your money is completely locked in. Do GICs offer a higher return to compensate for this lack of liquidity and lack of pricing? No, not usually. Government bonds often yield higher rates of return, are liquid, and have higher credit quality, generally speaking, than bank GICs, which offer only limited deposit insurance.

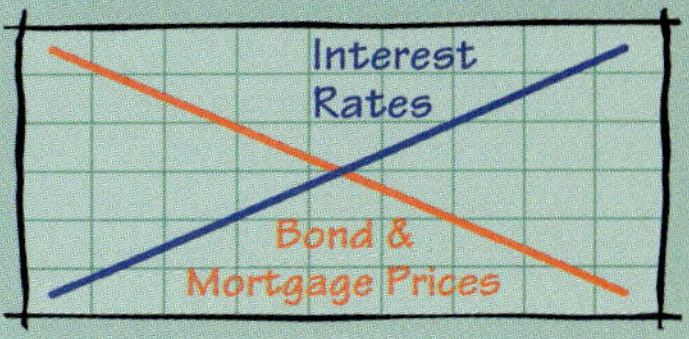

foreign economies that are in recession — where interest rates are likely to decline, in which case bond prices should rise.

Keep in mind, too, that Canada makes up only about 3% of the world's bond markets. And since a fixed-income component is important to any well-balanced portfolio, one should probably include international bonds as part of a sound investment strategy.

Mortgage Funds

Most mortgage funds concentrate on holding residential first mortgages. These generally include "conventional" mortgages, where the loan does not exceed 75% of the appraised value of the home. They may also include "insured" mortgages, in which the loan may exceed 75% of the appraised value but is insured against default by the Canada Mortgage and Housing Corporation (CMHC). Some mortgage funds also hold commercial mortgages.

These funds are generally very conservative and offer comparatively little risk. Returns are mostly in the form of interest income.

Dividend Funds

These funds traditionally invest in high-quality preferred shares (which pay fixed dividends) of taxable Canadian corporations. They may also invest in the common shares of banks and utilities, which also pay regular dividends.

The dividends paid allow investors to take advantage of the dividend tax credit, allowing for tax-favoured treatment over interest income. In fact, dividends represent the lowest-taxed form of income in every province except Quebec.

Because of the tax-favoured treatment, it's recommended that these funds be held in investment accounts and not as part of your RRSP or RRIF where the favoured tax treatment will be lost.

EQUITY FUNDS

If you own an equity (or growth) fund, you hope to see an increase in the value of your fund over a period of time. Most of that increase will be in the form of a capital gain.

As a result, equity funds are generally seen to be riskier in the short term. Over the longer term, however, they have historically produced better returns than other types of funds, and are generally more favourably taxed — two significant advantages.

I believe that as part of a well-balanced portfolio, ownership of some growth funds is absolutely essential.

Growth funds have one thing in common: they all hold stocks of Canadian and/or international companies. Beyond that, the differences can be bewildering. Here's how they can be organized to provide some order.

Canadian Equity Funds

This group invests in the common shares of Canadian corporations. Many of them are eligible for RRSP investing. Some invest in large, "blue chip" corporations ("big-cap" funds); others are more aggressive and invest in smaller companies ("small-cap" funds). Some are widely diversified, investing in many sectors of the economy; others specialize in energy or natural resources and are referred to as "sector funds." Some concentrate on stocks trading at near or below book value (value funds), while others seek stocks that (they believe) will continue to grow, even though they may be paying slightly higher prices (growth funds). Some invest only in companies that meet certain moral or ethical standards (ethical funds) — which generally precludes manufacturers of armaments,

Top Funds Scouting Report

Slamming the Doors on Labour Funds: What to Do Now

The deals were great — 40% cash back to invest in a high-growth asset class with important diversification benefits. But one fund abused the rules. Working Ventures invested too slowly and allowed money to still pour in, effectively creating a mostly T-Bill fund — subsidized at taxpayers' expense. Now, governments have cracked down on all labour-sponsored funds. Worse, they've changed the rules retroactively. The funds face a Dec. 31, 1997 deadline to become 70% invested. Many are closing their doors to new money, but will be OK with what they've got.

For Ontario-based investors, here are three high-quality venture capital funds with brief but strong track records, manageable size, and high-calibre management:

- C.I. Covington
- Capital Alliance Ventures
- Vengrowth

These funds remain attractive as holds or as new purchases, despite reduced tax credits (maximum combined credits now total 30%, depending upon the province, instead of 40%) and longer minimum holding periods (8 years, up from 5).

Top Funds Scouting Report

Real estate funds a bargain

Open-end real estate funds, most notable for their price collapse a few years ago, suffered from a fatal design flaw. Basically, it's this: real estate is not a liquid investment; so if investors want to get their money out, the fund is forced to sell assets — which, in a depressed market, is almost certain to be at a loss. This is exactly what happened in 1992 to a number of real estate funds, including **First City RealFund, Counsel Real Estate Fund, MD Realty Fund,** and others. The fund managers were unable to unload the properties without wiping out much of the value of the funds. So investors were stuck, and redemptions frozen. The situation changed, however, when these funds finally switched to a closed-end format and began trading on a stock exchange. There, they immediately offered liquidity to investors eager to get out since the redemption freeze. The key drawback for those sellers represents a key opportunity for investors in the exchange-traded funds today: they trade at a discount to their NAV, sometimes as much as 25% below their net aset value per share.

Smells like opportunity to me!

tobacco, or alcohol, or those companies that (directly or indirectly) carry on business in countries with oppressive or discriminatory regimes.

In general, equity funds have enjoyed good returns over the last few years after experiencing lower growth during the recession of the early 1990s.

US Equity Funds

These funds are varied in their approach, but invest almost exclusively in the US, the world's largest market. After 15 years of extraordinary growth, these funds seem unlikely to maintain their current pace for much longer.

International Equity Funds

These invest in the stocks of companies in several countries, and many roam the world looking for the "best of the best." Some limit themselves to investing in certain geographic areas (the Pacific Rim, Latin America, Europe), while others restrict themselves to investing in a specific country — Japan being one of the most popular.

Precious Metals Funds

Typically, these funds will invest mostly in gold — either by purchasing bullion directly or by investing in the shares of gold mining companies. Some funds also hold other precious metals such as platinum and silver, and generally invest worldwide. Precious metals funds are generally used to hedge one's savings from the risk of inflation.

Real Estate Funds/Real Estate Investment Trusts (REITs)

These funds specialize in buying income-generating commercial and industrial real estate. Investors benefit here from the income the properties generate, capital gains earned when properties are sold, and interest on short-term deposits a fund may hold.

Because of the negative impact of the recession on commercial property values in most parts of the country, several of these funds have been restructured to become closed-end funds which now trade on stock exchanges.

- ***Balanced Funds***

As the name suggests, these funds strive for a balance of assets: common stocks for growth and fixed-income instruments like bonds and/or cash to provide income. A balanced fund should be less volatile than an equities-only fund, and will appeal to investors who want a variety of asset categories in their portfolio.

The managers of a balanced fund will generally hold different weightings of asset types, depending on current or anticipated economic developments. Most work within a framework of holding not more than 60% or less than 40% in equities or fixed income at any given time.

Philosophically, a balanced fund makes sense and Canadians have responded very positively to the 100+ balanced funds available.

OPEN-END & CLOSED-END FUNDS

Although the emphasis in this book is on the more popular "open-end" fund, you may occasionally run across the "closed-end" type. These are not the same thing at all, and it's important to understand the differences.

In an "open-end" fund you can invest in, or take your money out of, the fund at any time. The money you invest is added to the money already contributed by others. The number of units you receive on purchase (or the amount you'll receive on sale) is determined by the value per unit (net asset value, or NAV, as it's called) when you buy or sell.

An open-end fund has an unlimited number of units and the NAV is determined by taking the current market value of all the assets of the fund, and dividing by the number of units or shares outstanding.

For example, if a fund had \$100,000 in net assets and there were 10,000 units outstanding, the NAV would be \$10. That's the price a seller would receive. Conversely, if someone had \$1,000 to invest in the fund, they'd receive 100 units.

A fund's NAV is generally calculated and published each day. Because the fund issues additional units on demand, the value of already outstanding units is not reduced ("diluted") as a result of new purchases. Depending on the fund type, the return to an investor comes from dividends or interest earned from investments made by the fund (usually reinvested to buy more units) and/or from an increase in the market value of the fund's portfolio.

So in our example, assume that the original number of units had been increased over time to 115 as a result of reinvesting dividends to purchase more units (the usual strategy) and that the NAV on the day of sale had increased to \$13 as a result of an increase in the underlying value of the assets. The amount received (ignoring possible redemption charges) would be $\$13 \times 115 = \$1{,}495$.

The vast majority of funds sold today are open-end funds, but let's take a quick look at the other type — closed-end.

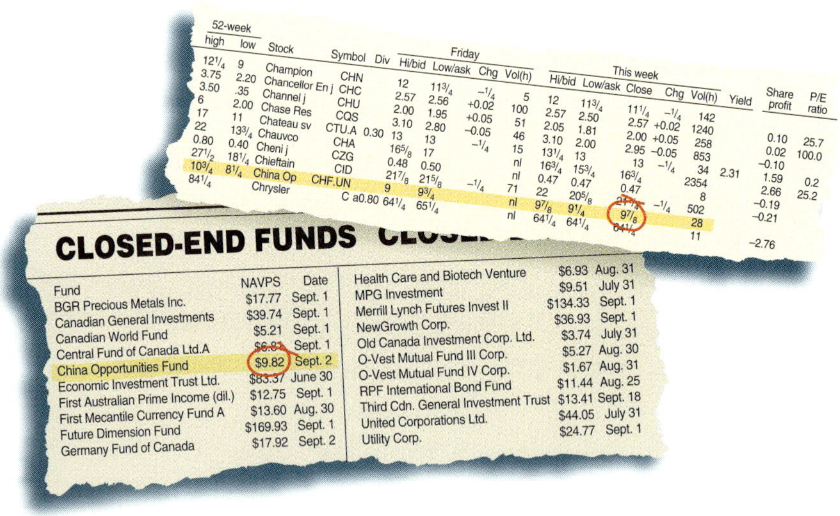

52-week high	52-week low	Stock	Symbol	Div	Friday Hi/bid	Friday Low/ask	Friday Chg	Friday Vol(h)	This week Hi/bid	This week Low/ask	This week Close	This week Chg	This week Vol(h)	Yield	Share profit	P/E ratio
12¼	9	Champion	CHN		12	11¾	–¼	5	12	11¾	11¼	–¼	142			
3.75	2.20	Chancellor En j	CHC		2.57	2.56	+0.02	100	2.57	2.50	2.57	+0.02	1240		0.10	25.7
3.50	.35	Channel j	CHU		2.00	1.95	+0.05	51	2.05	1.81	2.00	+0.05	258		0.02	100.0
6	2.00	Chase Res	CQS		3.10	2.80	–0.05	46	3.10	2.00	2.95	–0.05	853		–0.10	
17	11	Chateau sv	CTU.A	0.30	13	13	–¼	15	13¼	13	13	–¼	34	2.31	1.59	0.2
22	13¾	Chauvco	CHA		16⅝	17		nl	16¾	15¾	16¾		2354		2.66	25.2
0.80	0.40	Cheni j	CZG		0.48	0.50		nl	0.47	0.47	0.47		8		–0.19	
27½	18¼	Chieftain	CID		21⅞	21⅝	–¼	71	22	20⅝	21¼	–¼	502		–0.21	
10¾	8¼	China Op	CHF.UN		9	9¾		nl	9⅞	9¼	9⅞		28			
84¼		Chrysler	C	a0.80	64¼	65¼		nl	64¼	64¼	64¼		11		–2.76	

CLOSED-END FUNDS

Fund	NAVPS	Date
BGR Precious Metals Inc.	\$17.77	Sept. 1
Canadian General Investments	\$39.74	Sept. 1
Canadian World Fund	\$5.21	Sept. 1
Central Fund of Canada Ltd.A	\$6.8[illegible]	Sept. 1
China Opportunities Fund	\$9.82	Sept. 2
Economic Investment Trust Ltd.	\$83.37	June 30
First Australian Prime Income (dil.)	\$12.75	Sept. 1
First Mecantile Currency Fund A	\$13.60	Aug. 30
Future Dimension Fund	\$169.93	Sept. 1
Germany Fund of Canada	\$17.92	Sept. 2
Health Care and Biotech Venture	\$6.93	Aug. 31
MPG Investment	\$9.51	July 31
Merrill Lynch Futures Invest II	\$134.33	Sept. 1
NewGrowth Corp.	\$36.93	Sept. 1
Old Canada Investment Corp. Ltd.	\$3.74	July 31
O-Vest Mutual Fund III Corp.	\$5.27	Aug. 30
O-Vest Mutual Fund IV Corp.	\$1.67	Aug. 31
RPF International Bond Fund	\$11.44	Aug. 25
Third Cdn. General Investment Trust	\$13.41	Sept. 18
United Corporations Ltd.	\$44.05	July 31
Utility Corp.	\$24.77	Sept. 1

Source: Report on Business

Investor interest in China pushed up the market price of shares in the China Opportunities Fund to just over their net asset value per share (NAVPS). Such premiums are relatively rare among closed-end funds, which usually trade at a discount to NAVPS.

CLOSED-END FUNDS

Closed-end funds begin by raising capital from the public by offering shares in much the same way a public corporation does. The money raised is then invested by a fund manager as it is in an open-end fund.

However, once the money has been raised, the fund is "closed" and there are no more units offered. If you want to sell you can do so on a stock exchange or on the "over the counter" market; if you want to buy, you must buy from an owner of the fund's units who's willing to sell.

The NAV of these funds is generally calculated and published weekly in the Saturday edition of the Globe and Mail *Report on Business* and the weekend *Financial Post*. Keep in mind, however, that the NAV does not represent the selling price of a closed-end fund's units. The price is set by supply and demand in the market and, often, the market bids the price down below the NAV — often 10 to 30% below — mostly because they are harder to sell, and are therefore considered to have a lower investment value.

Thus, while there may be opportunities for a sophisticated investor to profit by dealing in closed-end funds, for most investors they are less attractive options than an open-end fund because of their lack of flexibility and liquidity.

COUNTING THE COST

There are two basic types of costs in the purchase of a mutual fund: sales charges and management fees. Both can have an impact upon your bottom-line returns. There may also be some miscellaneous charges that apply. In this section I'll provide an overview of these costs and offer some tips that may be helpful as you make these important decisions.

THE OBVIOUS COSTS: SALES CHARGES

Front-End Loads

If you opt for a front-load fund, an agreed-upon percentage of your total investment will be deducted. So if you pay 4% on a $10,000 purchase, the actual amount invested will be ($10,000 – 4%) = $9,600.

While it used to be normal to pay loads of up to 9%, the situation is quite different today. It's now extremely unusual to pay more than 5% on even a small investment; on larger amounts, a lower rate can usually be negotiated between you and your broker or advisor. Of course, when you purchase a front-load fund, there is no percentage charge when you sell.

One exception to negotiable front-end loads is in the discount brokerage community — although here the loads are already quite low. For example, one discount broker advertises a rate of 2.5% on mutual fund investments under $5,000, 2% on orders from $5,000 to $25,000 and 1% on orders larger than $25,000. Other discount brokers are in the same range.

One important note regarding front-load funds is that every dollar taken off your investment will have a negative impact on growth over time: the higher the load, the greater that impact will be (assuming all other things including rate of return, operating and management costs are identical).

Back-End Loads

Sometimes referred to as deferred sales charges (DSCs), these offer an advantage over front-load funds in that all of your money goes to work for you; nothing is deducted. This type of fund was introduced in 1987 and has become very popular over the intervening years.

Here's how it works. If you redeem these units before a certain period (usually about 7 years or so), you pay a fee based on the value of your investment. This percentage declines over time, as shown in the following example:

Several companies charge the redemption fee on the original amount invested; a few, however, charge on the market value of funds when you cash them. In most cases (specifically, where you redeem the fund units for more than you paid), the former approach is preferable for the investor.

REDEMPTION CHARGES					
Here's the way several of the larger fund companies currently handle their redemption charges:					
Redemption Policy	**Acquisition Cost**	**Redemption Value**	**Redemption Policy**	**Acquisition Cost**	**Redemption Value**
AGF	✘		Investors		✘
Canadian International	✘		Mackenzie		✘
Dynamic		✘	Templeton	✘	
Fidelity		✘	Trimark	✘	
Global Strategy	✘		20/20	✘	
Guardian	✘		United	✘	

Due to the popularity of back-end load funds, many funds that used to charge only a front-end load can now be purchased either way. **Trimark** set up a new "Select" group of DSC funds to mirror their successful front-load funds such as the **Trimark Fund** (**Trimark Select Growth**) and the **Trimark Canadian Fund** (**Trimark Select Canadian Growth Fund**).

While it appears at first glance that the back-load approach is the way to go, there are two additional factors that should be considered before making a final decision.

Distribution fees. Some fund companies have levied a distribution fee, but only on funds purchased on a back-load basis. It's based on the net asset value of your portfolio, so as the value of the holdings increases, so does this fee.

The fee is generally taken from any dividends or other distribution the fund may pay. But if the distribution isn't sufficient to cover the cost, the remainder will be taken from your holdings. Not surprisingly, investors haven't responded too well to this arrangement and, as a result, some companies (like **Bullock, Fidelity**, and **AGF**) have dropped it. And now, so has **Guardian**, who used to charge 0.625% for 10 years.

Management fees. Some fund companies charge higher management expenses if funds are purchased on a back-load basis than if they are purchased on a front-load basis — often tacking on an extra 0.25% to 0.5%. **Trimark** is a striking example. Their back-load funds cost as much as 0.8% more annually to own. So investors should always choose the front-load option at Trimark.

These costs fall directly to the bottom line, meaning that the difference in net return can be significant. When compounded over several years, this can make a big difference in the value of the fund.

Despite this difference, people still tend to resist "up-front" costs. Indeed, my research shows they are opting overwhelmingly for back-load funds — over 90% of load-fund sales in recent years has been of the back-load variety.

No-Load Funds

Until very recently, no-load funds were available predominantly from banks and trust companies, as well as a few management companies (most notably **Altamira**) which sold directly to the public. In dealing with these companies, one is usually speaking with a salaried employee rather than an independent financial advisor. Not surprisingly, these employees are able to provide information only about the funds offered by their company.

But there is growing evidence of ongoing change in the mutual fund industry. Only a few years ago, it was not unusual to pay a front load of up to 9% on a fund you purchased. Then came the back-end load funds and the practice of paying a front load on virtually any amount came abruptly to a halt.

There has been a similar trend toward no-load funds, though it comes in fits and starts. With nothing deducted on purchase and no redemption charges, this approach obviously has benefits for the investor. It is becoming increasingly popular in the US and there are a number of fund companies in Canada that have introduced no-load options.

In this situation, the broker, mutual fund salesperson, or financial advisor receives little or no up-front commission from the fund company; instead, he or she receives a (slightly higher than normal) ongoing service or trailer fee. (See *Top Funds Close Up*). This development will probably make life more difficult for newcomers to the business, since up-front commissions are likely to be significantly reduced. However, for those who have an established clientele, the increased trailer or service fees could generate substantially more ongoing income.

So it looks like we're soon going to see a situation that investors are really going to love: a much wider range of funds available on a no-load basis and ongoing financial advice at little or no direct cost.

WHAT YOU DON'T SEE: MANAGEMENT EXPENSES

The second, and less well understood, cost involved in the ownership of mutual funds is management fees. The first thing to recognize is that all mutual funds — including the no-load funds — charge these fees. They are the means by which the fund managers are reimbursed for their time, expertise, and (one hopes) the attractive returns they generate for their unitholders. They also reimburse the companies for costs incurred in establishing, maintaining, and promoting the fund.

Management fees generally range between 1% and 2.5% of the total assets under management. In some cases, this percentage will decline as the assets held by the fund increase. But most often the fees are determined by the type of assets held and, presumably, the work required to manage them — usually 2% for equity-based funds, and about 1% for cash management funds.

Management fees are charged directly to the fund, which means that investors do not receive a statement of the amount. But make no mistake — they do have an impact on the fund's return. For example, if a fund charges a 2% management fee and earns a 20% return in a given year, the investor's net return is 18%.

While some critics feel these fees are "too high," we are seeing growing numbers of people prepared to pay this amount in return for the prospect of receiving significantly higher returns than they could generate for themselves.

Investors should not pay as much attention to management fees as to the **management expense ratio**. This figure is expressed as a percentage of the fund's

Top Funds Close Up

The Dealer's Deal

On a front-load investment, the dealer (i.e., the investment company whose agent or representative sold the fund) receives the full amount of the load, which generally ranges from 2% to 5%. On a back-load investment, the range is about 4 to 5%.

Each dealer then pays its sales representatives a portion, generally from 40% to 80% of the dealer compensation. The remainder is retained to cover salaries and operating costs incurred by the dealer in carrying on business.

In many cases "trailer" or "service" fees are also paid to sales representatives. These are not paid by the investor, however (at least not directly), but are paid out of the management fees charged by the fund managers.

Critics of these charges say they could lead to increased management fees and/or higher expense ratios that affect an investor's return. While this is a possibility, it is not automatically true that an increase in management fees is charged to pay trailer fees.

To have the benefit of the skills and experience of several of the world's best money managers, combined with the ongoing advice and recommendations of a personal financial advisor is well worth 2% per year to growing numbers of investors.

total assets and totals **all management fees** (those referred to above) **as well as** other expenses charged to the fund. Typically, these include legal, accounting, custodial, and safekeeping costs, as well as the costs of producing prospectuses and other reports. All else being equal, the higher the management expense ratio, the more money is being spent by the manager and the lower the return to the investor, so be sure to examine these factors when considering any fund purchase.

Fund Fact

Rates of return published in the press are always **net** returns — that is, after deducting management expenses.

THOSE LITTLE "EXTRAS"

There are a few other charges that may apply to the fund you are considering. These include:

Set-Up Fees

This is a one-time fee often charged by "no load" companies. It's usually in the range of $40 or so.

Close-Out or Transfer Fees

You may be charged a modest fee for closing out your account with a particular fund company. Many fund companies charge $20 on the termination or transfer out of a tax plan for an RRSP or a RRIF. Growing numbers of financial institutions are also charging this fee.

Trustee Fees for RRSPs, RRIFs, or RESPs

For these types of accounts, an annual trustee fee may be charged, usually about $50. Some fund companies reduce or eliminate such fees from time to time as a promotional strategy.

Systematic Withdrawal Fees/Charges

A systematic withdrawal plan (SWP) allows investors to receive regular income from their fund. A few companies charge an annual fee, while others charge a fee for each withdrawal.

Preauthorized Chequing Fees

If you set up a regular investment program and invest monthly by preauthorized cheque, you may have to pay a service charge. If the identified bank account has insufficient funds to make the systematic investment, expect to pay a fee of about $15.

Switching Fees

Nearly all companies allow switching from one fund to another within the same family. Often the prospectus will allow for a negotiable charge of between 0% and 2%. You should not usually expect to pay for such a switch.

THE BIGNESS DEBATE: BIG IS BEAUTIFUL IN PICKING THE BEST FUNDS

Investors prefer large funds. In fact, two-thirds of fund industry assets are clustered in about 100 of the over 1200 funds sold in Canada.

And startling new research suggests that Canadians are on the right track. The big funds they patronize are indeed better performers. These giants beat the smaller funds hands down — sometimes by a little, sometimes by a lot.

Global equity funds are the most striking example. Just 11 funds, which make up a staggering 75 percent of the assets in this group, trounce the pack of 100 smaller also-rans with which they compete. These big funds earned 13.9% annually over the five years ended June 30, dwarfing the 9% earned by the rest of the group.

You also see this pattern in Canadian bond funds. Of 129 bond funds, the 13 biggest make up 60 percent of the assets. Over the past five years, these few big funds earned 11% annually, versus 10.5% for the small funds. A difference of half a percentage point a year may not sound like much, but in the world of bonds it's a big deal.

Jumbo US equity funds sold in Canada enjoy a similar performance advantage. Their annual return is half a percentage point higher than the little guys in their group. The fact that monster funds do better might shock investors who are fearful about bigness when it comes to equity funds. Many believe big funds won't be nimble enough to trade in and out of stocks at the best prices.

People also think big funds miss out on the sizzle from small-cap stocks — an area proven to offer higher returns — because their size makes a tiny small-cap position meaningless. The net asset value of a $2-billion fund won't even budge if a $1 million stock holding doubles in value.

But these fears are unfounded. Lipper Analytical Services, a US firm that monitors fund returns, says big-fund superiority has held true every year since it has been breaking out performance by size. Take the world's largest fund, **Fidelity Magellan**, with US $50 billion in assets (unfortunately not sold in Canada). This huge US equity fund keeps beating the market and 80 percent of its peers.

Toronto-based **Trimark** has about $5 billion in its Canadian equity funds, holding enough stocks to make up 1 percent of the entire domestic stock market. But you won't find a fund group with more consistently strong returns in Canada.

In doing my calculations, I went beyond a simple look at how today's biggest funds did over the last five years. Naturally, today's giants would have better track records — after all, that's why they became big.

Instead, I looked every month at what the biggest funds were holding that month. By rejigging the list monthly, I crafted a composite of what the returns of the biggest funds really were at various moments in time.

Why the performance gap between big and small funds? There are three key reasons, all having to do with success breeding success.

The first is simply great fund management. Not every big fund is superbly managed, or triumphs in every market climate. But consistency wins investor loyalty and builds a fund over time. While some funds balloon because of great marketing, lasting size is usually the result of investment success.

Second, lower expenses. Take bond funds, where expenses are so important. The average management expense ratio for the 13 largest bond funds is 1.5% — low, but still not low enough in my opinion — versus 1.7% for the rest of the pack. The economies created by size allow for a wider base across which to spread the fixed costs of managing a fund.

Mutual funds are a curious product: the highest quality is often found at the lowest price. Successful and established funds usually have lower expenses, while unproven upstarts often charge a bundle.

The third reason is trading and research economies. Bigger funds can afford more talent, whether in the form of more attention from brokerage analysts or more money for in-house analysts. And they pay even lower commissions on some trades than the already slim institutional rates.

You'd do well to stick to the big names, like most Canadians do, for the majority of your portfolio. But don't get me wrong. Lots of great small funds exist. Setting aside up to 20% of your mutual fund dollars for an undiscovered gem, especially a small-cap player, could be rewarding.

2 MAKING THE GRADE:

THE TOP FUNDS SELECTION METHOD

IN SEARCH OF "REAL" PERFORMANCE

Take a look at any mutual fund advertisement and chances are you'll find a lot of impressive numbers that attest to the fund's performance over the past six months, year, three years, or five years — all of which makes the fund look like a pretty attractive investment. But take a look at the fine print down near the bottom of the ad, which usually reads something like this:

"The performance data represents past performance and is not necessarily indicative of future returns..."

So what gives? Well, the disclaimer comes to you courtesy of your provincial securities regulator, who recognizes that performance figures can be deceiving.

Consider, for example, a fund that advertises an average annual rate of return of 65% over one year and 25% over three years. Sounds good, doesn't

Fund Fact

Do people really rely on past performance that much? Absolutely, yes! Consider this. The top 10% of Canadian equity funds, based on performance over the 3-year period ended December 31, 1992, enjoyed 90% greater sales during the boom of 1993 than all the other funds in that group. And this trend has persisted over the past couple of years as well.

it? But these figures could reflect a disturbingly roller-coaster performance record — say, a 30% loss followed by a 50% gain, followed by a 65% gain. In this scenario, you would have done fine if you had held the fund for the entire three-year period. But what if you'd panicked and sold after the first-year loss? Or if you'd sold out after two years for an average gain of 2.5%?

The fact is that just about any fund can make itself look good if it chooses the right measurement period.

So are the securities regulators right? Is past performance an unreliable indicator of future performance?

Well, most investors think that past performance is important. And so do I — but only if **the performance is measured properly**. The problem is that it's almost impossible to find that kind of performance data in conventional sources.

WHAT NEWSPAPER LISTINGS WILL (AND WON'T) TELL YOU

If you're one of the many people who spend hours comparing mutual funds in the monthly or quarterly surveys published by the Globe and Mail *Report on Business* or *The Financial Post*, then I needn't tell you how seductive past performance figures can be. Past performance is, after all, the only tangible, comparative thing investors have to go on. It's also the easiest yardstick for comparison, making it seem very easy to find the *best* mutual fund in the paper. Trouble is, you've then got a handle on what *was* the best fund, over

UPS & DOWNS

Most mutual fund reviews measure a fund's volatility by the extent to which its monthly returns deviate from the average. Month-to-month consistency may be easy on the nerves, but only if the fund is making money!

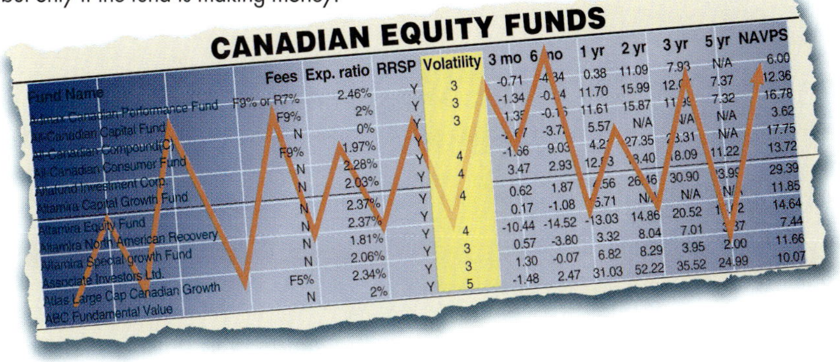

that particular period — whether that's six months or 10 years. You are by no means assured of having identified what fund is "best" for investors *now*.

The other problem that comes from looking at past performance figures is that we often compare them over the "wrong" time periods. My research into the use of standard time periods shows that this factor has a remarkable effect in blurring the line between good and bad funds. In some cases, I've found that reliance on these periods can be worse than useless — it can be hazardous to your wealth!

THE FATAL FLAW: END-DATE BIAS

The one-, three-, five- and 10-year rates of return typically listed in the newspaper are all tied to a single ending day. To illustrate (albeit somewhat unrealistically) the weakness in this approach, let's imagine that a fund tripled in value on the day just prior to June 30, 1996 — the ending date for all the data in this edition of *Top Funds*. Now, that incredible one-day return will exaggerate (upward) historic returns. It would suddenly look as though the fund had done much better over three, five and 10 years — all because of the heavy weighting unconsciously given to the most recent performance.

In fact, this example is not as far-fetched as it sounds: In mid-1996 some funds were posting six-month returns of nearly 100%! Their historical performance appeared (as in the case above) to suggest that these funds had done well over the long term. The result was that they attracted a lot of

Fund Fact

Past performance *is* indicative of future returns.

But only if you measure it right.

investors, many of whom were unaware of the cyclical market forces that were poised to cool down those super-hot funds in a big hurry.

THE SOLUTION: AVERAGE MONTHLY RANKS

To determine the Top Funds featured in this book, I've developed a simple mathematical model that eliminates end-date bias, and allows us to evaluate the past performance of funds in a fairer and much more informative way.

I call this approach the **Average Monthly Rank,** or **AMR** system, and it represents an evolution in my old multi-period composite (MPC) work. The new AMR is more refined, using monthly instead of yearly data, but the principles remain. It is not unlike the scoring system used to place athletes in multi-sport events such as the decathlon. Let's explore this analogy a little further.

In the decathlon we don't add up the number of seconds that an athlete spends running the 100 metres and 400 metres and compare that sum to that of the other athletes. We treat the events separately. Why? Simply because a one-second difference in time for the 100 metres is vastly more significant than a comparable difference in the 400.

Consequently, decathletes are awarded scores that reflect relative performance within each of their respective events. The overall winner is the individual whose average "place" is the highest.

Think of each month as a decathlon event and different mutual funds as decathletes and you have the essence of the AMR approach.

Not only does the AMR treat months as independent, incomparable events — which, after all, they are — it ranks only similar types of funds.

For example, each Canadian equity fund is ranked against other Canadian equity funds for as many months as the fund has been in existence. Then we just average the accumulated rankings to find the Top Funds.

In the decathlon, the best athletes are those who are consistent. It's tough to win the decathlon with a first in jumps but a last-place finish in sprints. Likewise with mutual funds. It's better to do pretty well in most periods, and eventually earn a rank that is better than most, than it is to do spectacularly some times then horribly in others. Slow but steady wins the race.

So past performance, properly measured, really does provide useful clues about the future.

But is that it? Is that all there is to finding tomorrow's best funds? Certainly not, although it's the first and most important step — if only because it eliminates over 80 percent of mutual funds from eligibility for *Top Funds*. The result is that, even before refining our shortlist with more qualitative tests (which we'll get to later), we now have a nucleus of funds that have proven themselves to be consistent performers, and as such, represent strong investment choices.

Top Funds Close Up

Putting AMRs to the Test

The Average Monthy Rank (AMR) method sounds logical enough. But how does it work in the real world? To find out, I tried a little back testing. Here are the results.

I studied 154 Canadian equity funds between the years 1980 and 1993. My hypothesis was that top funds selected by the AMR model would do better than others. The control group was the market itself — the (unmanaged) TSE 300 Total Return Index.

The study needed to start at some point that would allow for both adequate back data and adequate subsequent data to evaluate the merit of these 'dumb' or mechanical decisions. So I started the investing in 1988. That provided enough information to make informed AMR choices and to monitor them for 5 years. The rule was simply that the funds required a three-year minimum track record up to 1988.

Sure enough, the AMR-selected top funds outperformed the returns of the AMR-selected median and bottom funds by a significant margin. Performance was improved further by taking a more active role, redoing the multi-period composite annually and trading into those funds newly suggested by the AMR study.

Past performance, if measured properly, can be a good indicator of future returns. Though not everything, this quantitative framework is a useful first step in fund selection.

SORTING OUT THE WINNERS

THE TOP FUNDS RANKING SYSTEM

Every fund that appears in the *Top Funds* listings can quite justifiably be described as a "winner" within its category. But as you might expect, some funds have scored better than others. For this reason, I have devised a rating system that distinguishes those funds.

Here's how the system works. For each category of funds, we look at the best and worst AMR scores. Then each fund is assigned a certain number of *Top Funds* stars, ranging from three stars (remember, even the "worst" of our selected funds is still better than most of the funds you can buy) up to a maximum of five stars. In the *Monster Fund Tables*, I've applied the system to **all** the funds.

Now, having said all this, I should point out that the number of stars a fund receives is not the whole story. The star system is based entirely on AMR scores. And while this provides an exacting, objective measure of fund performance, it provides only a certain amount of information about any given fund. To make a truly informed investment choice, you need to supplement the AMR rankings with more qualitative data. I categorize these qualifiers under the headings of consistency, risk, efficiency, and style.

TOP FUND QUALIFIER #1: CONSISTENCY

Consistency involves performance in both good and bad markets. It also has to do with consistency of people — that is, the people at the helm of the fund. Ideally we're looking for no turnover at all (or very little turnover) among managers, research assistants, and others.

Let's examine each of these consistency factors in turn.

PERFORMANCE

The AMR system evaluates a fund's performance history. Consequently, an older fund that had a few rough years in the beginning may not score as well as a younger fund — even if both funds performed equally well in more recent years. How do we overcome this "unfairness"? One way is to "deconstruct" the AMR formula, examining the performance rankings of each Top Fund relative to those in the same group for a given number of recent time periods.

For each category in the Top Funds listings, we provide comparative performance rankings for the years 1987 to 1995 and the first half of 1996. This is shown graphically as a matrix consisting of ten columns, each representing the aforementioned time periods, and four rows, each representing the "performance quartile" for the time period. Consider the following example:

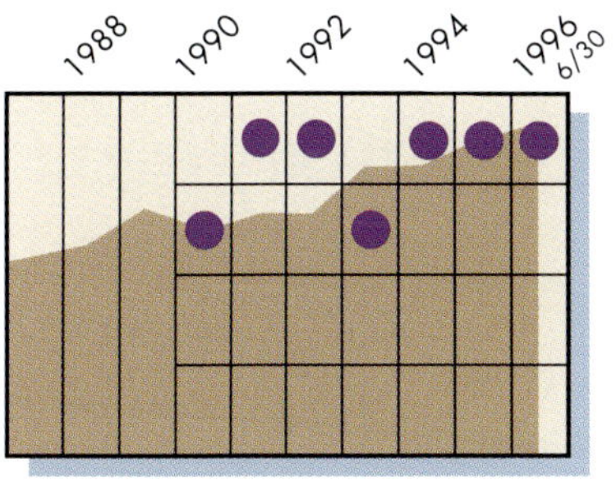

Here we see that in 1990, the fund started in the second performance quartile. In other words, it performed better than 50% of the funds (those in the third and fourth quartiles), but not as well as the 25% in the first quartile. In 1991, however, the fund moved up to the first quartile, outperforming 75% of funds in the same category. Note, too, the absence of horizontal grid lines (and data) prior to 1990. This indicates the fund did not exist before this date.

Another benefit of comparing performance over discrete (that is, non-overlapping) time periods is that it allows us to see how similar funds fared in good and bad markets. Referring back to the figure above, note the shaded graph in the background — indicating, in this example, the relative performance of the TSE 300. (This index is used as a benchmark for Canadian equity funds; other types of funds are shown against the most appropriate index; where no sufficiently meaningful index exists, no graph is shown.) Here we see that the fund's performance has been relatively consistent through a variety of market conditions.

Top Funds Close Up

Why Rookies don't Rate

With the almost exponential rate of growth that has taken place in the Canadian mutual fund industry, it's not surprising that many funds are relative newcomers. And while a number passed through the AMR "filter" with flying colours, they didn't make our *Top Funds* list. The reason: in my judgement, performance data for anything less than 36 months is not sufficiently meaningful.

This isn't to say that some "rookie" funds don't appear highly promising — they do. And I'm confident that they'll appear in future editions of *Top Funds*.

Top Funds Close Up

Why Quartiles Change

There is a logical reason why some funds' historic quartile rankings change. I've gotten letters on this, where a fund was given a 3rd quartile for 1990 in one edition, then a 2nd quartile for that same year in the next edition. Since the fund's performance didn't change, what did? — The comparison universe. As the fund world keeps exploding, more and more narrow peer-group universes can be created for comparison. Fund mergers affect historical comparisons also.

Simply stated, the markets were bad in 1990 and 1994. So our hypothetical fund's first-quartile performance in both 1991 and 1994 demonstrates an impressive degree of consistency throughout changing market conditions.

Examining relative performance over successive time periods also allows us to note any meaningful trends that may not be obvious from a fund's AMR score alone. For example, the data may show that the performance of a highly ranked fund has declined marginally over the past few years, or that of a not-so-highly ranked fund has improved. Either may have an effect on your investment decision.

MEASURING MANAGEMENT STRENGTH

Talent or Luck?

Will a .400 batter hit the ball every time at bat? Probably not. And yet such a hitter would be among the very best in the game.

Similarly, mutual fund managers provide no guarantees. But overall, a long-term investor will do well to stick with a manager or management team that has done well in the past (assuming a proper method of measurement, of course).

Poker, too, is a game of chance. On any given hand a professional player is as likely to get a great hand as is a novice. And yet over time, the professional will win more frequently.

I think talent exists. I believe that over the long term it manifests itself in superior fund performance. How do we know that talent exists? Well, let's take an example: Sir John Templeton turned $10,000 invested in the **Templeton Growth Fund** in 1954 into $3.7 million by 1996. George Soros, manager of the offshore-based **Quantum Fund** turned US$10,000 in 1969 (at the top of the market — just before the biggest bear market in history) into more than US$20 million by 1996.

Pure luck? I don't think so.

I believe that good managers (and good funds) can be identified by three fundamental characteristics:

1. consistently beating the market,
2. depth of talent in the management team,
3. solid research applied in a clear process.

Many institutional investors have given up looking for good money managers who are capable of beating the market; they simply try to do as well as the market. These institutions are hiring "passive" money managers who simply "buy the market" — that is, they buy every stock that makes up the TSE 300 Composite Index (in the case of Canadian equity funds) or Standard & Poor's 500 Index (for US equity funds) in proportion to the stock's weighting in that index.

Nevertheless, I believe that good managers can be identified on the basis of past performance. I think that reasonable judgment can determine whether a good manager still seems to have everything in place for future success. On the other hand, it is also possible to spot, and avoid, bad managers.

How do you spot bad fund managers? They exhibit all the opposite characteristics of the *Top Funds* manager. They have

1. performance that has been consistently below average or swings wildly between hot and cold,
2. high turnover of personnel because of poor environment, compensation, or structure,
3. funds with high fees,
4. no depth of personnel and few analysts, usually relying on second-hand research from others instead of conducting their own.

Top Funds Close Up

Skill Benchmarks

Some types of funds are so specialized (single-country funds come to mind here) that they are virtually alone in their category, making peer-to-peer comparisons almost impossible. So how do you determine the relative skill of the fund manager?

One method is to create a benchmark portfolio — essentially, an imaginary portfolio which is identical to that of the fund in question, and remains unchanged over, say, a one-year period. After the fund manager has done a year's worth of buying and selling different securities for the portfolio, I compare its value with that of the benchmark, thereby allowing me to see whether the manager was able to add value through his or her efforts. It's an instructive exercise: In some cases I've found that a fund's manager (and its unitholders) would have done better by locking up the portfolio and taking a year's vacation!

Top Funds Close Up

PH&N Priorities

Looking for fund managers who are motivated by investment — not just business — goals? A good example is **Phillips Hager & North**, who closed off their **Vintage Fund** in 1993 because they felt that more assets would impede its ability to trade in illiquid small-cap markets.

The fund has subsequently continued to soar for the lucky few who own it. If it were available, it would be featured as a Top Fund.

Management Consistency

Since the performance of a mutual fund depends so much on its people, consistent management is one of the most important things to look for in a potential investment. After all, when you buy a mutual fund you're buying the talent of the team running it. If the team leaves, then everything that you've bought has changed.

In the *Top Funds* listings you'll find information about who manages each fund, and for how long. Investors should generally avoid **those funds with recent, significant changes in management**, just to see how the new "hot shot" settles in.

Of course, management changes are not always a bad thing. And the fund listings include some cases where new management has actually improved the fund's relative performance. Such was the case of **United Canadian Equity Fund**, which saw the departure of Gerry Coleman and Jerry Javasky in 1992, and the arrival of manager Kiki Delaney. In less than 4 years, Kiki's earned half again as much as her two predecessors have earned at their new fund.

Remember that the *Top Funds* qualification system is strictly quantitative — if a fund has big numbers, it makes the list.

For any Top Fund listed in this book, you can read my opinion of the management team and whether it's stable enough to make it a *reasonable* choice within its category. Other information that space does not allow me to include here — but which you may wish to look into yourself — includes things like whether the fund manager owns a piece of his or her investment firm. Such managers tend to seek the best long-term results for the fund (and its investors), rather than shooting for a terrific quarter to make a good bonus.

Evaluating the Management Firm

Most often when we refer to a "fund manager" we tend to think of an individual who makes all the investment decisions. But even the most talented individuals rarely work alone; they are part of a team that works collaboratively within a management firm.

In addition to the qualities identified earlier, how do I identify a superior management firm?

Ten or more years in business. Generally, it's a good sign if the firm has been in existence for at least 10 years.

Large asset base. The firm should have enough assets under administration to buy and sell securities efficiently, and to attract the people that it needs. Look for total assets of $3 billion or more for bond managers and $1 billion or more for equity managers.

Low turnover. A firm should not lose more than one senior investment professional every five years. The reasons for any turnover should be closely investigated.

Local expertise. This is particularly important for specialized funds that buy stocks or bonds in overseas markets, where conditions are often quite different from those at home. Look for a firm that has investment management offices and/or advisors located in the markets where it does business.

Efficient management structure. Although difficult for non-professionals to measure, this is something I examine very closely. In an ideal situation, an individual fund manager should have full and immediate discretion — within the limits of the fund's overall investment objectives — to react to rapid market changes. In more bureaucratically structured firms, a manager might have to wait for a committee meeting before taking action. Meanwhile, buying or selling opportunities could be missed.

TOP FUND QUALIFIER #2: RISK

While properly constructed performance statistics provide a good measure of how well a fund has done (and may do), they're less informative about the likelihood of the fund doing badly at any given time. This type of worst-case evaluation is now being pioneered in the US by academics and investment practitioners. It's called "downside risk" and I believe that in a few years it will be as popular an investment buzzword as "asset allocation" is today.

In the *Top Funds* listings I've laid out some easy-to-understand indicators of a fund's downside risk:

- how often a fund has provided a lower return than 5-year GICs,
- how often a fund has lost money,
- a fund's worst annual return.

top of their interest income. While offering a higher potential return, these funds are appropriate only for someone with investment experience and sufficient assets to have diversified into other, less aggressive instruments.

3 HOW THEY RATE:

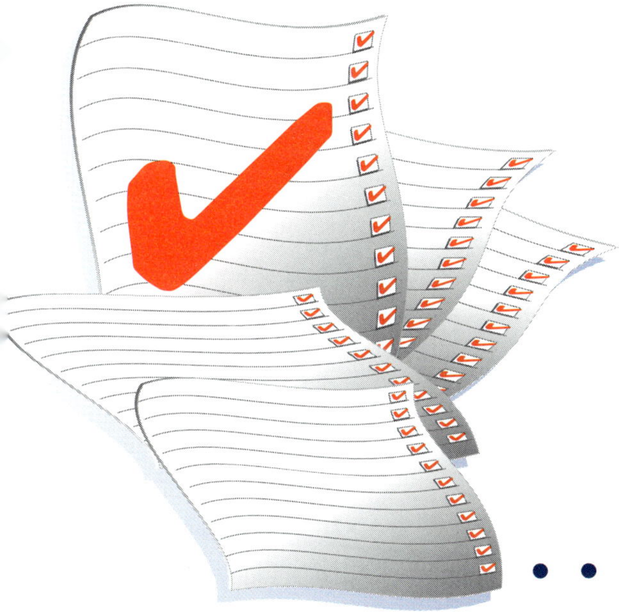

TOP FUNDS 1997

Here's where it all comes together. The numbers have been crunched, the trends analysed, and the final cuts made. What remains is an admittedly elite group — funds that have proven themselves as the best of the best.

In this section you'll find the *Top Funds* selections for 1997, grouped according to fund type (this is indicated by a tab in the margin), and presented in order of their AMR scores — from outstanding to merely impressive.

THE TOP FUNDS LEGEND

Each full-page listing is provided in a concise, standardized format. Here's how to navigate your way through:

Fund Name

Fund Manager/Firm

New in '97

RRSP Eligibility

NEW

SCOTIA EXCELSIOR TOTAL RETURN FUND

André Marsan (inception)/Scotiabank

RRSP

Top Funds Rank

RATING

★★★½

Performance Trend

CONSISTENCY

Performance Trend

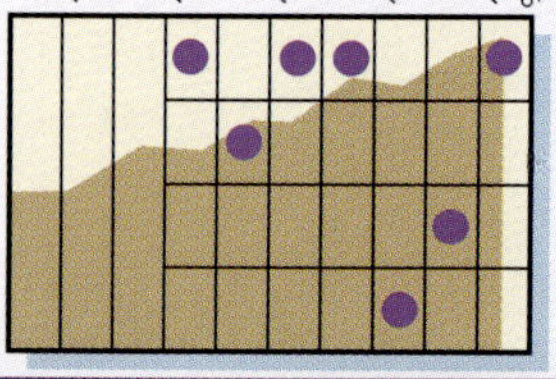

Risk Indicators

RISK

How often GICs performed better	2 years in 6
How often fund lost money	1 year in 6
Worst year's rate of return	-4.8% (1994)

Management Expenses (MER)

EFFICIENCY

Management expense/ $100 $2.32

Style Grid

Sector Rotation (SR)

Value Growth

Company Size: Small Medium Big

STYLE

This Fund
Blend/Big

Complement
Value/Small

You won't find many balanced funds that are steadier than this one. While it never overwhelms, Marsan's active approach to adjusting the stock/bond/cash mix is one that manages nicely to avoid bad markets – like 1990, when stocks and bonds lost money. In that tough year, Marsan managed to make about 7%, thanks to heavy cash holdings. You won't make a killing in this fund, but if you're new to the mutual fund scene and you are a Scotiabank client, this is a great place to get started.

The Fund Review

RRSP eligibility. An unstroked maple leaf indicates that the fund meets Revenue Canada's "Canadian content" rules, and can therefore make up to 100% of the total value of your RRSP or RRIF. A maple leaf with an oblique stroke indicates that the fund is considered "foreign content," which must not exceed 20% of the value of your RRSP or RRIF.

New in '97. Funds listed for the first time are labelled "new."

Fund manager (where applicable). The manager's name and the year when he or she assumed responsibility for the fund, plus the name of the fund management company. "Inception" means that the manager has looked after the fund since it began.

Top Funds rank. Funds are ranked on the basis of AMR scores, from a maximum of five stars to a minimum of three. Remember, a three-star fund is still better than most comparable funds available.

Performance trend. This graphic shows the fund's rankings by quartile for the calendar years 1987 to 1995 and the first half of 1996. A first-quartile position indicates that the fund beat 75% of its direct competitors. A second-quartile ranking means that it beat 50% of the others, but was beaten by 25%. The graph in the background indicates the relative performance of the most appropriate market index with which the fund can be compared.

Risk indicators are pretty much self-explanatory.

Management expenses (MER), shown as the amount charged by the fund managers for every $100 in assets managed. Since different categories of funds require different levels of managerial effort, the colour-coded bar shows whether the MER for a given fund is high or low relative to other funds in the same category.

Style grid categorizes the fund by investment approach. Here, the style leans toward large companies representing a blend of value and growth. The smaller style grid shows the complementary style to this fund. Labels indicate what each square means. For simplicity, however, I have omitted labels on the actual listings. Note that the sample style grid is for funds that hold primarily equity (stock market) investments. A different grid is used for fixed-income (bond, mortgage, money market) funds. Labels for this grid are shown at right.

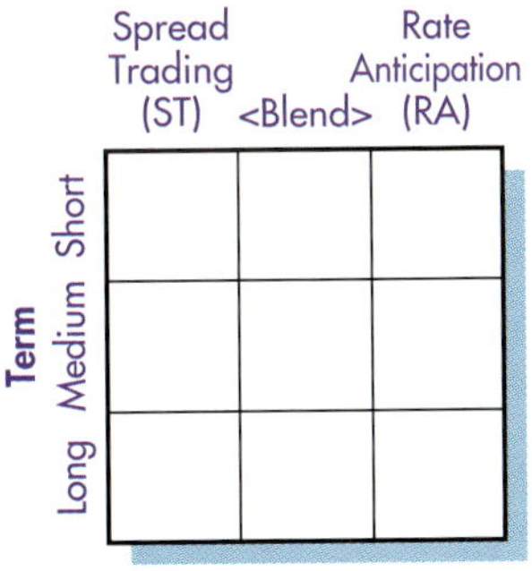

TOP FUNDS 1997

The following is a list of the Top Funds for 1997, arranged by category. Within each category the funds are listed in the order I've ranked them.

RRSP

ALTAMIRA GROWTH & INCOME FUND

Cedric Rabin (inception)/Altamira

RATING

★ ★ ★ ★ ★

CONSISTENCY

Performance Trend

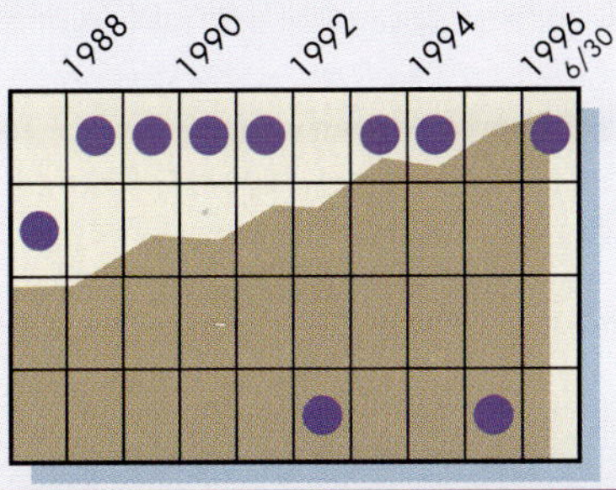

RISK

How often GICs performed better	5 years in 9
How often fund lost money	0 years in 9
Worst year's rate of return	0.9% (1992)

EFFICIENCY

Management expense/ $100 $1.41

STYLE

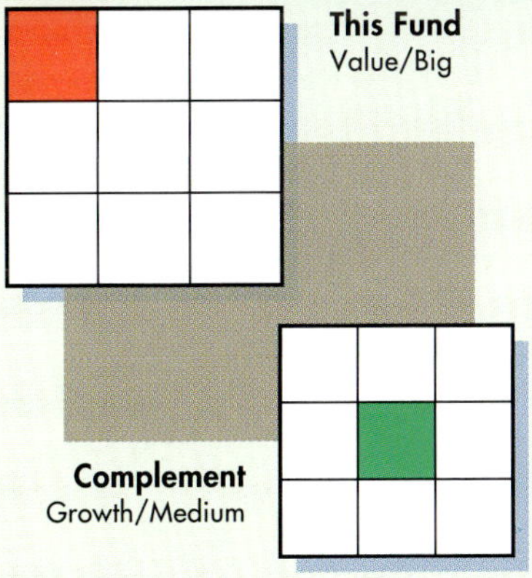

Ted Rabin manages to deliver a conservative fund with unique positioning today. Proof that it's conservative lies in the fact that this fund never lost money in a calendar year and scores better than 75% of all balanced funds during down markets generally.

The unique take on things now is that Rabin's bullish on stocks, especially those in the resource group – a sector he argues is cheap. In fact, the 74% stock weighting (at time of writing) was an all-time high for the fund.

Why's he so bullish? Simple, he says. Commodities are dirt cheap, demand for gold in particular is far outstripping supply, and oil stocks are due for some "multiple expansion" (higher price to cash flow ratios).

But Rabin doesn't bet the farm. About 10% of the stocks are currently optioned for a cash premium. That's a conservative move to trade away some upside potential for cold hard cash now and it's helped this fund earn steady returns historically.

NEW

BEUTEL GOODMAN PRIVATE BALANCED FUND

Stephen Clements (1990)/Beutel Goodman

RRSP

RATING

CONSISTENCY

Performance Trend

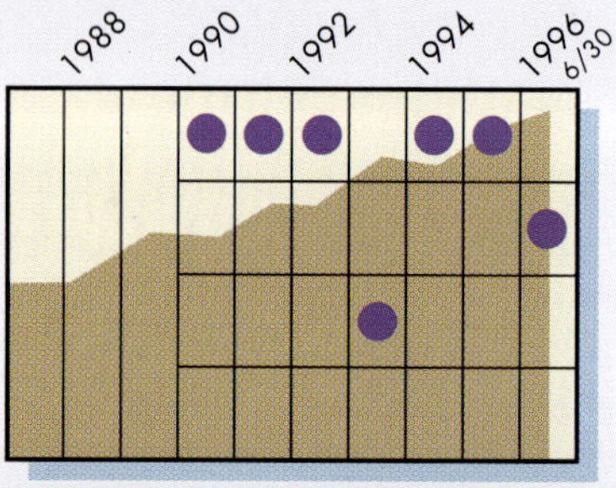

RISK

How often GICs performed better	2 years in 6
How often fund lost money	1 year in 6
Worst year's rate of return	-0.1% (1994)

EFFICIENCY

Management expense/ $100 $2.20

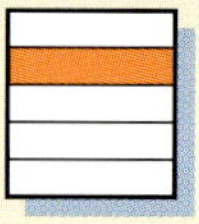

STYLE

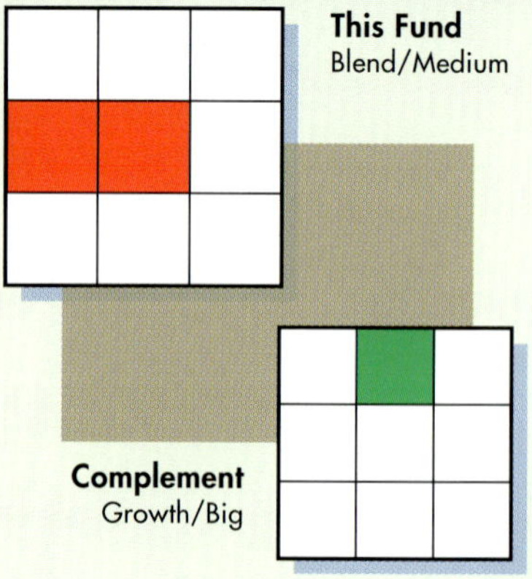

I suppose it's a good sign that a quality balanced fund management team would be a touch bearish – and would be postured (as usual) in cheap stocks. That's because balanced funds tend to appeal to the conservative crowd. And this balanced fund should impress, if indeed the market struggles in the coming year.

The Beutel team uses an entirely bottom-up approach to buying a few good businesses – cheap. While lots of firms say that, it has more credibility from these guys. Their stocks really are cheap.

This fund will, however, miss out on rallies in glamour stock areas like technology and junior mining – one reason it underwhelmed during part of 1996.

RRSP

BISSETT RETIREMENT FUND

Michael Quinn (1991)/Bissett & Assoc.

RATING

CONSISTENCY

Performance Trend

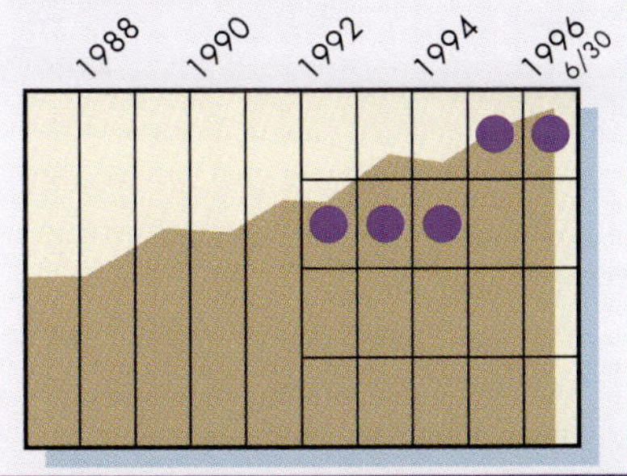

RISK

How often GICs performed better	2 years in 4
How often fund lost money	1 year in 4
Worst year's rate of return	-1.8% (1994)

EFFICIENCY

Management expense/ $100 $0.36

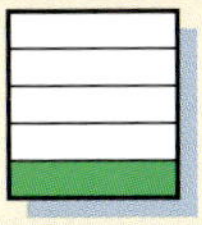

STYLE

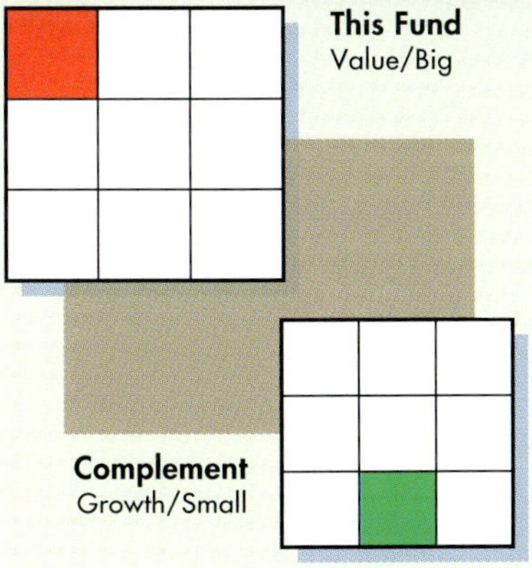

This is a fund of funds from a great family. It charges an extra 0.36% annually for the job of allocating among the funds. That's in addition to the regular expense ratios on the underlying funds. Still, this bundle has been a winner for investors. And why not? The team offers some of the best Canadian equity management around.

There aren't wild shifts in the asset mix in this fund. But the team does have a view on where interest rates and stock prices are headed: down and up. With Canada making such impressive fiscal gains, our high real interest rates are bound to fall, providing support for stocks. Add in maximum foreign exposure for diversification (mostly in the US market), and you've got a balanced portfolio. While this is one of the best one-decision funds around, investors are probably still better off to diversify by management style, and get a Top Fund for global exposure – like Sceptre International. Indeed, the foreign holdings in Bissett Retirement Fund have been a relative weak spot for the fund as bets on solid US blue chips were outpaced during much of the 1996 rally.

BALANCED-CANADIAN

TRIMARK INCOME GROWTH FUND

Walter Kusters (1995) + Patrick Farmer (1993)/Trimark

RRSP

RATING

CONSISTENCY

Performance Trend

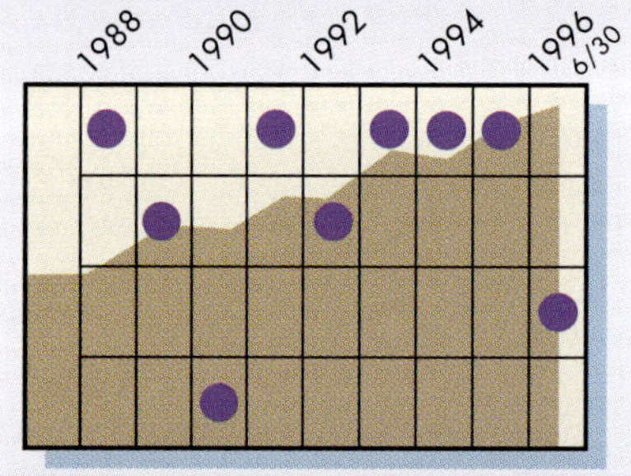

RISK

How often GICs performed better	3 years in 8
How often fund lost money	1 year in 8
Worst year's rate of return	-7.2% (1990)

EFFICIENCY

Management expense/ $100 $1.73

STYLE

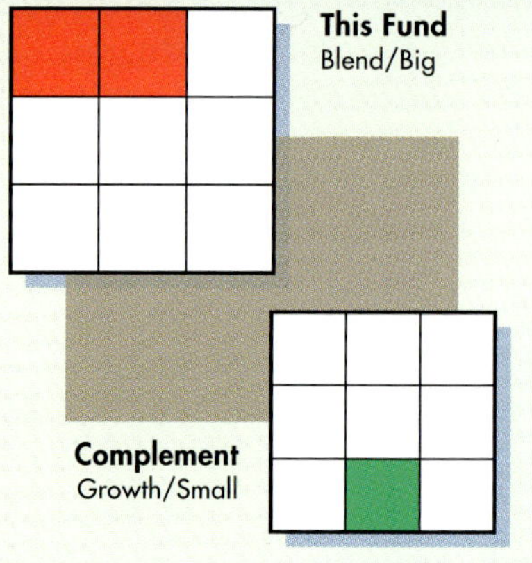

Bond ace Patrick Farmer has called the bond market just right over the past couple of years and has added return to this strong fund. His shifts are subtle, as he's gone from bullish in 1995 to more bearish in 1996. In '95 he held bonds of an average 7-year duration, versus 5 years for the market index. Those incremental moves add return without betting the farm.

He thinks central banks have lowered interest rates far too much, given our healthy economic growth rate. Accordingly, he fears inflation, which could drive up bond yields and hurt prices. So at writing, he was lighter on bonds, and leaned toward the shorter maturity variety.

The Trimark approach is less about stock picking and more about business buying. Before any purchase they do more legwork on a company's business than would a consultant. They meet everybody – managers, competitors and executives – before and after buying.

At 1.73%, the management expense ratio of this fund is 0.48% cheaper than the rear-end load version of the same fund. Investors are better off paying a front-end load to buy this fund and reaping the cost savings year after year.

DYNAMIC PARTNERS FUND

RRSP

N. Bengough + J. Goodman (inception)/Goodman & Co.

RATING

★★★★

CONSISTENCY

Performance Trend

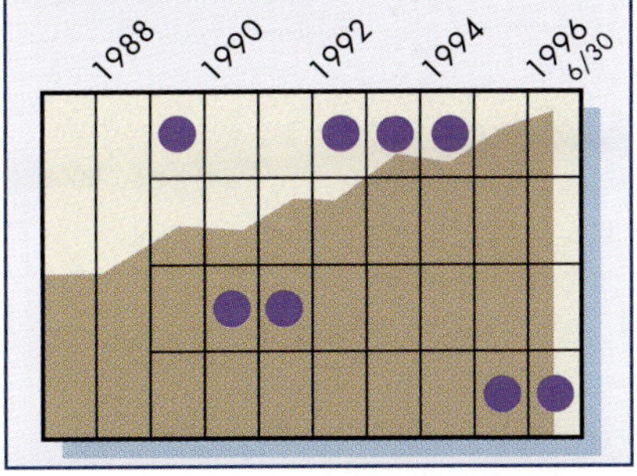

RISK

How often GICs performed better	2 years in 7
How often fund lost money	2 years in 7
Worst year's rate of return	-2.5% (1990)

EFFICIENCY

Management expense/ $100 $2.45

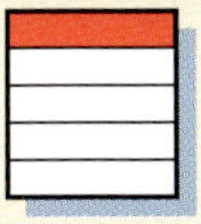

STYLE

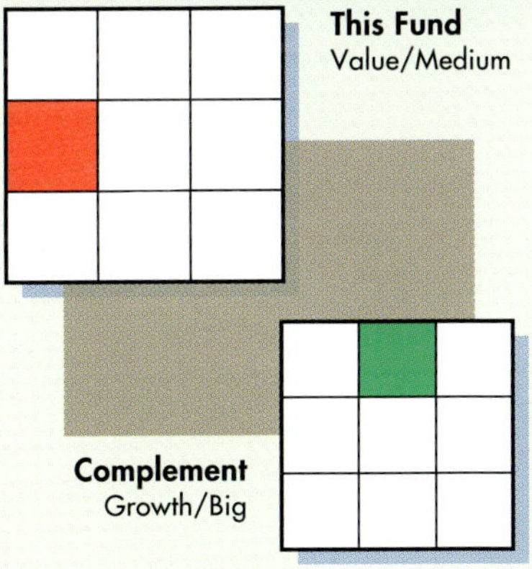

Bond ace Norm Bengough isn't wild about the prospects for making big profits in Canadian bonds any time soon. But surprisingly, that's exactly why investors should consider this fund: interest rates are likely to remain stable (and low). A low inflation/low interest rate environment is great for investors generally – and for stocks in particular.

With a cash build-up of 15% at writing and a neutral 35% bond weight, it's up to the stocks in this conservative fund to drive returns in 1997. Resource stocks tend to be the focus as Goodman & Co. team members are counting on synchronized world growth in 1997. That growth will pump demand for Canada's natural resources – and hopefully the mining sector in particular – where Partners Fund owns a few standouts.

PHILLIPS HAGER & NORTH BALANCED FUND

Tony Gage and Ian Mottershead (inception)/PH&N

RRSP

RATING

CONSISTENCY

Performance Trend

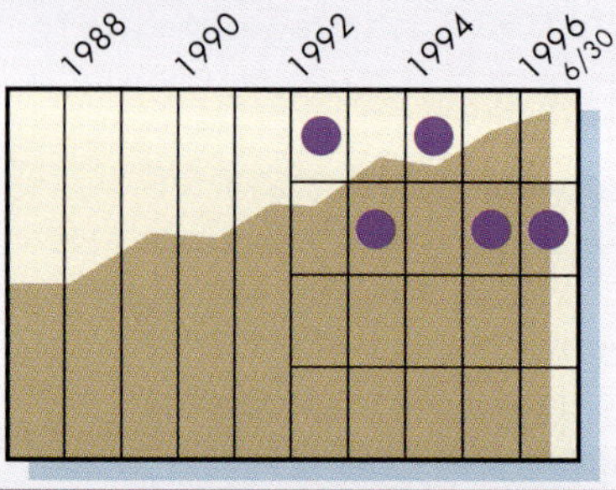

RISK

How often GICs performed better	2 years in 4
How often fund lost money	0 years in 4
Worst year's rate of return	0.4% (1994)

EFFICIENCY

Management expense/ $100 $0.92

STYLE

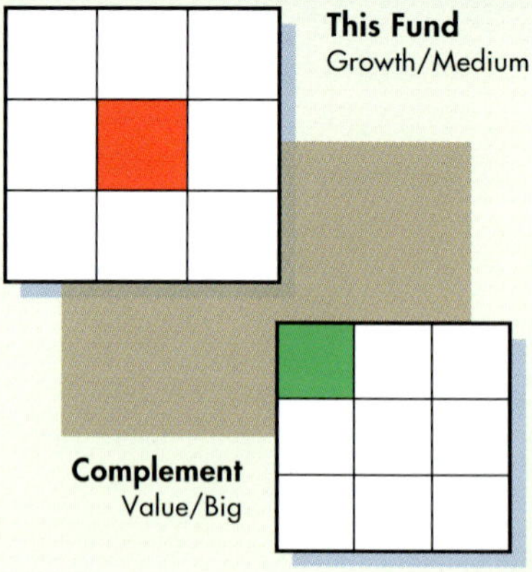

This fund brings together the bond expertise of a five-member team and the stock-picking savvy of eleven equity professionals. It employs an active approach to varying the portions of stocks and bonds in the fund within relatively narrow bands. It's managed to appeal to conservative investors and sports a typically low 0.92% management expense ratio. Its conservative appeal comes from terrific performance in up and down markets.

With a neutral stance on Canadian bonds (mostly Governments) and a bullish outlook for stocks, this fund appears ready for continued good returns for investors in any market.

RRSP

TRIMARK SELECT BALANCED FUND

Walter Kusters (1995) + Patrick Farmer (1993)/Trimark

BALANCED-CANADIAN

RATING

CONSISTENCY

Performance Trend

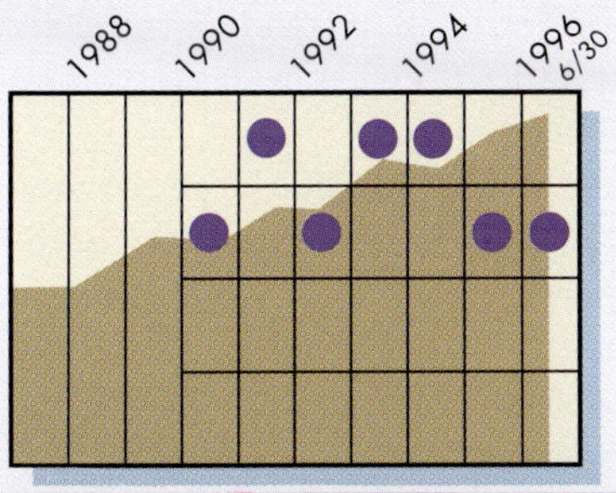

RISK

How often GICs performed better	3 years in 6
How often fund lost money	1 year in 6
Worst year's rate of return	-0.1% (1990)

EFFICIENCY

Management expense/ $100 $2.21

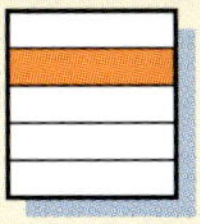

STYLE

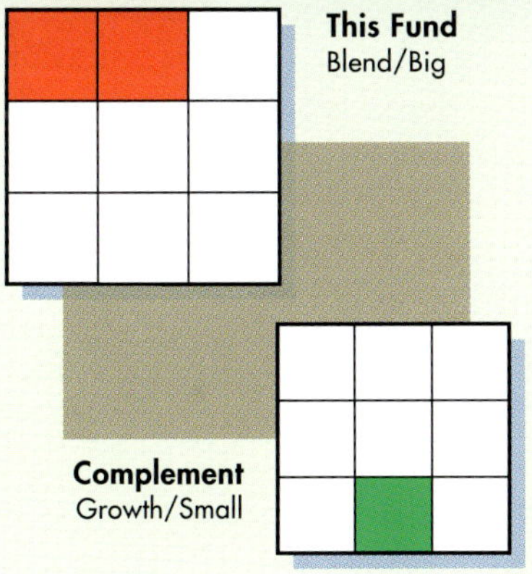

This is the rear-load version of the Trimark Income Growth Fund. But this one costs 0.48% more annually than its sister fund. For this reason, investors are better off to simply pay a front-end load and reap the benefits of owning the cheaper fund year after year.

But even with its higher MER, this fund has had handsome returns. Bond ace Patrick Farmer may be the best-kept secret on a much-lauded investment team. He's called the bond market just right over the past couple of years and has added return to this strong fund. His shifts are subtle, as he's gone from bullish in 1995 to more bearish in 1996. He thinks central banks have lowered interest rates far too much, given our healthy economic growth rate. Accordingly, he fears inflation, which could drive up bond yields and hurt prices.

The Trimark approach is less about stock picking and more about business buying. Before any purchase they do more legwork on a company's business than would a consultant. They meet everybody – managers, competitors, and executives – before and after buying. When they like a company they buy a big piece of it. They recently held more than 10% of Canfor, Crestbrook, and Co-Steel, to name just a few. Each exemplifies their goals by being an attractively priced, low-cost leader.

NEW

C.I. CANADIAN BALANCED FUND

John Zechner (inception)/J. Zechner Associates

RRSP

RATING

★★★½

CONSISTENCY

Performance Trend

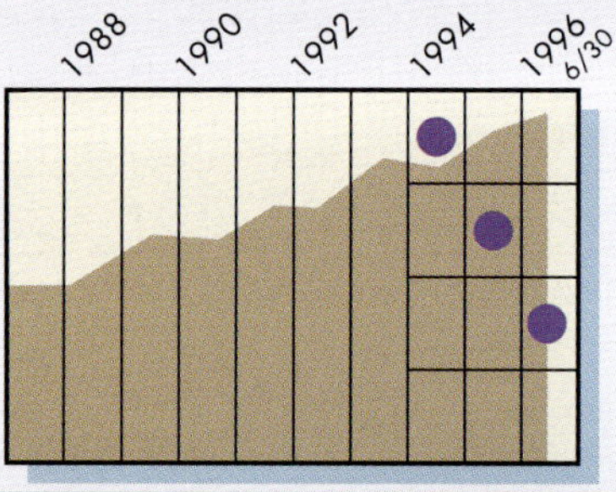

RISK

How often GICs performed better	1 year in 2
How often fund lost money	0 years in 2
Worst year's rate of return	1.1% (1994)

EFFICIENCY

Management expense/ $100 $2.35

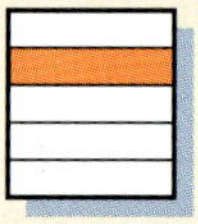

STYLE

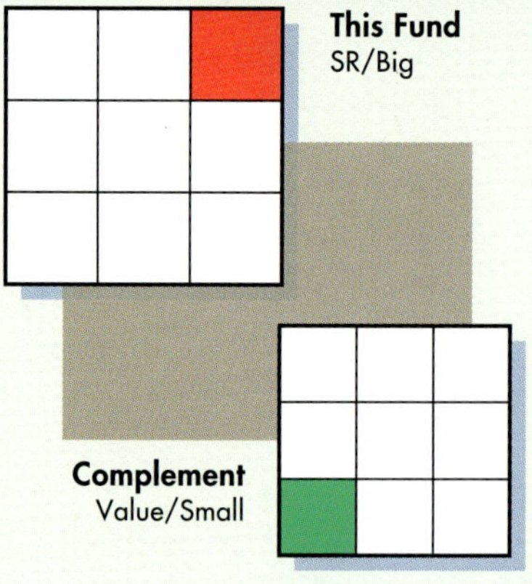

John Zechner is at it again. He's holding cash – plenty of it. At a recent 35% weighting, cash is sure to seal the fate of this fund – for better or worse – in the near term. It's important to understand his motivation to learn what makes this active manager tick.

On the bond side he's been motivated by fear in the early part of the year, although he was more neutral at writing. He's holding 5- to 10-year issues with a goal of capital protection, not capital gains. He's nervous about longer US bonds in what is likely to be a stronger economy.

In the stock market he's been acting defensively, selling cyclicals and some pricey gold and base metals stocks. Zechner argues that market sentiment has been far too positive, and that some earnings disappointments are coming in as a result of wage gains. He's holding and adding to growth names, especially in the technology area, as well as defensive groups like oils, where his biggest name is CanOxy.

His only mistake in the past few years has been holding cash levels in the high teens a couple of times during what continued to be a rising market. Today's higher cash levels could make or break this fund, but history suggests that Zechner is never wrong for long.

NEW

RRSP

AGF GROWTH & INCOME FUND A

Gerard Ferguson (1996) + Clive Coombs/AGF

RATING

CONSISTENCY

Performance Trend

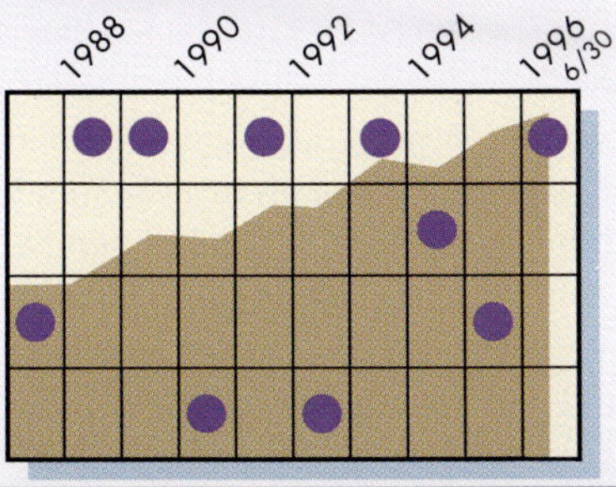

RISK

How often GICs performed better	6 years in 13
How often fund lost money	2 years in 13
Worst year's rate of return	-12.5% (1990)

EFFICIENCY

Management expense/ $100 $2.00

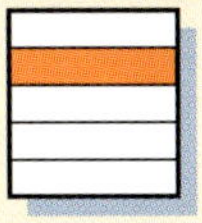

STYLE

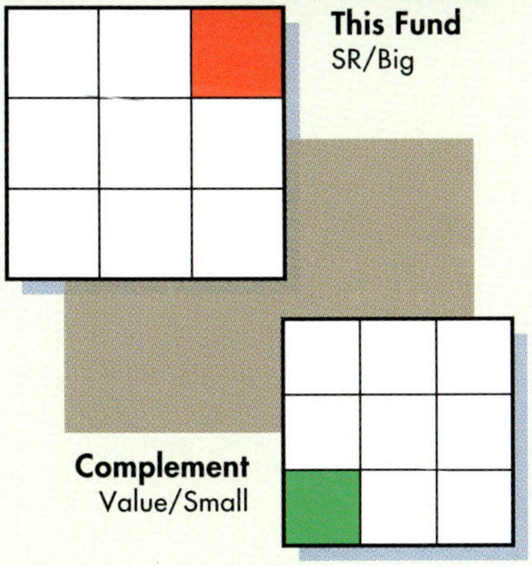

Exactly how this fund will fare in the wake of Veronika Hirsch's departure is anyone's guess. AGF is looking for another top-notch stock picker, and is relying in the meantime on a capable, younger manager.

Even with all of our progress on debt and deficits, bond ace Clive Coombs isn't yet jumping at the chance to buy bonds. Our yield premiums are slim and our currency is under pressure, he thinks. At the time of writing, the fund had a large cash reserve of 20% and a typically low foreign exposure of just 5%.

I'm counselling investors who own this fund to hold it. Newcomers, though, should wait until the management has settled in before committing to this fund.

NEW

SCOTIA EXCELSIOR TOTAL RETURN FUND

André Marsan (inception)/Scotiabank

RRSP

RATING

CONSISTENCY

Performance Trend

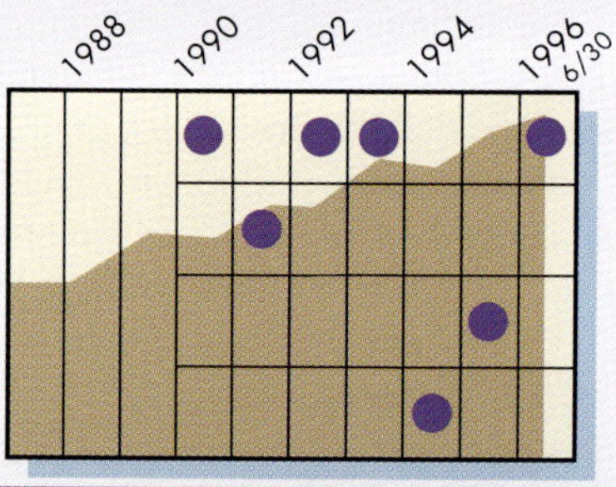

RISK

How often GICs performed better	2 years in 6
How often fund lost money	1 year in 6
Worst year's rate of return	-4.8% (1994)

EFFICIENCY

Management expense/ $100 $2.32

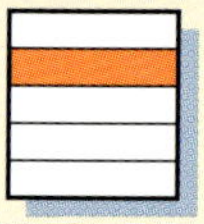

STYLE

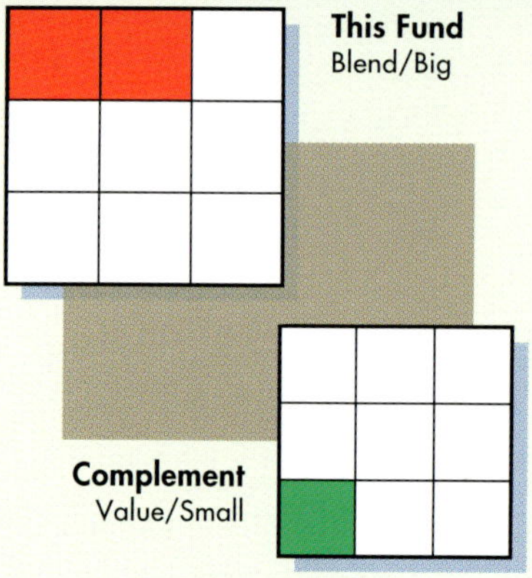

You won't find many balanced funds that are steadier than this one. While it never overwhelms, Marsan's active approach to adjusting the stock/ bond/cash mix is one that manages nicely to avoid bad markets – like 1990, when stocks and bonds lost money. In that tough year, Marsan managed to make about 7%, thanks to heavy cash holdings. You won't make a killing in this fund, but if you're new to the mutual fund scene and you are a Scotiabank client, this is a great place to get started.

BALANCED-CANADIAN

RRSP

ABC FULLY MANAGED FUND

Irwin Michael (inception)/I.A. Michael Investment Counsel

RATING

★★★½

CONSISTENCY

Performance Trend

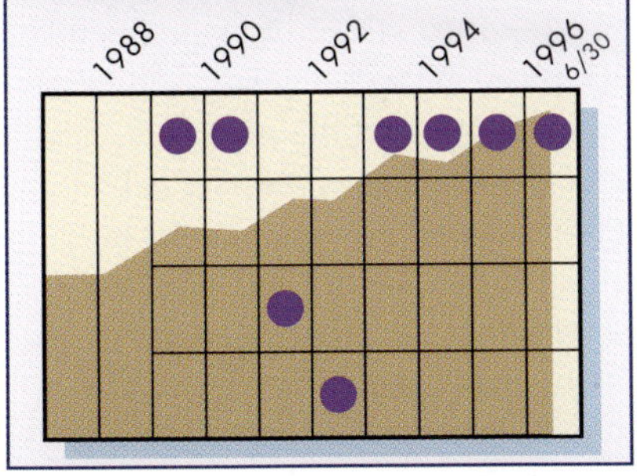

RISK

How often GICs performed better	3 years in 7
How often fund lost money	1 year in 7
Worst year's rate of return	-1.5% (1992)

EFFICIENCY

Management expense/ $100 $2.00

STYLE

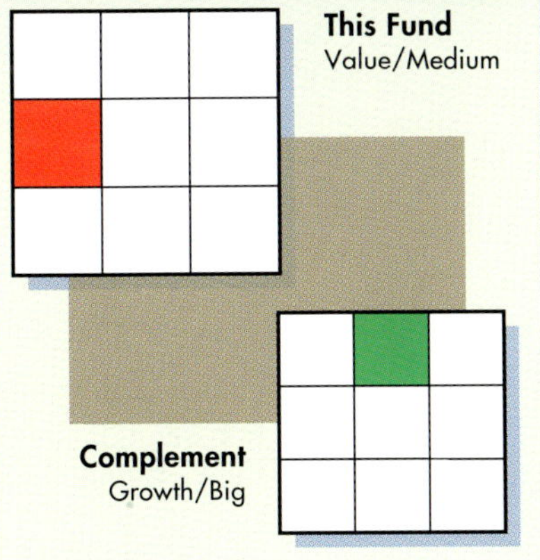

The venerable Irwin Michael is boosting his average capitalization and his cash level in anticipation of a choppy market for the remainder of this economic cycle. The good thing, though, is that he sees it as a trader's heaven: a market with sharp, fast changes in direction. Michael's not afraid to take profits fast. He's so decisive that he makes decisions in black and white, seldom making subtle moves. When he likes bonds he buys a whack of them – long ones. And when he doesn't like them, he dusts all of them – as he did in March of 1996. He's a freak for value – a true contrarian who's often able to find stocks trading at cash value.

In a year of debate on the ethics of trading for their own account, most managers are under pressure now to disclose or limit their personal trading, but Michael has always had a policy of investing all his nickels only in his mutual funds. He's honest and he's smart, but to invest in this fund, you'll need at least $150,000. Hopefully you'll have much more, so that you can adequately diversify from his unique investment style.

NEW

SCEPTRE BALANCED FUND

Lyle Stein / Sceptre

RRSP

RATING

CONSISTENCY

Performance Trend

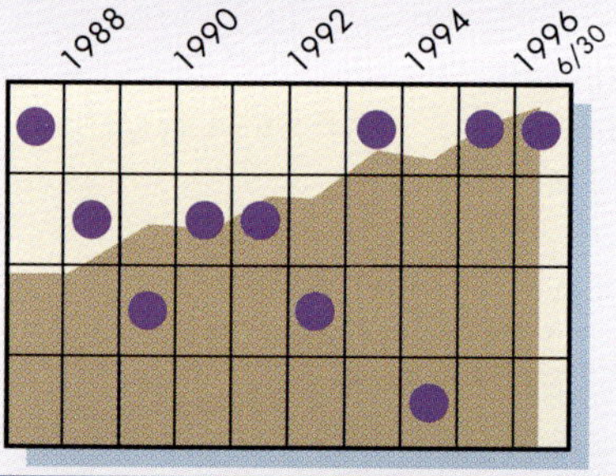

RISK

How often GICs performed better	4 years in 10
How often fund lost money	2 years in 10
Worst year's rate of return	-4.2% (1994)

EFFICIENCY

Management expense/ $100 $1.57

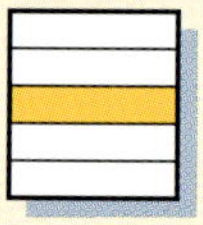

STYLE

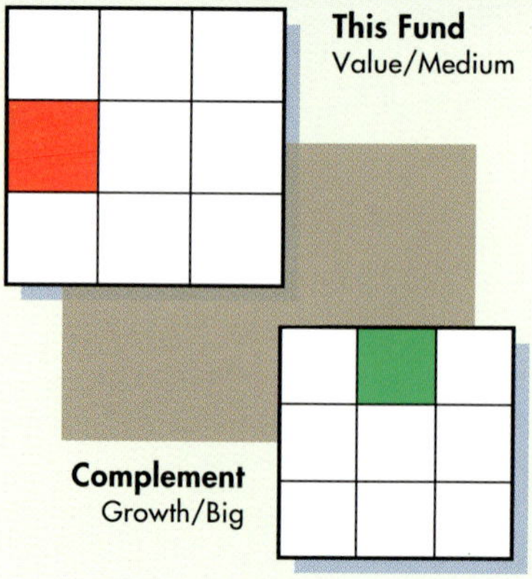

You've got to love a consistent balanced fund like this. It's actively managed, making shifts into and out of stocks or bonds mostly to avoid losses – rather than to make a killing.

Of course, this fund benefits from a typically low management expense ratio and good stock selection. The stock/bond mix moves made by Stein have so far been adroit: he sidestepped the bond market meltdown in early 1996 and has profited from an overweight position in industrial product stocks.

The fund has done well in both good markets and bad and has never had a blow-out (its worst twelve-month stretch saw it lose just 8.8%). So, it's appropriate for conservative investors.

RRSP

BATIRENTE–SECTION OBLIGATIONS

Carmand Normand (inception)/St Laurent Financial

RATING

CONSISTENCY

Performance Trend

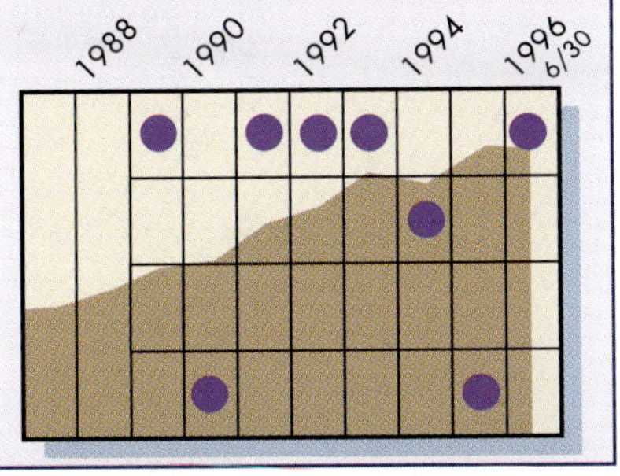

RISK

How often GICs performed better	2 years in 7
How often fund lost money	1 year in 7
Worst year's rate of return	-4.6% (1994)

EFFICIENCY

Management expense/ $100 $1.61

STYLE

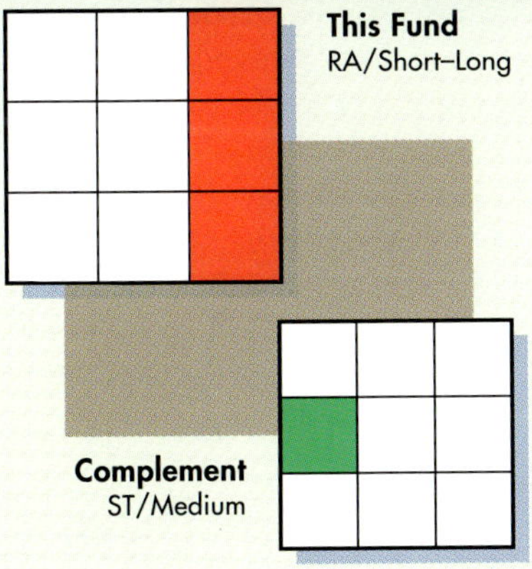

If St Laurent is smart, they'll hire Carmand Normand to continue to manage this fund once he opens his own shop in late 1996. He is a bond trading superstar. At time of writing he had announced his intention to form his own firm (Addenda Capital), and had confirmed that his team was moving with him.

Normand's approach is novel; he sees bonds as investment, not income vehicles. They are meant to be bought low and sold high; the interest earned along the way is just the icing. For him, the average 1.5% swing in interest rates annually that Canada has experienced translates into a hefty 8% price band around which bonds move. He buys long bonds when he figures rates will fall, like now.

Now, he insists, supply and demand factors will drive down bond yields. More savings by individuals and less borrowing by governments will boost demand and crimp supply – an ideal situation for bond holders. About 80% of his returns come from his interest rate anticipation calls (the term of the bonds held). At writing, he was one and a half times as long as the benchmark index in terms of duration, with an average term of about 10 years.

The remaining 20% of this fund's returns come from yield enhancement. He typically holds one-third of the portfolio in Quebec bonds, which offer better-than-average yields.

PHILLIPS HAGER & NORTH BOND FUND

Tony Gage + team (inception)/PH&N

RRSP

RATING

★★★★

CONSISTENCY

Performance Trend

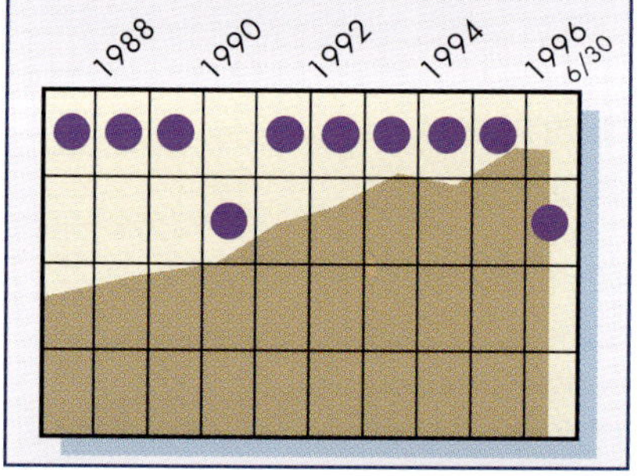

RISK

How often GICs performed better	4 years in 14
How often fund lost money	1 year in 14
Worst year's rate of return	-4.1% (1994)

EFFICIENCY

Management expense/ $100 $0.60

STYLE

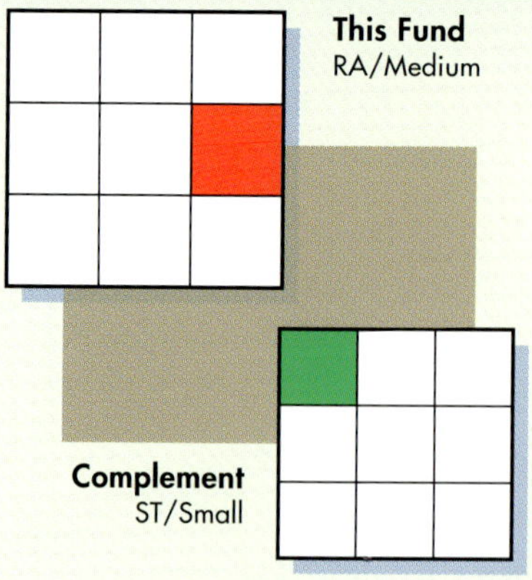

I generally recommend that investors ignore bond funds, and opt for their own passive (buy-and-hold) portfolio of a few laddered stripped-coupon bonds. It's simple and it saves the average 1.6% in management expenses charged by bond fund managers. The expenses weren't so burdensome back in the era of double-digit (and falling) bond yields. But today, most funds' MERs gobble up a disproportionate share of their fund's gross income.

But that argument doesn't hold water with PH&N Bond fund. This one's different. It's cheap, it's active, and it delivers for investors.

The MER is just 0.6% annually – putting it head-and-shoulders ahead of the pack. An eclectic management style helps to add value not just by making the right term decisions (long- or short-term bonds in anticipation of falling or rising interest rates), but also by making the right moves on term mixture. Finally, Gage and his 7-member fixed income team are sharks when it comes to picking up the best high-grade corporate bonds. A typical 35% exposure to corporates adds some one-quarter of a percentage point in annual yield to the fund, which has never suffered materially from a credit downgrade thanks to the two credit analysts on staff. At time of writing, Gage was light on corporates – whose yield spreads have narrowed considerably – producing a big win for the fund.

RRSP

MD BOND FUND

John Braive (inception)/TAL Investment Counsel

RATING

★ ★ ★ ★

CONSISTENCY

Performance Trend

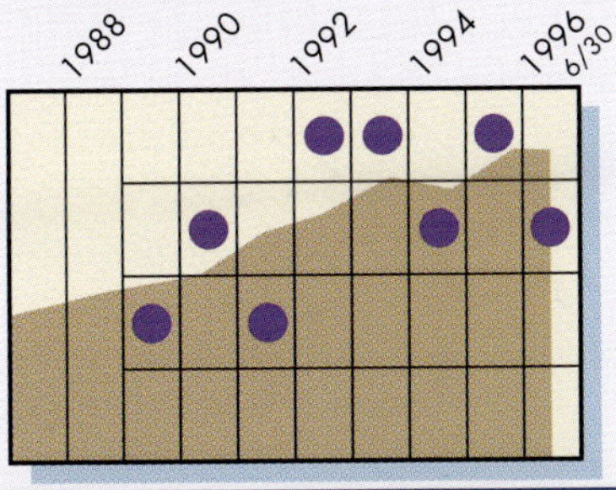

RISK

How often GICs performed better	2 years in 7
How often fund lost money	1 year in 7
Worst year's rate of return	-5.4% (1994)

EFFICIENCY

Management expense/ $100 $1.03

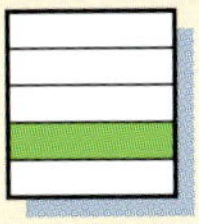

STYLE

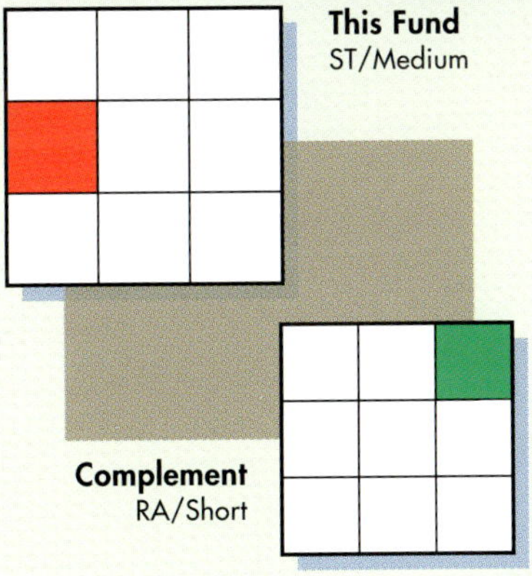

Again, MD proves that med school can pay off. Braive's lower-risk pension fund style of management works in just about every environment for the investors in this fund – which is only available to doctors and their families.

The style involves actively trading among and between different types of bonds (Governments, corporates) to capitalize frequently on small incremental yield advantages and to capture little capital gains. Add those trading gains to the regular coupon income and this has been a winning fund for investors – even in years of falling rates, when most of the gains are to be made in longer-dated bonds. Braive can go long if he sees rates falling. With spreads (or yield advantages) tight for corporates, this fund has already squeezed about as much out of the economic cycle as one would think possible. It's profited from lower rates and tighter spreads. Future gains will likely be harder won.

NEW

McLEAN BUDDEN FIXED INCOME FUND

Craig Barnard + team (inception)/McLean Budden

RRSP

RATING

CONSISTENCY

Performance Trend

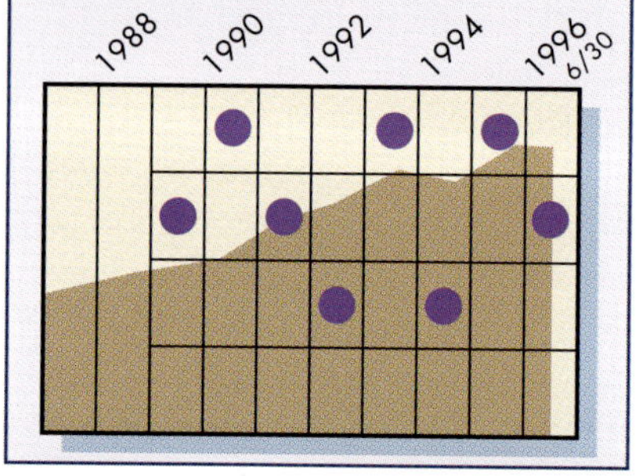

RISK

How often GICs performed better	2 years in 7
How often fund lost money	1 year in 7
Worst year's rate of return	-6.2% (1994)

EFFICIENCY

Management expense/ $100 $1.00

STYLE

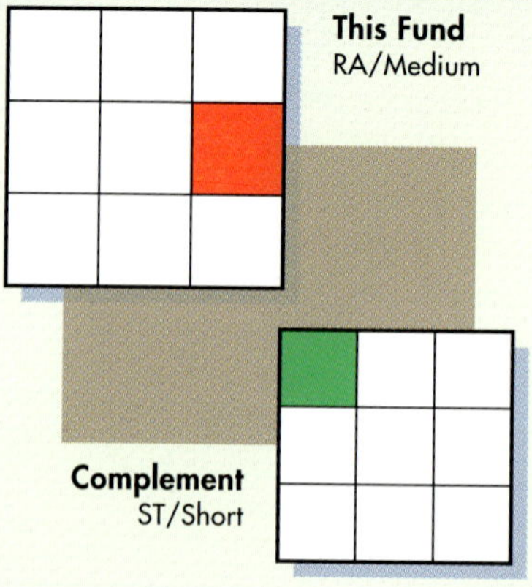

You won't find a bond team as similar to PH&N as these people. Like PH&N, McLean Budden generally buys plenty of corporates (minimum A credit rating) and provincials. In fact, such issues often make up half the fund or more. But today's razor-thin yield premiums hardly reward investors for the extra risk of such bonds. So, McLean Budden is light on these higher-yielding issues today.

McLean Budden is a powerhouse in the pension world but is little known to retail investors. They employ a rate anticipation style – varying duration (a measure of term) of the portfolio within strict limits (about 4 to 6 years). Unlike PH&N though, this fund has no credit analysts *per se*, charges a pricier 1% annually, and occasionally dabbles in US-pay bonds (up to 15%).

NEW

RRSP

EQUITABLE LIFE SEG. ACC. INCOME FUND

Ian Grant (1992)/Equitable Life

RATING

CONSISTENCY

Performance Trend

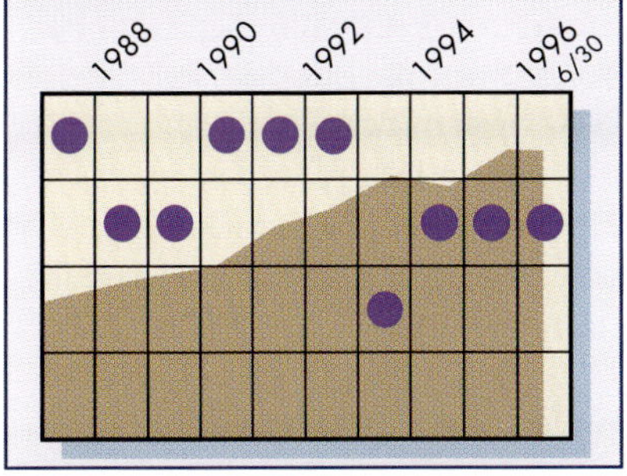

RISK

How often GICs performed better	4 years in 13
How often fund lost money	1 year in 13
Worst year's rate of return	-4.7% (1994)

EFFICIENCY

Management expense/ $100 $0.50

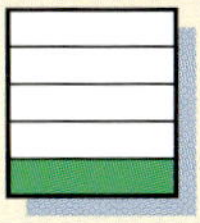

STYLE

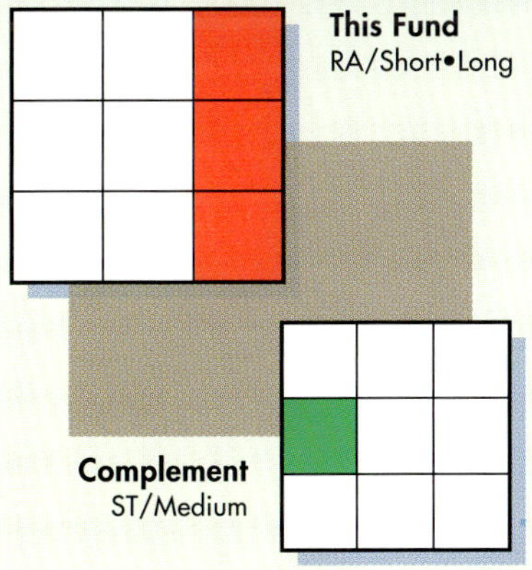

Surprisingly, Grant's rate-anticipation style of management can still keep up with the ScotiaMcLeod Universe Bond Index (a very tough benchmark), even after paying its steep 1.56% management expense ratio. This is a pricey fund that has managed to deliver for investors. But now it's only available to existing unitholders.

BOND-CANADIAN

BOND-INTERNATIONAL

AGF GLOBAL GOVERNMENT BOND FUND A

Clive Coombs + Warren Goldring (inception)/AGF

RRSP

RATING

★ ★ ★ ★ ★

CONSISTENCY

Performance Trend

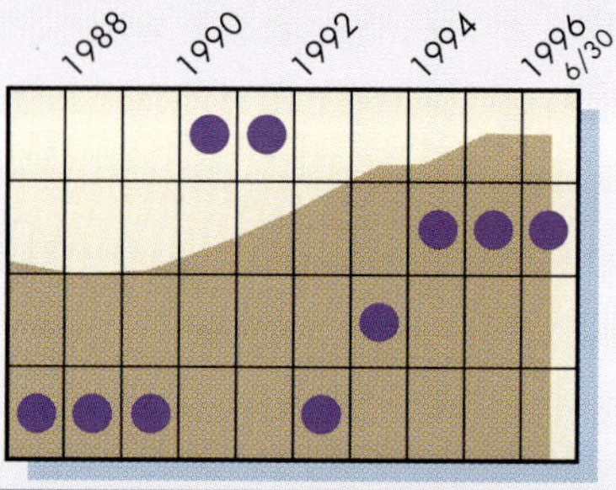

RISK

How often GICs performed better	3 years in 9
How often fund lost money	1 year in 9
Worst year's rate of return	-6.4% (1988)

EFFICIENCY

Management expense/ $100 $1.28

STYLE

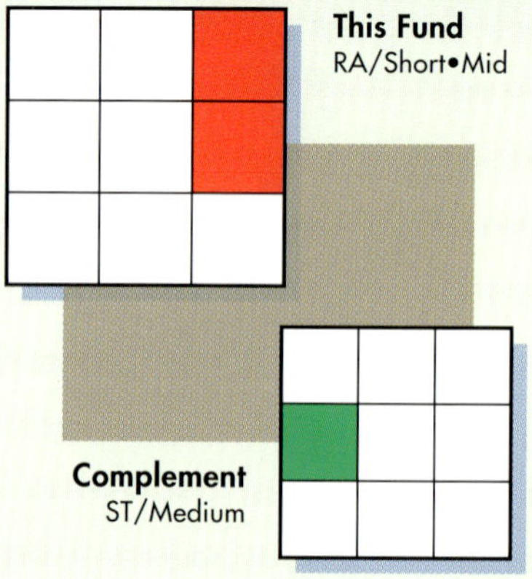

The US bond market is the world's pacesetter. It's the biggest and most liquid. In addition, US Fed policy influences that of other central banks. That's why it's so key to understand the US market psychology in global bond investing. Besides, AGF Global Government Bond holds about half its assets in US Treasuries.

But the US bond market is driven by psychology first and actual data second.

In 1996 manager Clive Coombs could see that investors were considering recession inevitable and were certain of a US rate cut – against all economic odds. So he positioned the portfolio to gain from steeper US yields, and as the long bond yield climbed from 6.2% to 6.6% he outperformed his peer group. Long term, he sees Treasuries as very attractive securities.

The fund has been served well by a policy of only occasionally hedging currency exposure to be defensive, not speculative. At the time of writing, there is only a small hedge on sterling, a currency the managers think could come under pressure. With that exception, the fund will excel when and if the C$ falls.

NEW

RRSP

ROYAL TRUST INTERNATIONAL BOND FUND

Barry Edwards + team (1994)/Royal Bank

RATING

★ ★ ★ ★

CONSISTENCY

Performance Trend

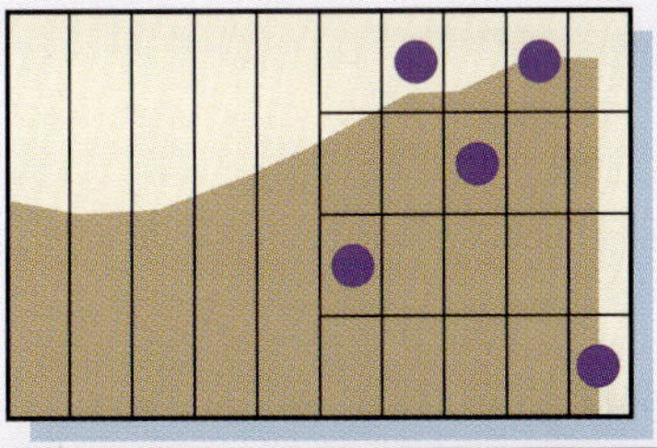

RISK

How often GICs performed better	1 year in 4
How often fund lost money	0 years in 4
Worst year's rate of return	1.1% (1994)

EFFICIENCY

Management expense/ $100 $1.86

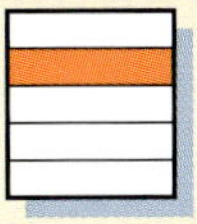

STYLE

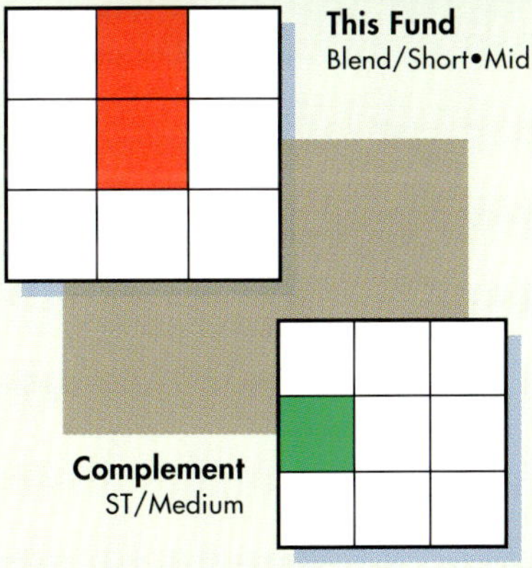

There are always trade-offs in investing. This fund offers full RRSP eligibility, good past performance, and no load. It's limited, though, to buying mostly Canadian or so-called 'supranational' issues – bonds of entities like the World Bank denominated in, say, Sterling. Trouble is, such issues aren't as widely available as regular foreign government bonds. That's why Edwards missed out on a rally early in 1996 in Europe's secondary markets (Spain, Netherlands, and Italy) where yields are high – and so are the risks.

Generally, the fund managers believe that hedging a fund like this is not productive for investors. After all, to hedge is to negate the benefits of foreign currency diversification. And diversification is the reason for buying this fund. Still, sometimes currency opportunities arise. So, lately, Edwards has worked in some exposure to the Japanese yen, for example, without owning Japanese bonds. That way, when interest rates rise in Japan as Edwards expects, unitholders will benefit from an appreciating yen without suffering from a crumbling bond market. He's bullish on Canada and Germany but he is more negative on the US market. For this fund to continue to be sucessful, we will require a decoupling of bond markets that have so far been slaves to US Fed interest rate policy.

NEW

GLOBAL STRATEGY WORLD BOND FUND

Ceris Williams (1992)/Rothschild Asset Management

RRSP

RATING

CONSISTENCY

Performance Trend

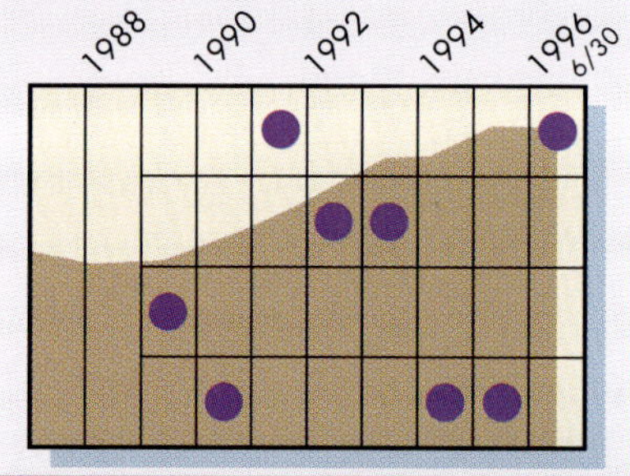

RISK

How often GICs performed better	3 years in 7
How often fund lost money	1 year in 7
Worst year's rate of return	-8.8% (1994)

EFFICIENCY

Management expense/ $100 $2.26

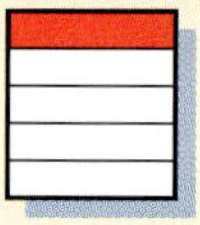

STYLE

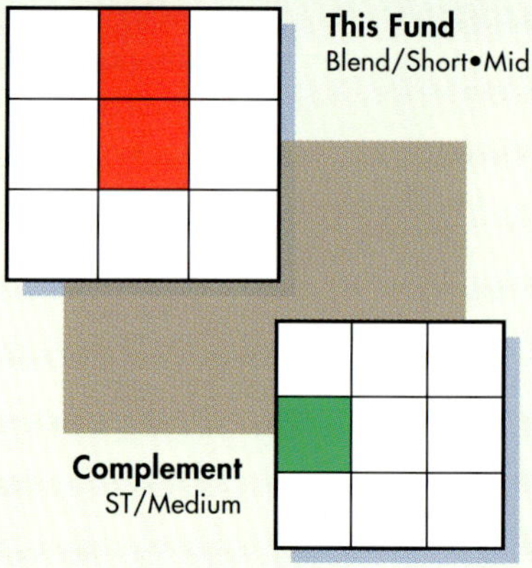

This fund has generally been a market beater. Investors, however, haven't noticed. Too many of them bought in during the heady 1993 season on the basis of strong past performance and were disappointed by the results that followed. Mistakes during the weak years were errors of conservatism – and miscommunication. The fund had been sold as the 'get-the-hell-out-of-Canada' fund for some time, with reams of data supporting the argument to diversify outside Canada's bond market.

After investors piled in, currency hedges (a conservative move to protect the C$ value of the fund) effectively reduced the fund's diversification out of Canada. While the managers got the currency wrong a couple of times, the Rothschild team are steadfastly committed to seeing this cycle through, and making big bond gains for Canadian investors.

They're sure those big gains will come from Europe. High unemployment and slow growth make for little inflation pressure in Europe, so rates can – and should – fall, says Williams, who has geared the fund toward longer-maturity bonds. That will lead to bond market gains in Europe, where three-quarters of the fund is invested. If rates fall in Europe, and rise in Japan (where the fund has a short position), investors in this fund will continue on the top-performance tear that this fund has had for over a year.

RRSP

DYNAMIC GLOBAL BOND FUND

Norm Bengough (inception)/Goodman & Co.

RATING

CONSISTENCY

Performance Trend

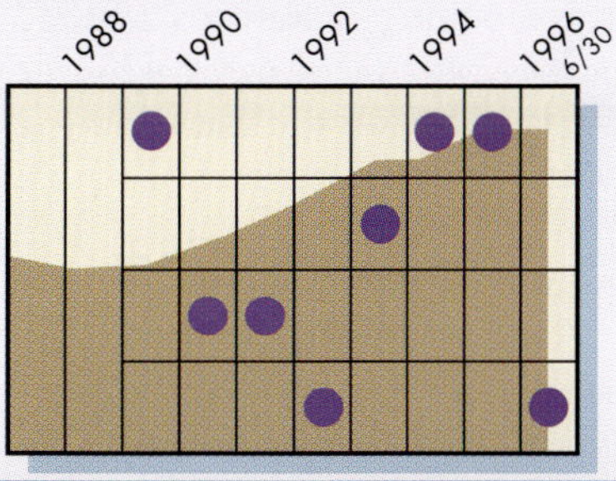

RISK

How often GICs performed better	3 years in 7
How often fund lost money	0 years in 7
Worst year's rate of return	4.9% (1994)

EFFICIENCY

Management expense/ $100 $1.94

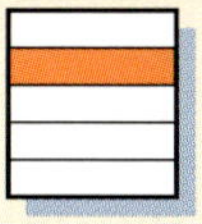

STYLE

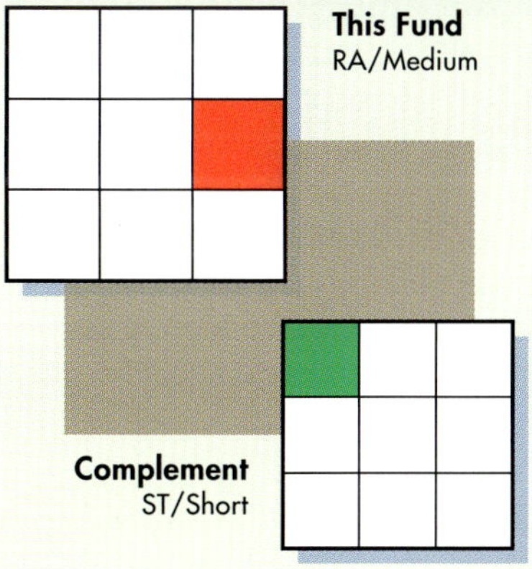

Norm Bengough hasn't posted a losing year yet for investors in this fund. In absolute value, his remarkably consistent profits stand in sharp contrast to other global bond fund peers.

Bengough has excelled, in relative terms, over the past three years through a combination of adroit country and, more importantly, good currency decisions. Stubbornly tied to US interest rate policy in 1995 and 1996, European bond yields are higher than they should be – hurting the fund. It can't last forever, so he's redoubling his conviction that the market will eventually bear him out.

One move that's worked out well for the fund is the move into the Australian and New Zealand markets, where both bonds and currencies have appreciated.

If Bengough underperforms – as he did early this decade – it's likely to be in a good market. In that way, this is a conservative fund for investors who are less than enthusiastic about Canada's bond market prospects.

BOND-INTERNATIONAL

ALTAMIRA EQUITY FUND

Frank Mersch (inception)/Altamira

RRSP

RATING

★ ★ ★ ★ ★

CONSISTENCY

Performance Trend

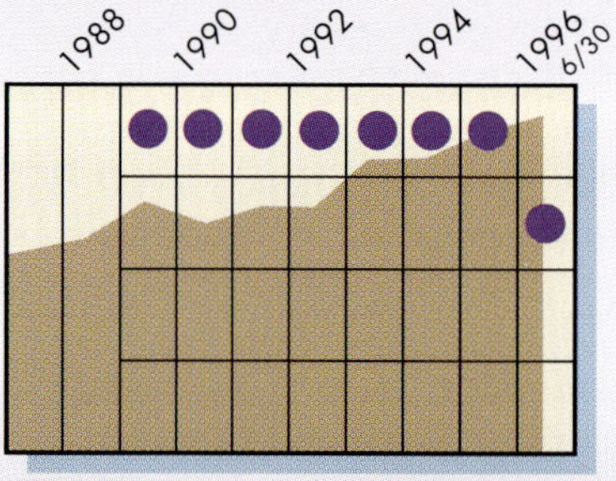

RISK

How often GICs performed better	2 years in 7
How often fund lost money	1 year in 7
Worst year's rate of return	-1.8% (1990)

EFFICIENCY

Management expense/ $100 $2.31

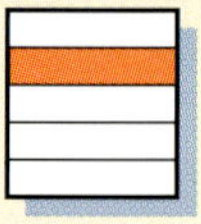

STYLE

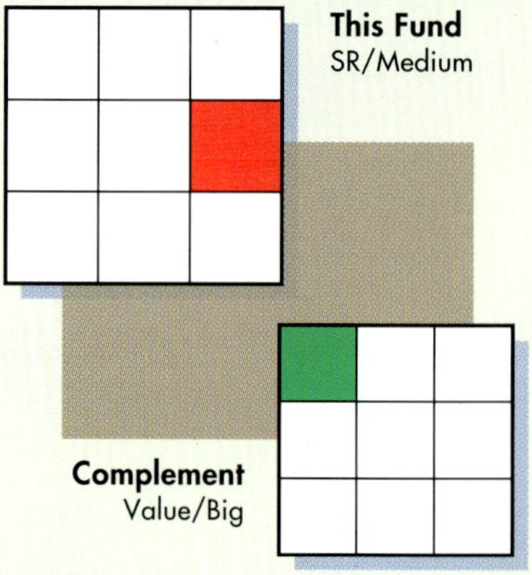

In four separate years out of the last eight Frank Mersch has made over 30% for investors in this fund. His worst year was only –1.8%.

But now some argue that he manages too much money to beat the market, because he must become the market. Support for that argument comes from the fact that he hasn't beaten the market by as much lately, as his assets have swelled.

That argument is flawed. Mersch isn't the passive type. Even with a fund as big as this he's owned plenty of small to mid-sized companies, and his sector shifts are still huge. He started out 1995, for example, with 23% in banks and no golds. At the time of writing that situation had completely reversed. He's a confident, bold manager who makes at least an extra 1% annually by occassionally owning more junior companies – like before the referendum, when he bought some junior gold stocks which later led a bullion rally.

He believes that Canada is experiencing a mid-cycle slowdown, so he's positioned the portfolio in the deep cyclicals (still waiting their turn) and out of the interest-sensitive stocks.

With a recent 18% cash under the pillow, Mersch is set to attack in any market pullback. But if the market rises, he could miss out on the party. That's unlikely, because after being early with the gold bet in 1995, Mersch is out to prove that he can still beat the market.

ABC FUNDAMENTAL VALUE FUND

RRSP

Irwin Michael (inception)/I.A. Michael Investment Counsel

RATING

★★★★★

CONSISTENCY

Performance Trend

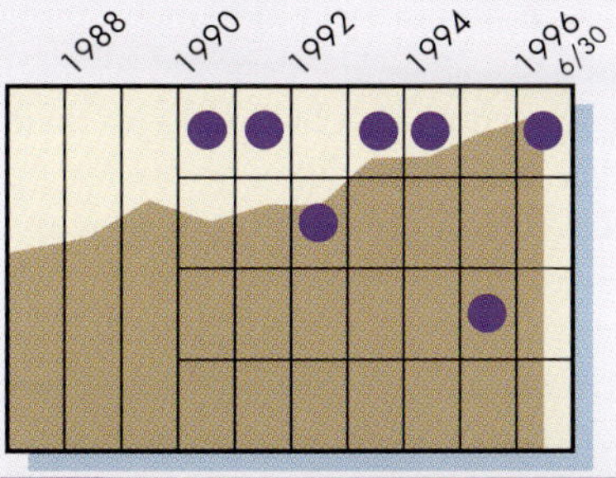

RISK

How often GICs performed better	3 years in 6
How often fund lost money	1 year in 6
Worst year's rate of return	-2.0% (1990)

EFFICIENCY

Management expense/ $100 $2.00

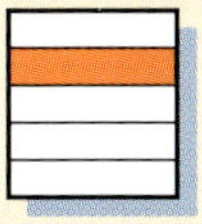

STYLE

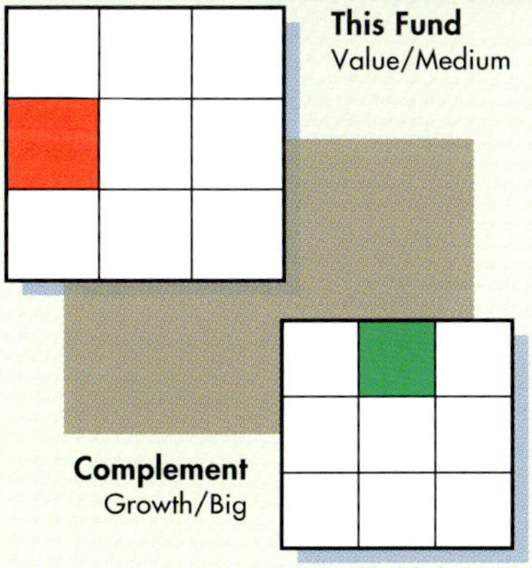

If investing in mutual funds is only about hiring the best people then look no further. Irwin Michael has it all: ethics, trading savvy, a sharp value discipline, and confidence. Personal trading is banned at his little shop. He invests only in his own funds. He doesn't buy promotional stocks, though he does look at and buy lots of IPOs (initial public share offerings).

This fund requires a minimum $150,000 investment. But you'll need much more than that – maybe half a million – to adequately diversify by geography and management style.

It's a year of change for the fund, which is moving up-market – to the bigger-name cyclical companies – in anticipation of a strengthening Canadian economy. Michael is a contrarian manager – he's generally made a lot of money buying obscure, underfollowed stocks at low, low prices. But the froth in small caps in early '96 put him off.

You'll often hear Michael saying things like "Take Richland Petroleum. Everybody loved it at $10. Now they hate it at $4.50." That's classic Michael. At writing, he was bearish on the bond market (not a great sign for stocks) and had moved into bigger, higher-yielding defensive stocks. Michael usually gets such big-picture calls right – which explains why he earns a top grade in weaker markets. Protecting capital is a key element of this fund's strategy.

UNIVERSITY AVENUE CANADIAN FUND

Jonathan Baird (1995)/Baird Asset Management

RRSP

RATING

★ ★ ★ ★ ★

CONSISTENCY

Performance Trend

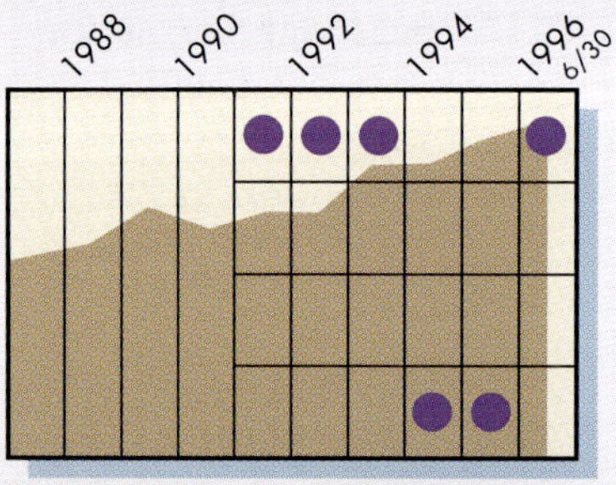

RISK

How often GICs performed better	2 years in 5
How often fund lost money	1 year in 5
Worst year's rate of return	-9.5% (1994)

EFFICIENCY

Management expense/ $100 $2.54

STYLE

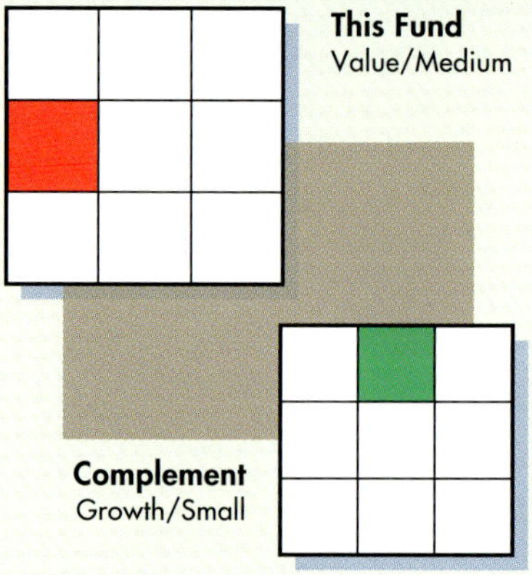

Jonathan Baird is a study in contrasts. Just when you think that a heavy resource tilt means he's focusing only on this sector, he changes everything around so that there's no sector theme at all. When you think he's lost all of his ideas and research support because he no longer manages the $600 million he ran last year at Dynamic, he surprises you with news that the institutional brokers still pay him a great deal of attention. He's an active trader for whom stock price valuations are absolutely key. He believes that even the best company's stock can be a bad investment if you overpay.

He's not a timer at all, but stickhandled the summer '96 correction quite nicely; he went into June with just 8% in cash, and within weeks had raised it to 45%.

Jonathan Baird is on a mission. I really believe that he's swinging for the fences with this fund. He's certainly working harder than ever – and making more money for his clients. All, I think, to prove that he can be a success on his own – without Ned Goodman. The breakup with Dynamic wasn't smooth, and he's out to prove his worth.

In typical Baird style, he soared in his first 8 months on the fund (through May, '96) by overweighting resources and banks for example. Then, during the thumping he took in June, '96, he sold two-thirds of his vast gold exposure – though he remains bullish on the shiny metal.

RRSP

ALTAFUND INVESTMENT CORP.

David Taylor (1995)/Altamira

RATING

CONSISTENCY

Performance Trend

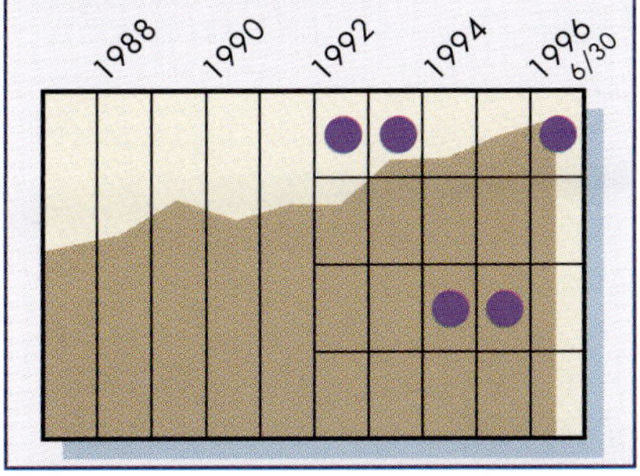

RISK

How often GICs performed better	1 year in 4
How often fund lost money	1 year in 4
Worst year's rate of return	-2.9% (1994)

EFFICIENCY

Management expense/ $100 $2.38

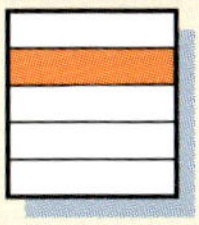

STYLE

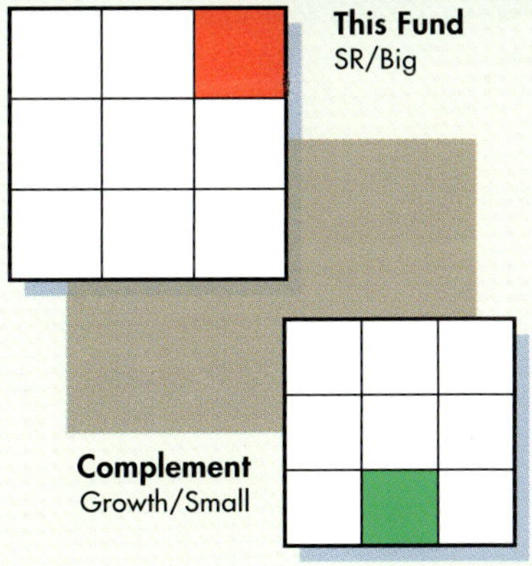

This is a very different fund from a couple of years ago. Where previous manager Norm LaMarche made forecasts about commodity prices, then bought a basket of companies poised to benefit, today's AltaFund is set to deliver a more enduring satisfaction. Taylor is highly risk-averse.

It would have been a glorious1996 for this fund had LaMarche stuck around: Most of the market action was in junior golds – an area Taylor simply avoids. He won't pay for potential finds – that's too risky, he insists. Rather, he'll pay a comparatively and historically low price for first-class management, assets, and track record. This strategy will considerably mute the fund's ups (which used to be dramatic: the fund made over 170% in the two years ended 1993) and downs.

GUARDIAN GROWTH EQUITY FUND A

John Priestman (inception)/Guardian

RRSP

RATING

★ ★ ★ ★

CONSISTENCY

Performance Trend

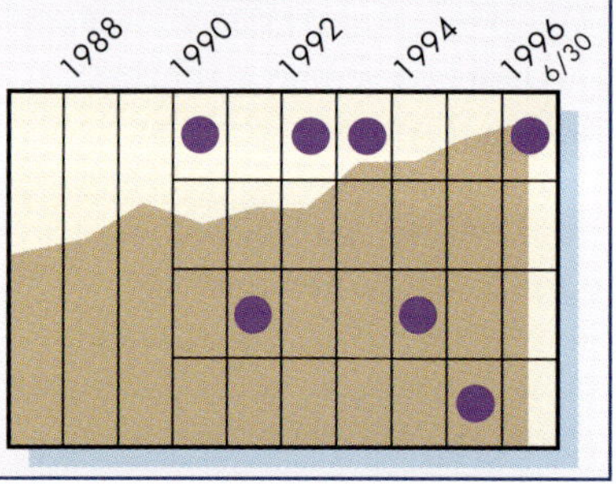

RISK

How often GICs performed better	2 years in 6
How often fund lost money	2 years in 6
Worst year's rate of return	-4.5% (1994)

EFFICIENCY

Management expense/ $100 $2.15

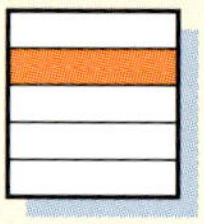

STYLE

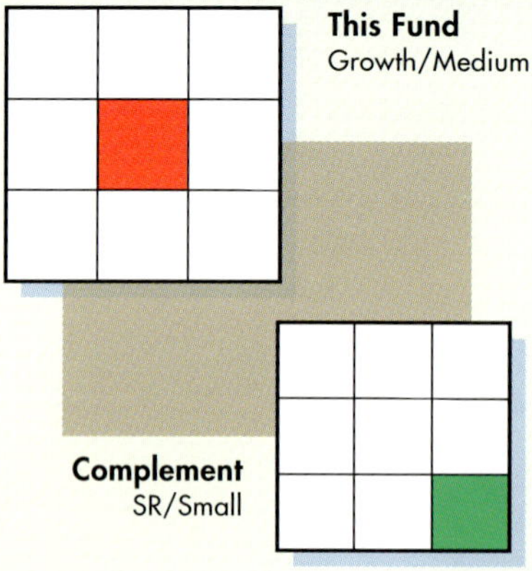

This Fund
Growth/Medium

Complement
SR/Small

This fund seldom makes the 'top' lists in mutual fund rankings over any short period. Its beauty lies in its ability to preserve capital. Priestman manages it with the goal of delivering steady results in markets both good and bad. He's no ace, though, at making money in rising markets. Over the past four rising markets for the TSE it has, in fact, placed in the bottom one-fourth of all Canadian equity funds.

But by not losing big – even in market droughts – Guardian Growth Equity manages to amass real growth over time. The fund lost just 1.2% during the savage 1990 market meltdown that shaved 14.8% off the TSE.

Now Priestman is positioning the fund for modestly higher interest rates in Canada, thanks to a US economy that's clipping. There's a two-barreled effect of the economic surge south of the border for investors in this fund. First, a play on cyclical stock groups like oil and gas, as well as forest products. Second, protection from higher rates through fewer bank and utility stocks. An idle 10% cash reserve is another defensive tool for this fund, which is suitable for investors who should be in stocks, but are leery of market swings.

RRSP

TRIMARK CANADIAN FUND

Vito Maida + Wally Kusters (1995)/Trimark

RATING

★ ★ ★ ★

CONSISTENCY

Performance Trend

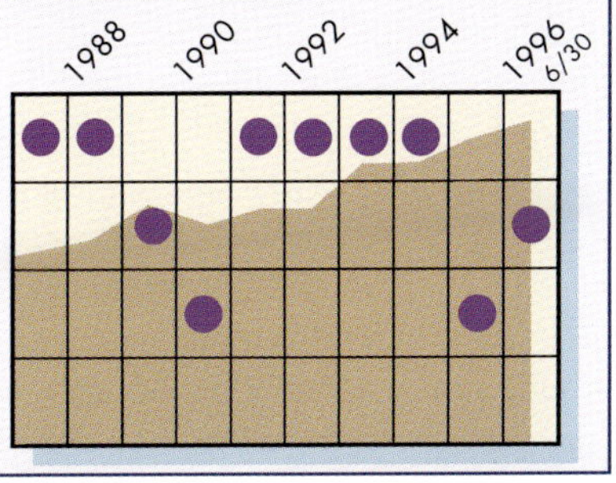

RISK

How often GICs performed better	6 years in 14
How often fund lost money	1 year in 14
Worst year's rate of return	-12.1% (1990)

EFFICIENCY

Management expense/ $100 $1.54

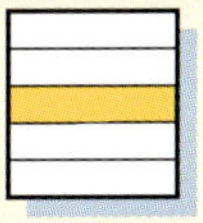

STYLE

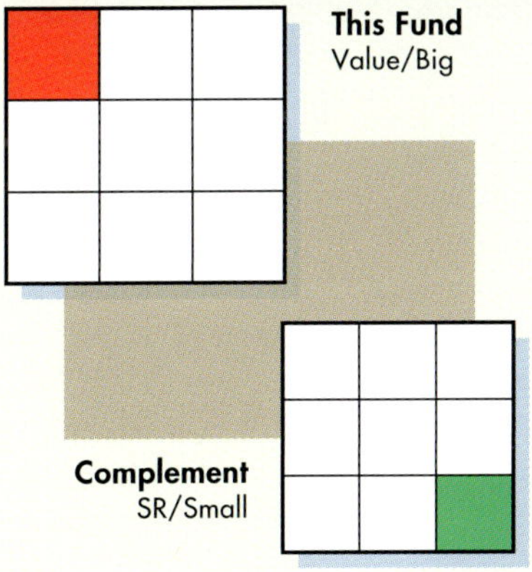

Is Trimark too big to beat the market in Canada? No.

True, the Trimark team manages some $5 billion in Canadian equities across all funds. So investors wonder how the team, which is largely new in the past few years, will be able to excel as they grow. At some level, of course, size does become an issue.

But there's no evidence of it yet. The new team members have successfully rejigged the portfolio since their arrival in 1995. They've replaced about 10 names and reduced cash levels in addition to handling the torrent of cash from spectacular unit sales – all while improving returns. In fact, they're beating departed manager Dina DeGeer.

The Trimark approach is so research intensive that on balance they've benefited from a net increase in research talent. When they like a company, they buy a big piece of it. They recently held more than 10% of Canfor, Crestbrook, and Co-Steel, just to name a few. Each exemplifies their goals by being an attractively priced, low-cost leader.

This low-cost version of the popular Trimark domestic equity product is particularly appealing because of its much lower management expense ratio – just 1.54%.

NEW

TRIMARK SELECT CANADIAN GROWTH FUND

Vito Maida and Wally Kusters (1995) + team/Trimark

RRSP

RATING

CONSISTENCY

Performance Trend

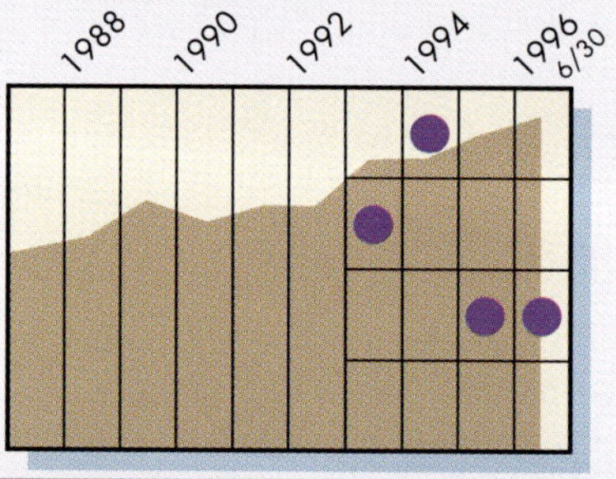

RISK

How often GICs performed better	1 year in 3
How often fund lost money	0 years in 3
Worst year's rate of return	3.8% (1994)

EFFICIENCY

Management expense/ $100 $2.30

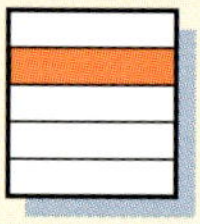

STYLE

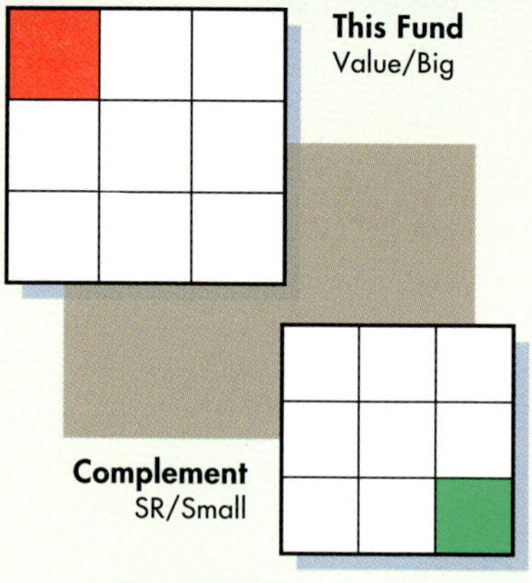

At an annual expense clip of 2.3%, this is the most pricey of Trimark's Canadian offerings. It has a shorter, 6-year declining redemption schedule, but is otherwise very similar to Trimark Canadian – a front-end powerhouse with a 14-year track record.

Some think Trimark is too big to beat the market in Canada. They're wrong. It's true, the Trimark team manages some $5.2 billion in Canadian equities across all funds. So investors wonder how the team, which is largely new in the past few years, will be able to keep a tight list of just 40 investments as the money keeps pouring in. At some level, of course, size does become an issue.

But there's no evidence of it yet. New team members Vito Maida and Wally Kusters have replaced about 10 names and reduced cash levels, in addition to handling the torrent of cash from spectacular net unit sales.

The Trimark approach is less about stock picking and more about business buying. Before any purchase, they do more legwork on a company's business than would a consultant. They meet everybody – managers, competitors, and executives – before and after buying. When they like a company, they buy a big piece of it. They recently held more than 10% of Canfor, Crestbrook, and Co-Steel, to name just a few. Each exemplifies their goals by being an attractively priced, low-cost leader.

RRSP

AGF GROWTH EQUITY FUND A

Bob Farquharson (inception)/AGF Management

RATING

CONSISTENCY

Performance Trend

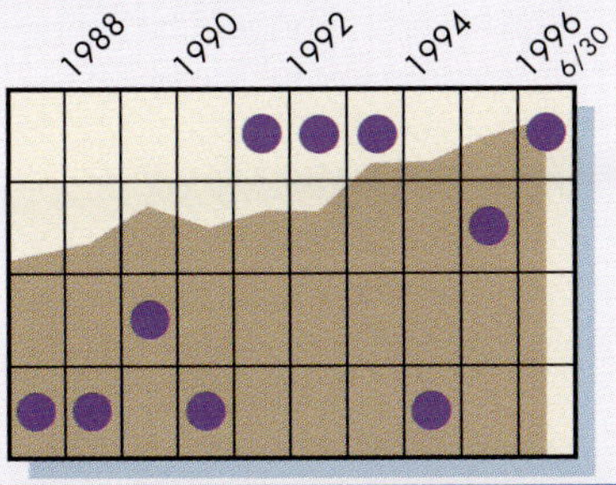

RISK

How often GICs performed better	5 years in 13
How often fund lost money	4 years in 13
Worst year's rate of return	-16.3% (1990)

EFFICIENCY

Management expense/ $100 $2.44

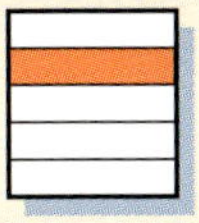

STYLE

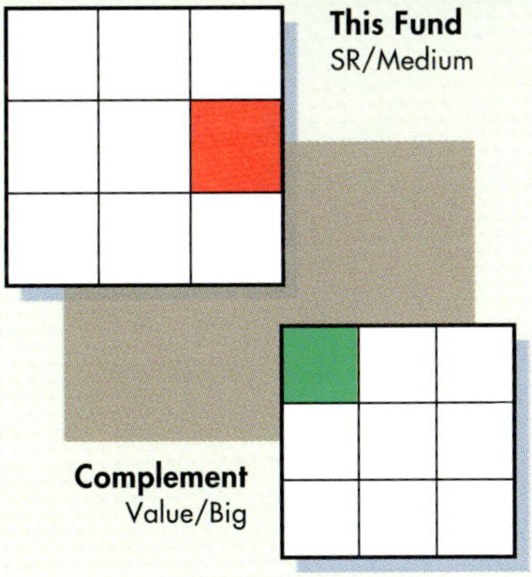

Here's a fund in flux. AGF Growth Equity has made most of its gains in resource moves, especially in smaller companies. After a great rally for small resource stocks in early 1996, this fund has retooled for the next move and at writing is actually underweight resources. That's odd for a team who believe now is the time to favour later-cycle names (like resource stocks). But resources have had such a run – especially the smaller golds. Understanding why they've sold those stocks is key to understanding this management team.

They were overweight in golds last summer, favouring (as usual) the lower-cost producers with proven deposits and sound management. Then the sector exploded in price – to a point where some small companies had amassed market values of $300 million or more without a single hole in the ground. AGF sold into the strength and now holds only smaller positions in the premium companies.

The fund's mandate is to make aggressive investments in aggressive companies. But don't take that to mean they'll take a flyer at the top of the market. As this year's moves have shown, Farquharson's savvy is knowing when to ratchet the risk level down. Indeed, the fund has stood up well in the three bear markets over the past decade, beating half its peers.

AIC ADVANTAGE FUND

Jonathan Wellum (1990)/AIC

RRSP

RATING

CONSISTENCY

Performance Trend

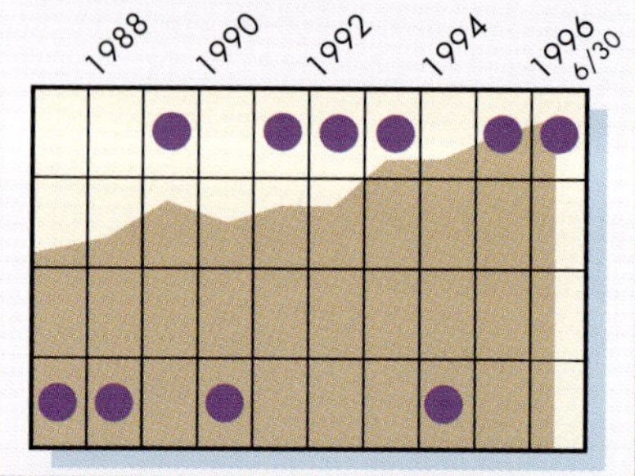

RISK

How often GICs performed better	4 years in 10
How often fund lost money	3 years in 10
Worst year's rate of return	-18.0% (1990)

EFFICIENCY

Management expense/ $100 $2.70

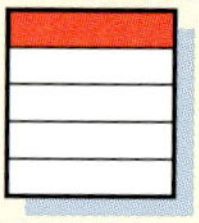

STYLE

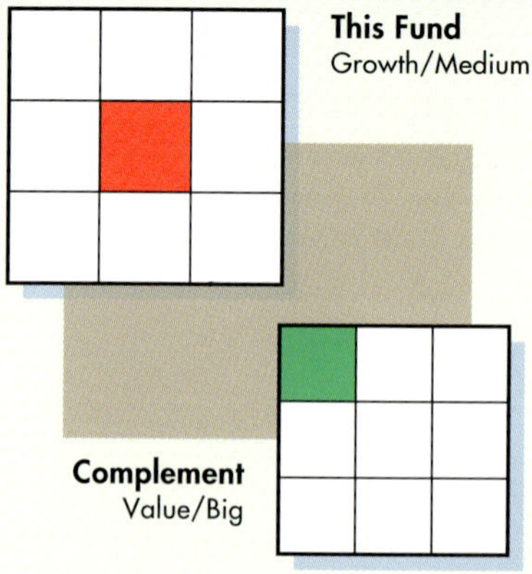

This fund focuses on wealth management companies in the Canadian marketplace. The growth of this industry lies in the strong fundamentals of

- a growing, aging population that's more affluent and financially knowledgeable, and
- a long-term trend of low inflation and low interest rates.

By buying and holding, the fund's never paid a distribution – making it very tax-efficient. But that's just it: for 2.7% annually, you'd expect them to do more than buy and hold.

But it works. This is the number-one performing fund in Canada in rising markets – though it's the third-worst in falling markets.

BISSETT CANADIAN EQUITY FUND

RRSP

Michael Quinn (1986) + Fred Pynn/Bissett & Associates

RATING

★★★½

CONSISTENCY

Performance Trend

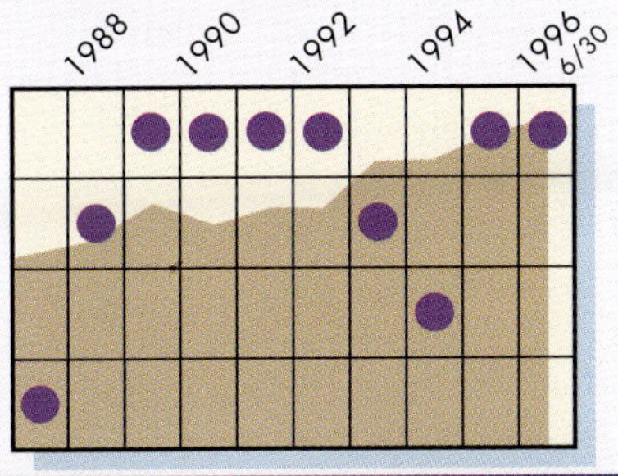

RISK

How often GICs performed better	5 years in 12
How often fund lost money	5 years in 12
Worst year's rate of return	-8.5% (1990)

EFFICIENCY

Management expense/ $100 $1.35

STYLE

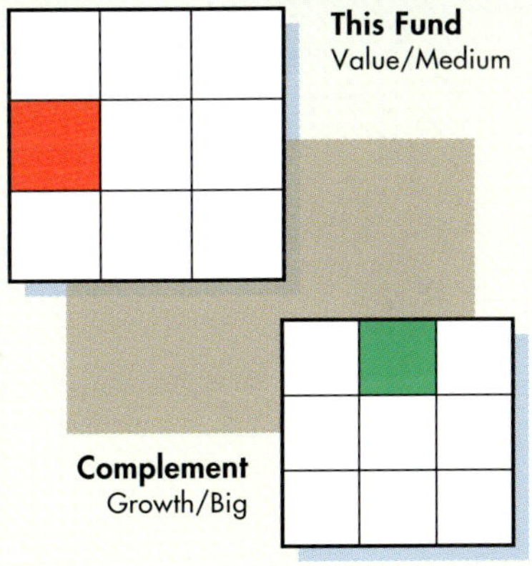

How to achieve the competing goals of growth and stability? Diversify, says this Calgary-based team. This is an odd mid-cap fund: It owns a slew of high-growth, low-priced companies in the $150-$500 million market cap range. But it also keeps a chunk of money in stable, higher-yielding big cap companies. On average, the fund ends up with the best of both worlds. It's holdings sport impressive profit margins (18% return on equity versus 15% for the TSE) with low debt and greater stability.

They're not market timers, but the team does have a view on where interest rates, corporate profits and, ultimately, stocks, are headed: down, up, and up. With Canada making such impressive fiscal gains, our high real interest rates are bound to fall – providing support for stocks. Trouble is, many good stocks are overpriced now. That's especially true in the US (this fund generally maximizes the foreign content at just under 20%). Indeed, the US holdings have been a relative weak spot for the fund. Big wins at home have come from oil service stocks, more obscure growth companies like Apex Land, and a few junior oils. That's an area that promises to deliver the big returns in the future for this stellar, efficient, all-season fund.

ELLIOTT & PAGE EQUITY FUND

Nereo Piticco (1993)/PCA Associates

RRSP

RATING

CONSISTENCY

Performance Trend

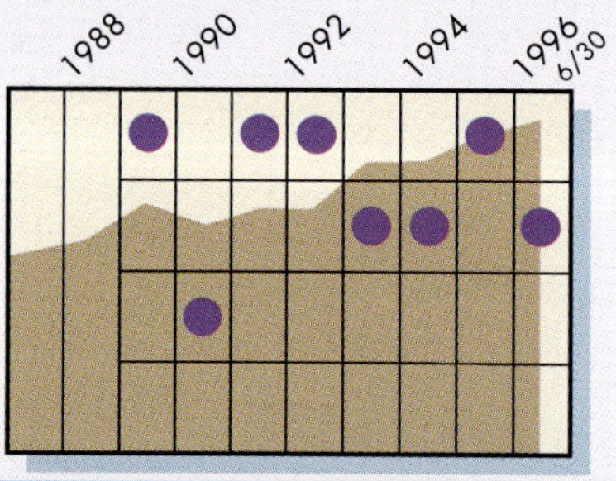

RISK

How often GICs performed better	2 years in 7
How often fund lost money	2 years in 7
Worst year's rate of return	-12.5% (1990)

EFFICIENCY

Management expense/ $100 $1.89

STYLE

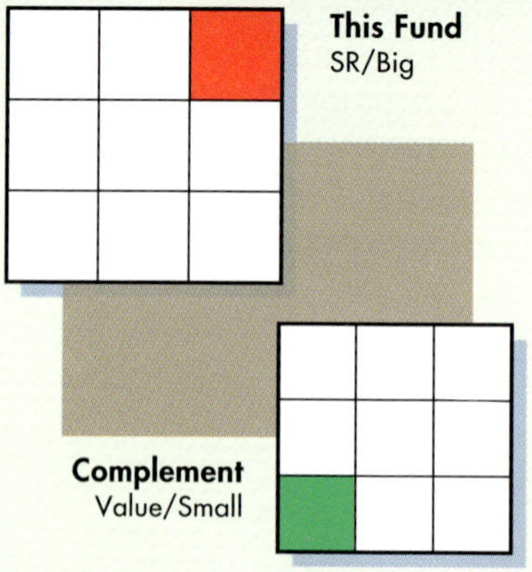

The team at Elliott & Page believe that they can grow this domestic fund without growth in our domestic economy. They won't do it by investing abroad or holding cash like some funds. If history is any indication, they'll do it by trading the right big-company stocks at just the right time.

These active stock traders are thematic sector rotators – a big difference from traditional value or growth funds. So Elliott & Page can offer powerful diversification from other fund families.

Their late-cycle theme today is premised on little or no domestic economic growth, thanks to severe government spending cuts. So growth will only come from exports as our southern neighbours' economy revs up again. Export-oriented cyclicals and resource plays dominate the equity side of this fund.

As usual, there's almost no idle cash in the fund to mess up investors' asset allocation plans. Interestingly though, a fifth of the fund is held in defensive stocks (Seagram, Loewen Group, NorTel, and others) just to hedge the rest of the fund from downturns. But that could all change in a heartbeat because these managers turn their portfolio over 4 times annually.

The only constant is a short list of big-cap names – and a big tax bill from all the profits realized – making this an ideal RSP fund.

NEW

TRADEX EQUITY FUND

RRSP

Ian Mottershead + team (inception)/PH&N

RATING

CONSISTENCY

Performance Trend

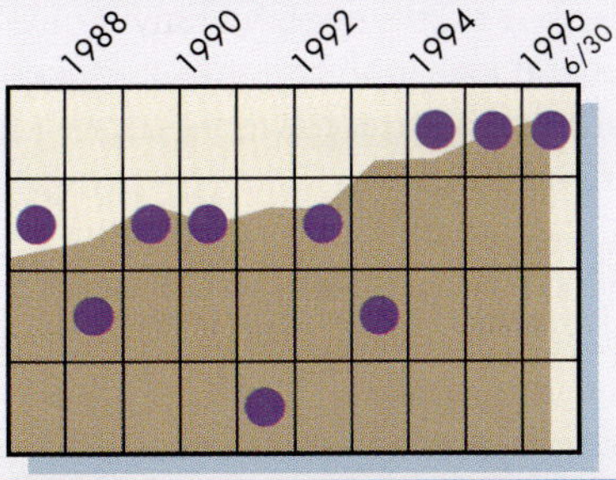

RISK

How often GICs performed better	5 years in 13
How often fund lost money	1 year in 13
Worst year's rate of return	-9.4% (1990)

EFFICIENCY

Management expense/ $100 $1.39

STYLE

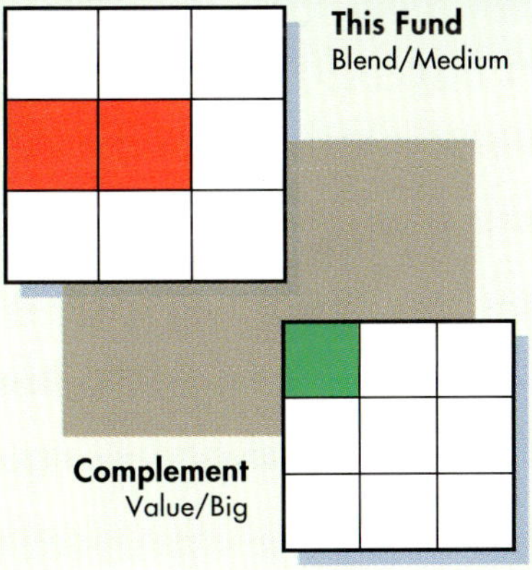

Tradex Funds are available only to civil servants in Canada. This one qualified for this edition of the book before an announcement came out that it would be closed to new investors. PH&N, the fund's advisor, announced that it was no longer interested in adding new clients in any third party arrangement (like the one with Tradex). Too bad. If you hold this fund, keep it. If you're a civil servant, get to know Tradex. They've got a quality line-up of other managers.

This one qualified because of steady wins with moves like remaining fully invested, owning funeral and wealth management companies, and timing some technology stocks just right.

NEW

EMPIRE PREMIER EQUITY FUND 1

Catharina van Berkel/Empire Life

RRSP

RATING

★ ★ ★

CONSISTENCY

Performance Trend

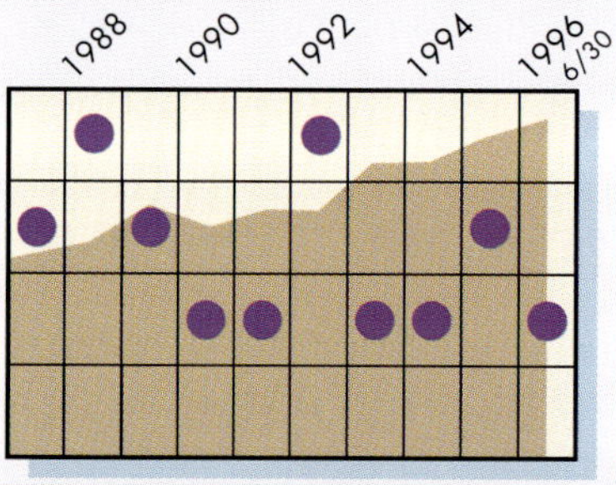

RISK

How often GICs performed better	5 years in 13
How often fund lost money	3 years in 13
Worst year's rate of return	-12.8% (1990)

EFFICIENCY

Management expense/ $100 $1.54

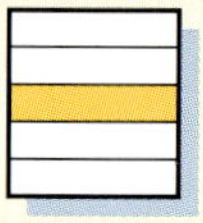

STYLE

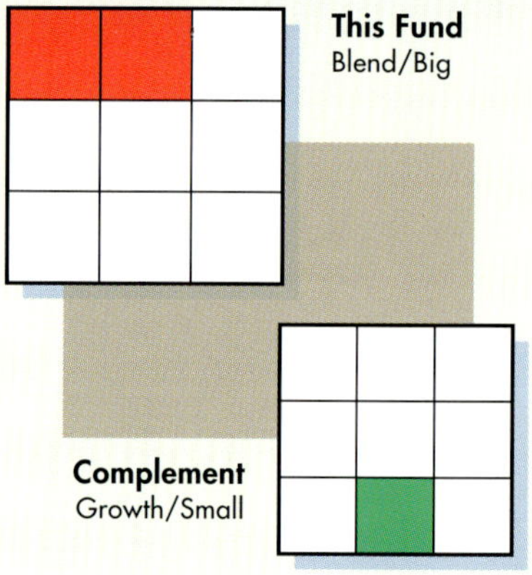

Insurance companies tend to really deliver with a particular style of fund in the Canadian marketplace: well diversified (but actively managed), big cap, conservative, and with low expenses. This book highlights several that fit this mould, and the two funds featured from Empire Life are no exception. This one's available on a front-end load basis only. Van Berkel is a bottom-up manager who likes to think of her own approach in much the same way as Trimark's TV ads portray their managers – diligent company investigators. She too buys businesses, not stocks, a distinction that may be lost off Bay Street. The expression simply means that she is not troubled by near-term perceptions of a company. She believes in a longer holding period, thinking that eventually true value can be realized. The fund offers a good index alternative for the conservative insurance company client.

RRSP

UNITED CANADIAN EQUITY FUND

Kiki Delaney (1992)/C.A. Delaney Capital

RATING

★ ★ ★

CONSISTENCY

Performance Trend

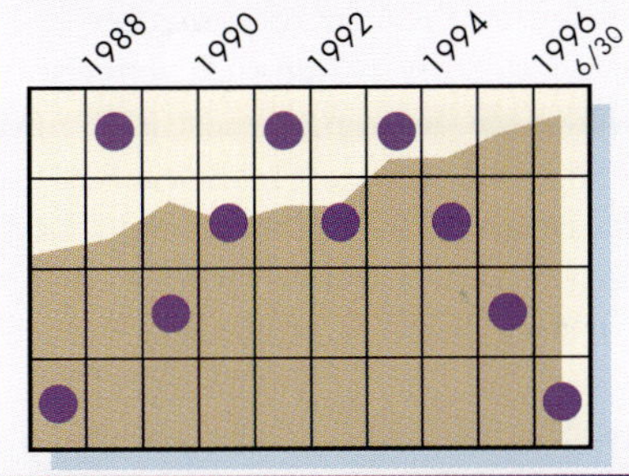

RISK

How often GICs performed better	5 years in 14
How often fund lost money	4 years in 14
Worst year's rate of return	-9.3% (1990)

EFFICIENCY

Management expense/ $100 $2.34

STYLE

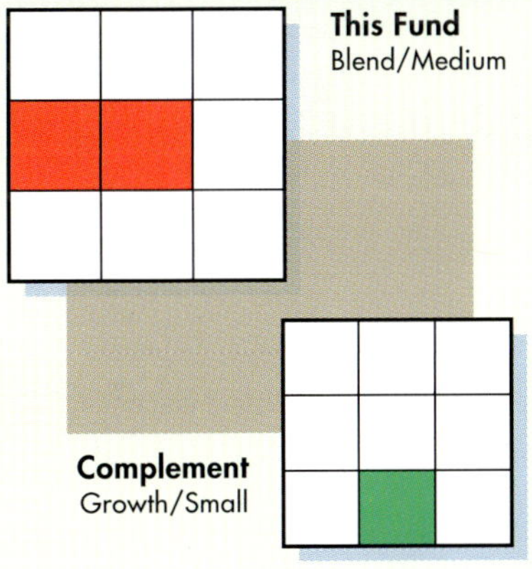

Spending 90% of her time on specific company research leads Kiki Delaney to enough growth companies that she can find a few that are bargains. But her definition of value is flexible; a 'buy' must have an attractive relative price versus competitors or substitutes and versus history. Take Cameco, the Saskatchewan uranium producer whose success is well known. Most strict P/E or price/book value shoppers avoid the stock because it's expensive in those terms. But Delaney and her team say the scarcity value of Cameco's rare and precious uranium isn't reflected in the company's book value. They've sold part of the fund's big position into the strength as the stock has climbed.

Still, the lesser time spent on macro thinking is critical. From analysis of big-picture trends she gleans insights about themes that will drive stocks. Current themes or trends include cost containment, emerging market growth, and agriculture. These ideas drive the stock research and have produced wins in John Deere and Agrium, for example.

Note that this fund's excellent record under its prior managers (Gerry Coleman and Jerry Javasky, now with Mackenzie's Ivy family) has helped it earn a place on the *Top Funds* list.

NEW

EMPIRE ELITE EQUITY FUND 5

Catharina van Berkel/Empire Life

RRSP

RATING

★ ★ ★

CONSISTENCY

Performance Trend

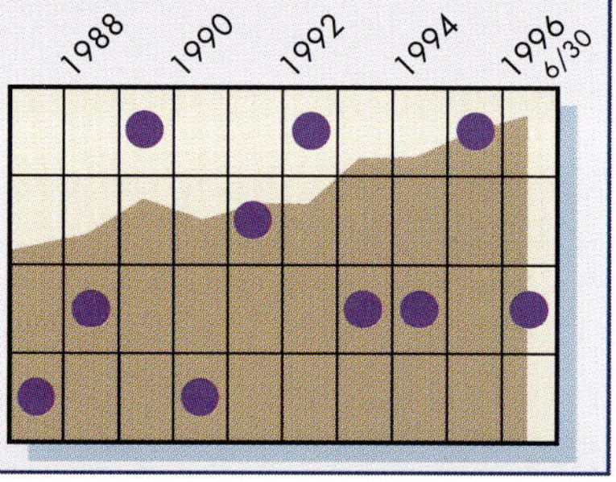

RISK

How often GICs performed better	5 years in 13
How often fund lost money	3 years in 13
Worst year's rate of return	-18.2% (1990)

EFFICIENCY

Management expense/ $100 $2.57

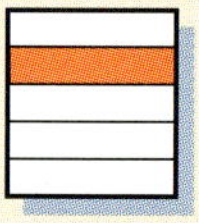

STYLE

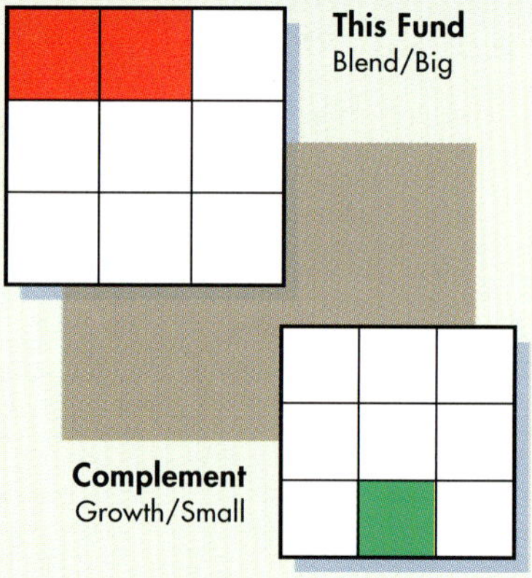

This one's much the same as Equity Premiere Equity Fund 1, except that it's available only on a back-end load basis. Insurance companies tend to really deliver with a particular style of fund in the Canadian marketplace: well diversified (but actively managed), big cap, conservative, and with low expenses. This book highlights several that fit this mould, and the two funds featured from Empire Life are no exception. Van Berkel is a bottom-up manager who likes to think of her own approach in much the same way as Trimark's TV ads portray their managers – diligent company investigators. She too buys businesses, not stocks, a distinction that may be lost off Bay Street. The expression simply means that she is not troubled by near-term perceptions of a company. She believes in a longer holding period, thinking that eventually true value can be realized. The fund offers a good index alternative for the conservative insurance company client.

NEW

RRSP

C.I. CANADIAN GROWTH FUND

John Zechner (inception)/J. Zechner Assoc.

RATING

★ ★ ★

CONSISTENCY

Performance Trend

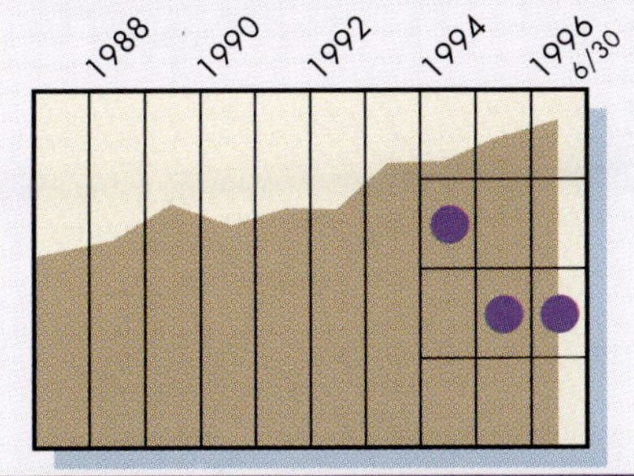

RISK

How often GICs performed better	1 year in 2
How often fund lost money	0 years in 2
Worst year's rate of return	0.4% [1994]

EFFICIENCY

Management expense/ $100 $2.40

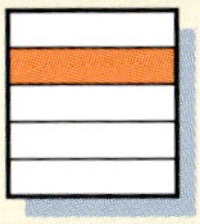

STYLE

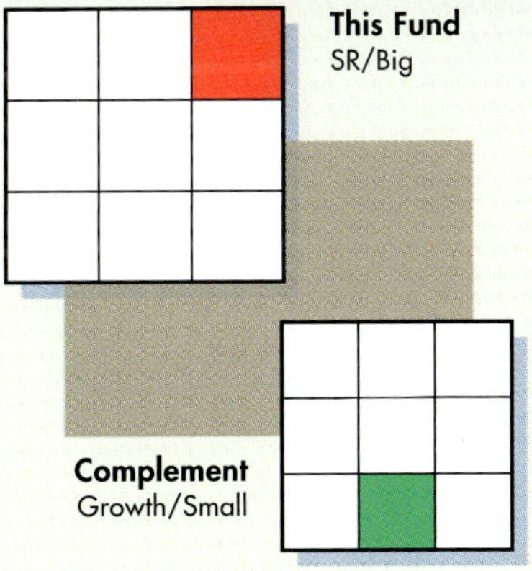

If the market falls soon, John Zechner's clients will be riding high. He's armed this opportunistic fund with a recent 30% cash war chest to buy stocks cheap, if he gets the chance. That's a bold move because the fund would likely lag a market rally right now.

His defensiveness is a function of the liquidity infusion our markets have received, both locally and from abroad. Now, he foresees diminished liquidity in the stock market.

So he's been selling cyclicals and some pricey gold and base-metals stocks. Zechner argues that market sentiment is far too positive, and that some earnings disappointments are coming in as a result of wage gains. He's holding and adding to growth names, especially in the technology area, such as PC Docs, Mitel, and Newbridge Networks. He's also holding on to defensive groups like oils, where his biggest name is CanOxy.

But gold stocks are trading at higher-than-normal valuations to cash flow, so he's out of most, except for Kinross Gold. Not that he's bearish on the shiny metal, he just thinks some of the names have become too pricey.

His only mistake in the past few years has been holding cash levels in the high teens a couple of times during what continued to be a rising market. Today's higher cash levels could make or break this fund, but history suggests that Zechner is never wrong for long.

TRIMARK RSP EQUITY FUND

Vito Maida and Wally Kusters (1995) + team/Trimark

RRSP

RATING

CONSISTENCY

Performance Trend

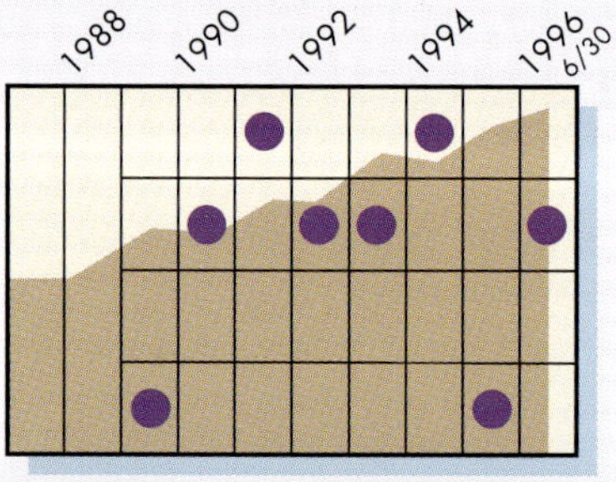

RISK

How often GICs performed better	3 years in 7
How often fund lost money	1 year in 7
Worst year's rate of return	-11.2% (1990)

EFFICIENCY

Management expense/ $100 $2.00

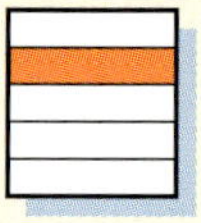

STYLE

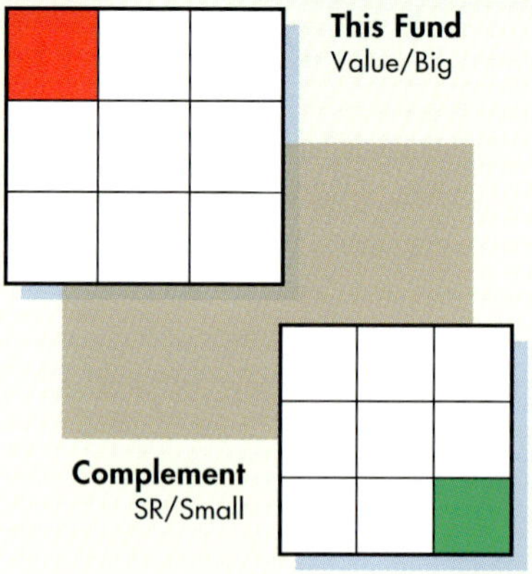

At an annual expense clip of 2.0%, in line with industry averages, this is a rear-load fund with a 9-year declining redemption schedule, but is otherwise very similar to Trimark Canadian – a front-end powerhouse with a 14-year track record.

Some think Trimark is too big to beat the market in Canada. They're wrong. It's true, the Trimark team manages some $5.2 billion in Canadian equities across all funds. So investors wonder how the team, which is largely new in the past few years, will be able to keep a tight list of just 40 investments, as the money keeps pouring in. At some level, of course, size does become an issue.

But there's no evidence of it yet. New team members Vito Maida and Wally Kusters have successfully re-jigged the portfolio since their arrival in 1995. They've replaced about 10 names and reduced cash levels, in addition to handling the torrent of cash from spectacular net unit sales.

The Trimark approach is less about stock picking and more about business buying. Before any purchase they do more legwork on a company's business than would a consultant. They meet everybody – managers, competitors, and executives – before and after buying. When they like a company they buy a big piece of it. They recently held more than 10% of Canfor, Crestbrook, and Co-Steel, to name just a few. Each exemplifies their goals by being an attractively priced, low-cost leader.

PHILLIPS HAGER & NORTH CANADIAN EQUITY FUND

RRSP

Ian Mottershead + team (inception)/PH&N

RATING

★ ★ ★

CONSISTENCY

Performance Trend

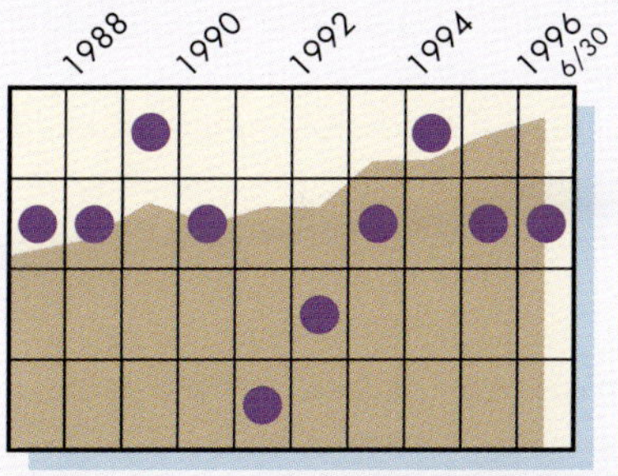

RISK

How often GICs performed better	7 years in 14
How often fund lost money	3 years in 14
Worst year's rate of return	-10.4% (1990)

EFFICIENCY

Management expense/ $100 $1.13

STYLE

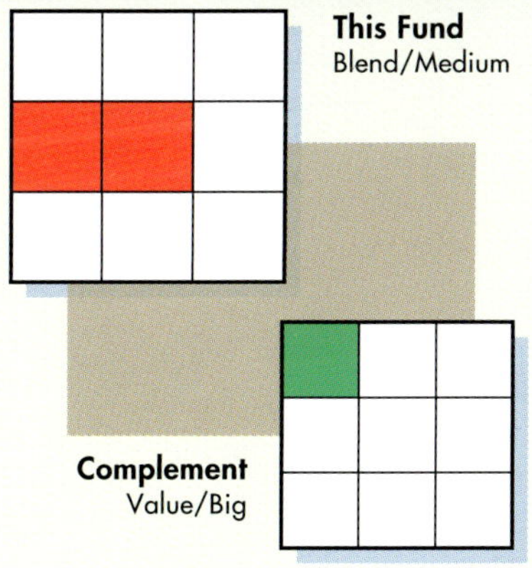

It's rare to see a domestic stock team embody so many positive qualities – and execute them all well. PH&N's Canadian equity team, led by Ian Mottershead, really do use both top-down and bottom-up approaches to finding themes – and then picking stocks.

And, they're contrarian at times – helping explain their better-than-most performance. Here is an example. They love the demographics of the wealth management industry, so they have made big gains on long holds like Mackenzie, Trimark, and AGF. And they're wild about technology, but sold Newbridge when it got a bit rich – only to buy it back cheap.

PH&N has always been active in the Oil & Gas sector, not because they think gas prices will soar, but because sometimes companies in this sector get mispriced – especially during times of market turmoil. The bargains that surface are fertile ground for the equity team. In many ways, they can be described as both growth and value in their approach to picking stocks. Add a low MER and this is a consistent fund from a strong family.

ALTAMIRA CAPITAL GROWTH FUND

Ian Ainsworth (1993) + Ian Joseph (1991)/Altamira

RRSP

RATING

★ ★ ★

CONSISTENCY

Performance Trend

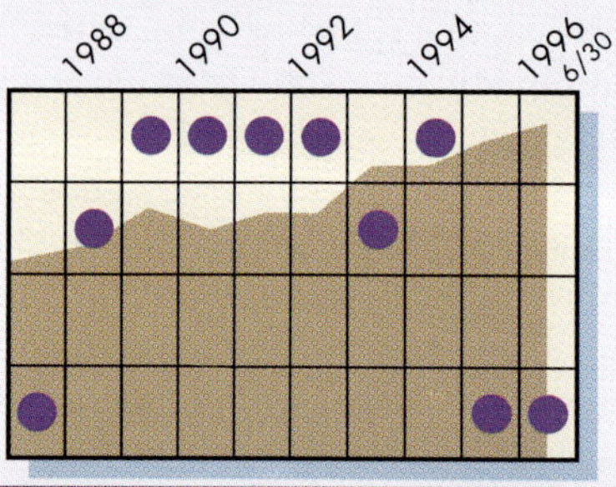

RISK

How often GICs performed better	5 years in 14
How often fund lost money	3 years in 14
Worst year's rate of return	-7.2% (1987)

EFFICIENCY

Management expense/ $100 $2.02

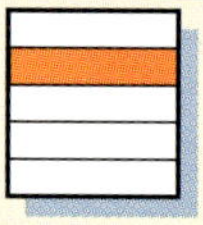

STYLE

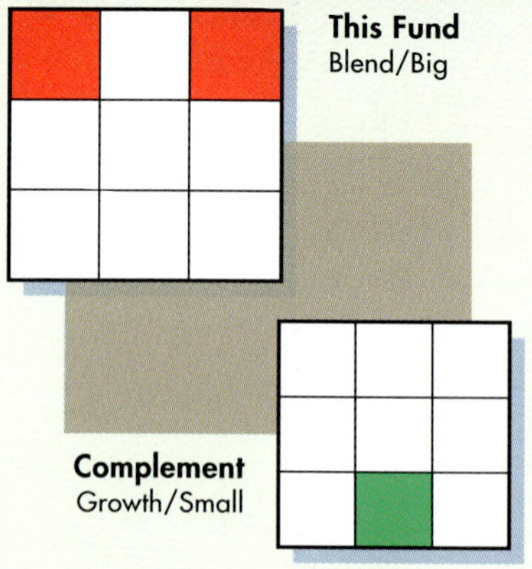

This is a decidedly more aggressive fund lately than it has been for much of its decade-long history. The current managers are bold movers, whose great bullishness on natural resources is manifested in a giant 67% exposure to the group as a portion of Canadian stock exposure. A couple of factors attract Joseph and Ainsworth to groups like metals, gold, and trees; first, a real surge in growth in the latter part of our economic cycle coming partly from growth in Europe and Japan. This sustainable economic uptick can provide real demand pressure for natural resources worldwide, they say. The second factor that will help Canada's natural resource stocks perform well is a cheap Canadian dollar, allowing for competitive exports. And with an efficient and productive group of resource companies here at home, Canada offers great leverage to global growth.

It's that heavy focus that hurt the fund for a time in 1996 – an overweight position in gold and cyclical stocks in particular. But it's times like these, when managers' convictions are tested, that funds tend to really slingshot back.

NEW

RRSP

ROYFUND CANADIAN EQUITY FUND

John Embry/Royal Bank Investment Management

RATING

★ ★ ★

CONSISTENCY

Performance Trend

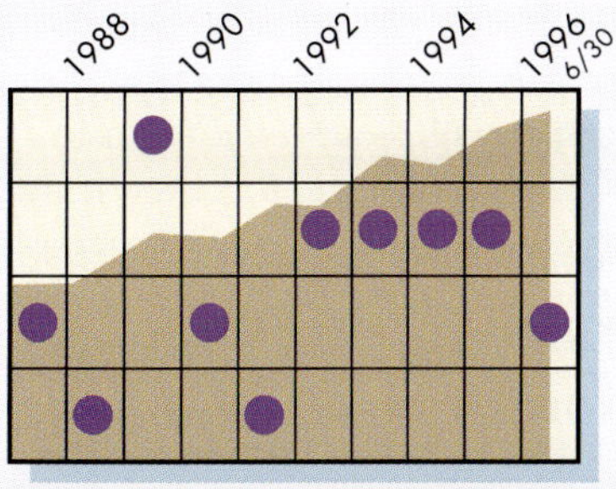

RISK

How often GICs performed better	6 years in 13
How often fund lost money	3 years in 13
Worst year's rate of return	-14.7% (1990)

EFFICIENCY

Management expense/ $100 $2.09

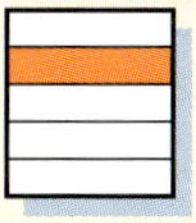

STYLE

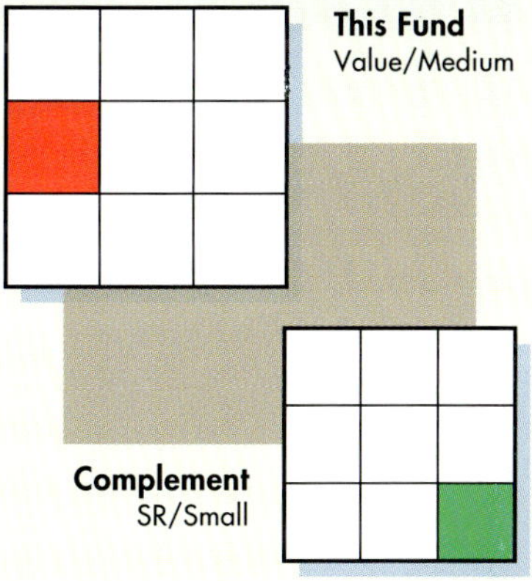

This Fund
Value/Medium

Complement
SR/Small

Like most bank funds, this fund is anything but exciting. But look closely and you'll see a fund whose performance has been remarkably consistent, especially compared to its true peer group of 'closet indexers' – funds whose sector weightings don't deviate much from the TSE weights. Embry and the 8-member team are essentially conservative. They stick to bigger-name companies, buy them at low prices, and reap handsome yields. They know that their clients are mostly savers, not aggressive investors.

But this fund is better at stock picking than big names like Trimark – not because it makes more money, it doesn't. Rather, RoyFund beats its benchmark by more – some 3 percentage points annually over the past 3 years – when compared to a cluster of 10 near-identical fund peers. The huge value added has come from both timely moves into gold and better stock picking within other sectors.

Even if they're wrong on the resource push, they won't be far off. This all-weather fund has sailed through good and bad markets consistently ahead of the pack – without ever being on top in any one year.

GBC CANADIAN GROWTH FUND

Ian Soutar + team (inception)/Pembroke Management

RRSP

EQUITY-CANADIAN SMALL-CAP

RATING

★★★★★

CONSISTENCY

Performance Trend

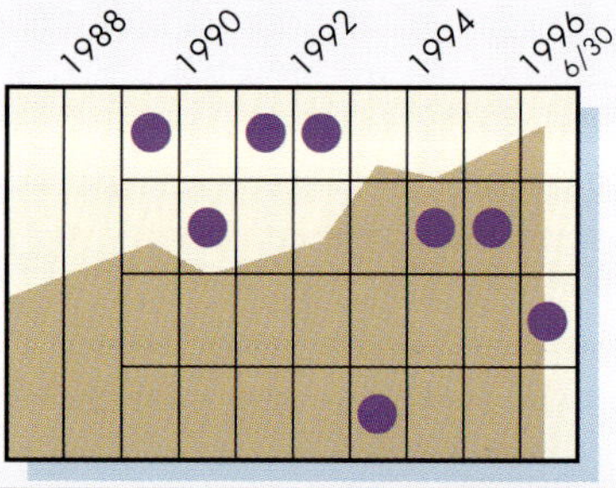

RISK

How often GICs performed better	2 years in 7
How often fund lost money	2 years in 7
Worst year's rate of return	-13.6% (1990)

EFFICIENCY

Management expense/ $100 $1.89

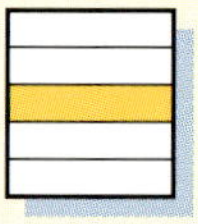

STYLE

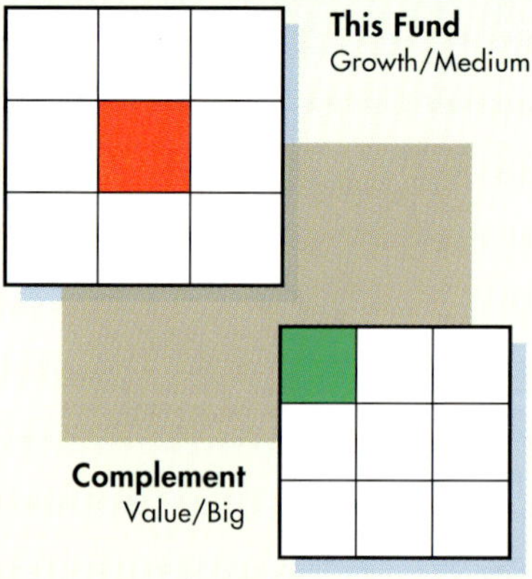

If you had the time, this is how you'd pick stocks for yourself. You'd stick to smaller companies, the ones that haven't yet attracted the attention of Bay Street analysts. There you'd find cheaper companies with faster growth rates, companies with real unit growth. You wouldn't waste your time trying to forecast the near-term direction of the stock market. And you'd diversify broadly so you weren't betting on the price of oil or some such thing.

Then, when you had a list of great companies, you'd hold them forever. Because the only way you really make money in Canada is if you keep it. Selling your winners forces you to pay tax, so less money's available to compound for you. In short, you'd emulate Ian Soutar's approach with this fund. Some of the winners he owns now include golds Franco-Nevada, Greenstone and Kinross. In the energy group there's Berkely, Cimarron, Morrison and Renaissance. Then there's lots of exciting stories in technology, health care and communications, including long-held winners GEAC, Hummingbird, AltaGenetics, ACTel and others.

This fund, with its broad diversification and typical 17%-20% US exposure, is uniquely able to mitigate the risk usually associated with small-stock investing.

RRSP

BISSETT SMALL-CAP FUND

David Bissett (inception)/Bissett & Associates

RATING

CONSISTENCY

Performance Trend

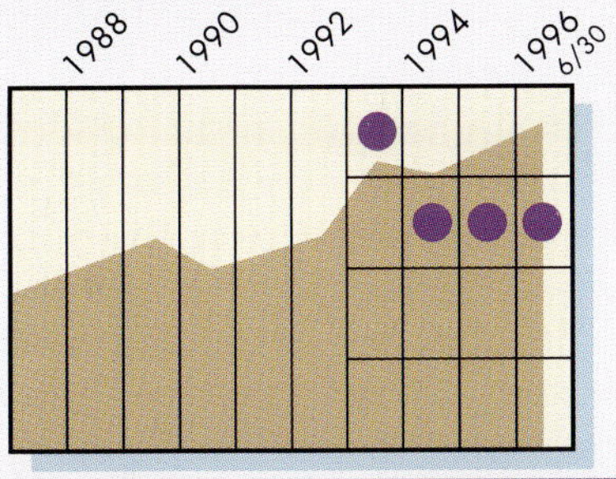

RISK

How often GICs performed better	1 year in 3
How often fund lost money	1 year in 3
Worst year's rate of return	-8.6% (1994)

EFFICIENCY

Management expense/ $100 $2.00

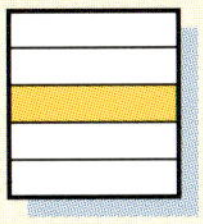

STYLE

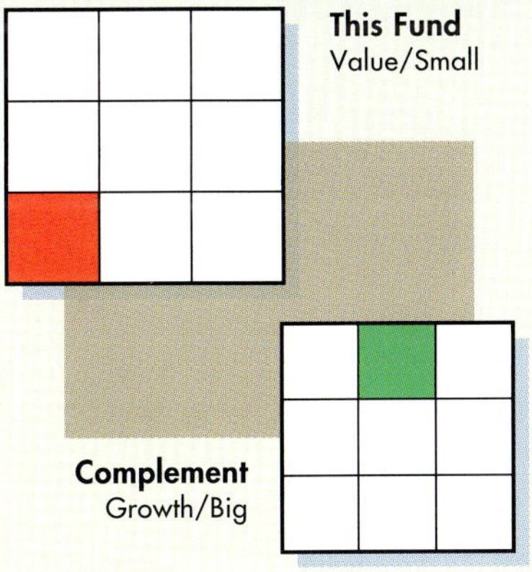

Everything's set for lower interest rates in Canada, and that's one of the positives reinforcing a great stock market outlook, says Dave Bissett. But stocks have already discounted all the good news, and at the time of writing, are pretty fully valued – even after the summer correction. So this small-stock fund has to search for growth in obscure, out-of-the-way places. Thankfully, there are a slew of high-growth, low-priced companies in the $150-$500 million market cap range.

But rather than dig too deep into the obscure, Bissett avoids the penny-stock hypes that were on a tear in 1996. He avoids the shell companies with turnaround promises and focuses on good businesses with a history of earnings and proven management – something not all small-cap funds do.

Ultimately, he ends up with companies like Winpak, ATS Automated Tooling Systems, and Mosaid Technologies. Since he's often early on these success stories, he typically sells into the strength that follows – as he did with a big win in Western Star Trucks. But that's what you pay him for; to hunt for quality businesses, and find them before Bay Street does.

This fund, now finally available in Ontario, is available from brokers with a modest 2% front-end load.

NEW

SCEPTRE EQUITY GROWTH FUND

Allan Jacobs (1993)/Sceptre Investment Counsel

RRSP

RATING

★ ★ ★ ★

CONSISTENCY

Performance Trend

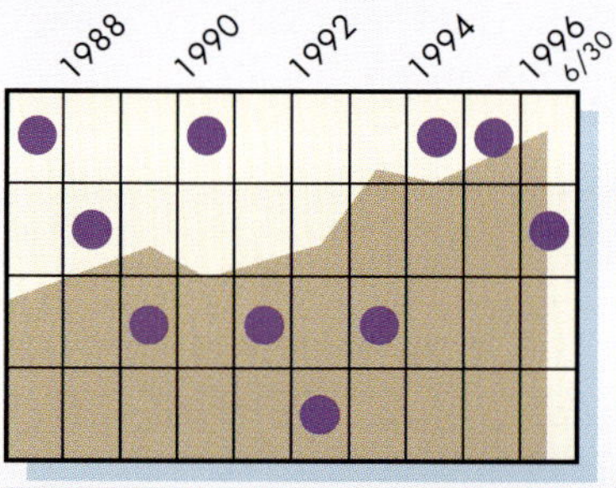

RISK

How often GICs performed better	4 years in 9
How often fund lost money	2 years in 9
Worst year's rate of return	-9.6% (1990)

EFFICIENCY

Management expense/ $100 $1.68

STYLE

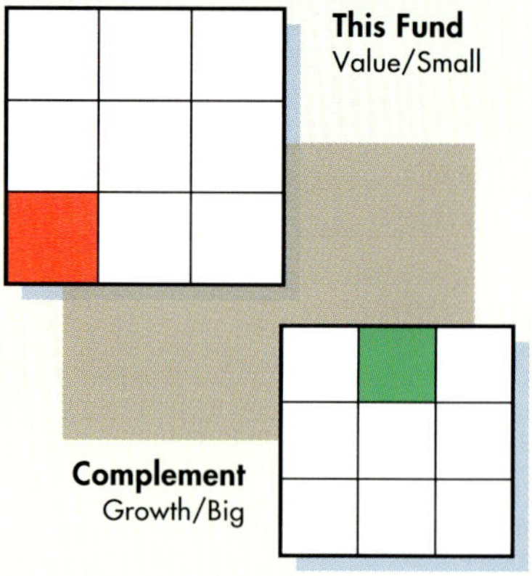

Don't expect these heady returns to continue forever, says Allan Jacobs. In his first three years at the helm, the fund grew at a 28% annual clip, just about triple the return of its benchmark small-cap index. And he didn't do it all in one hot year by owning mining exploration stocks.

The fund's success has been real; it's a steady performer in up and down markets, and it makes no big commodity price bets (it was underweight gold stocks during their spectacular 1996 rally). Instead, South African-born Jacobs screens the cheapest stocks for earnings momentum. He ends up with companies you've never heard of – all with impressive growth and relative obscurity on Bay Street.

One of his favourites still includes YBM Magnex, a magnet technology company doing business in Hungary and making fistfuls of money. Even after tripling, the stock (at time of writing) still trades at a P/E ratio of just 11 times trailing earnings – far less than the market and just half its annual earnings growth rate.

With single-digit P/Es and impressive growth rates, his holdings make one wonder why anyone would pay top dollar for some mature big-cap company with dim earnings growth prospects.

NEW

UNITED CANADIAN GROWTH FUND

RRSP

Lynn Miller (1992)/C.A. Delaney Capital

RATING

★★★★

CONSISTENCY

Performance Trend

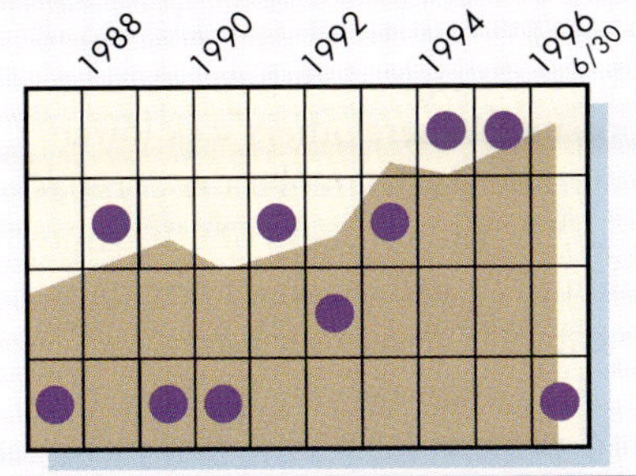

RISK

How often GICs performed better	4 years in 13
How often fund lost money	3 years in 13
Worst year's rate of return	-21.2% (1990)

EFFICIENCY

Management expense/ $100 $2.46

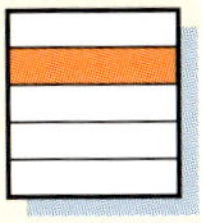

STYLE

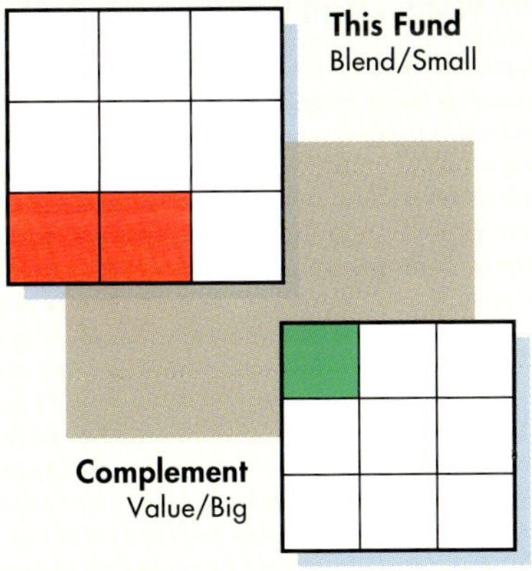

A few big-picture theme ideas and tons of bottom-up stock selection drive the impressive returns for this fund since its manager change in 1992. But holders should expect less impressive results going forward, says Miller, who's cautious on markets now and has built up an 18% cash reserve. The fund was closed to new investors in 1996.

Though improvements in Canada's fiscal situation (especially at the provincial level) are encouraging, Miller believes there's probably enough growth in the US to drive interest rates up in Canada. While that could be tough on stocks generally, there are always attractive names that can be found.

Energy and energy service stocks have been big winners for the fund and remain the most overweight group. Here's why. Natural gas prices are depressed now, partly because of delivery problems in meeting American demand. But more pipeline capacity is coming. And our supply is dwindling (depressed prices mean less exploration). When deliverable US demand picks up and supply tightens, prices should move up. Lynn Miller loves bargains, and our oil service stocks trade at just half the multiples of comparable US companies.

But there's much more to this story than a bet on gas prices. It's a bottom-up, stock-by-stock, value fund appropriate for growth investors.

PRUDENTIAL DIVIDEND FUND OF CANADA

Jackee Pratt (1995)/Prudential

RRSP

RATING

★ ★ ★ ★ ★

CONSISTENCY

Performance Trend

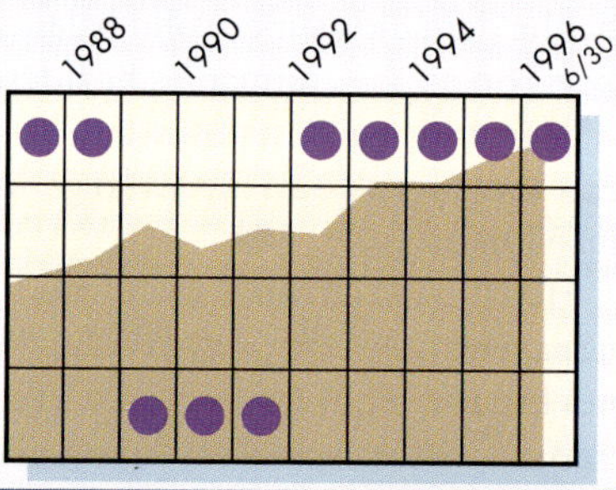

RISK

How often GICs performed better	5 years in 9
How often fund lost money	1 year in 9
Worst year's rate of return	-9.3% (1990)

EFFICIENCY

Management expense/ $100 $1.50

STYLE

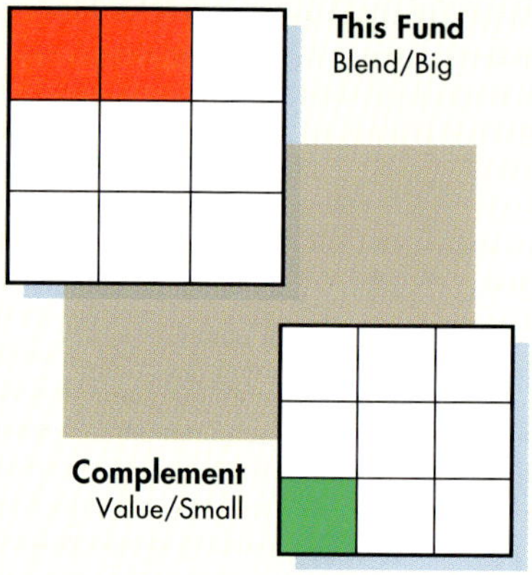

This is a total return fund for conservative investors. Pratt, who inherited this portfolio from departed star Veronika Hirsch, hasn't changed things much. There's still a focus on (mostly high-yielding) common stocks. Of course, you'll find big banks in the portfolio as well as some utilities and pipelines – standard fare for any dividend fund. But Pratt is looking for capital gains to drive this fund – dividends are a lesser consideration. The fund is also helped by a low management expense ratio – a boon that will come in handy during tough times – when interest rates creep up. While common stocks do generally have less sensitivity to rate changes, dividend funds that own bank and utility common shares can still feel the punishment from higher interest rates.

PHILLIPS HAGER & NORTH DIVIDEND INCOME FUND

RRSP

Ian Mottershead + team (inception)/PH&N

RATING

CONSISTENCY

Performance Trend

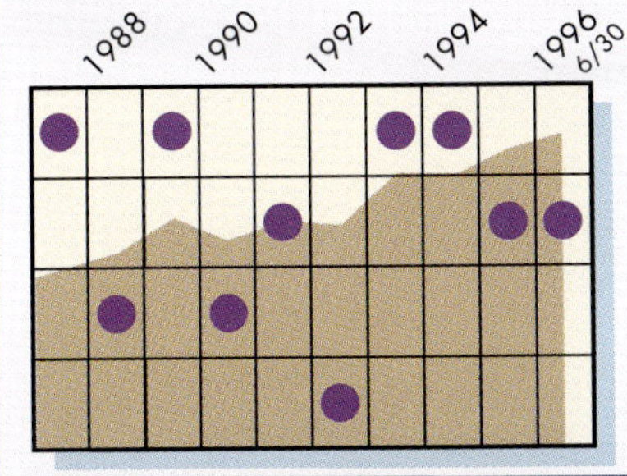

RISK

How often GICs performed better	6 years in 14
How often fund lost money	2 years in 14
Worst year's rate of return	-6.0% (1990)

EFFICIENCY

Management expense/ $100 $1.19

STYLE

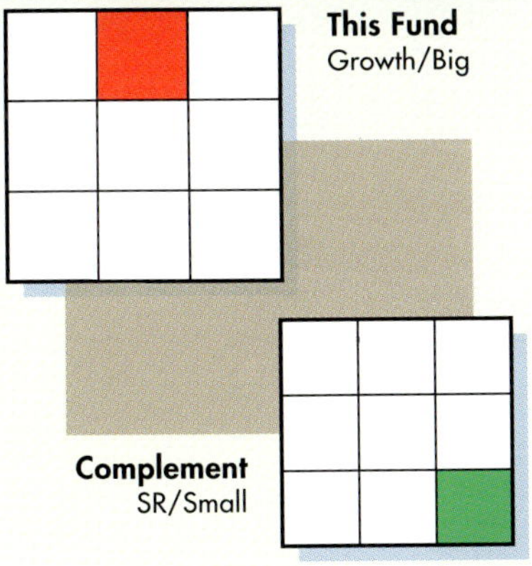

In this fund, you see the melding of a lot of different disciplines from PH&N: you get interest rate calls from Tony Gage and four other CFA fixed-income income team members (big by any standard). Plus, you get sector calls from natural resource experts and high-yielding stock picks from the rest of the equity team of 11 professionals.

All that expertise results in a steady, conservative dividend fund that prospers in good times and (perhaps more importantly to the conservative clients for which this fund is geared) excels in bad markets too.

The fund has earned a second quartile rank overall for performance through the past four falling markets in Canadian stocks. Holding up well in weak times is essential for the conservative investor. Typical of its group, this fund is rife with high-yielding common stocks. There is a measure of interest rate sensitivity in this fund and its managers are not all that bullish on interest rates just yet in Canada. As of the third quarter of 1996, they were a touch bearish on rates but felt that the low inflation environment of 1996 and 1997 would continue to be great for investors.

20/20 DIVIDEND FUND

Gordon MacDougall (inception) + Martin Gerber/CC&L

RRSP

RATING

★★★★½

CONSISTENCY

Performance Trend

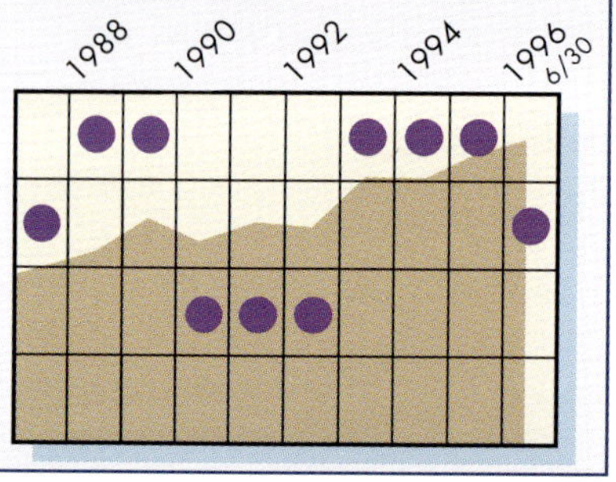

RISK

How often GICs performed better	4 years in 9
How often fund lost money	1 year in 9
Worst year's rate of return	-5.1% (1990)

EFFICIENCY

Management expense/ $100 $1.98

STYLE

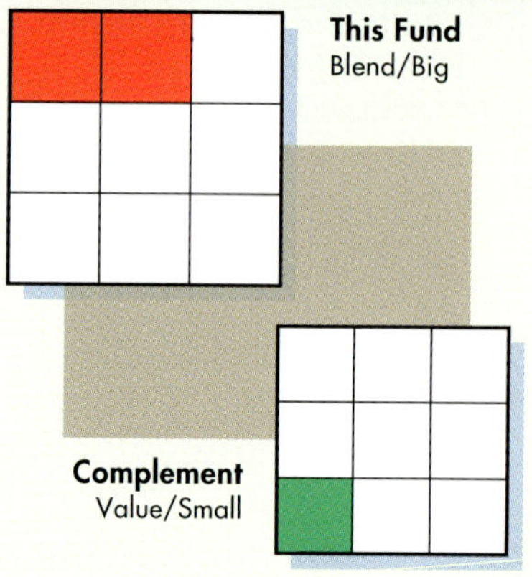

Utilities have lagged banks substantially during the Fall 96 rally. True to form, Connor, Clark & Lunn avoided the utilities and made out well. That's the kind of move this fund makes. It doesn't search for the highest-yielding issues, it searches for ways to beat the TSE modestly (after fees) with less risk.

It would be wrong to think that 20/20 Dividend is just a preferred-share fund. It's really a conservative common-stock fund with a little kick from a US high-yield component. Regardless of its category, the fund is impressive. The managers make no explicit interest-rate calls, but do exercise a cash build-up when attractive stocks can't be found.

As for the US portion, here's the thinking. California-based Riverside Capital Management runs a specialist high-yield bond mandate with about 15% of the fund's assets. The arrangement, which is rare in this category, adds currency and market diversification as well as annual expected returns on the order of 10% to 12%. The current yield on that portion of the fund is a steep 12% in US dollar terms.

Every stock in the portfolio pays a dividend, and all have better growth and value characteristics than the market generally. That's why the fund holds up well in comparison to the TSE, although its gross yield of just 4.2% hardly makes it an income fund.

RRSP

DYNAMIC DIVIDEND FUND

Lesley Beech (1991)/Goodman & Co.

RATING

★★★½

CONSISTENCY

Performance Trend

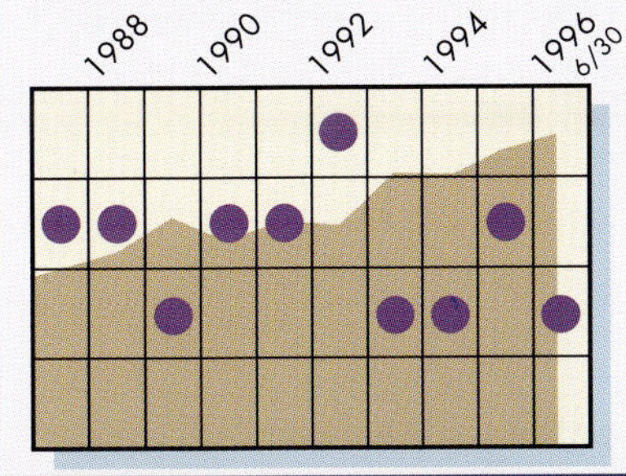

RISK

How often GICs performed better	5 years in 10
How often fund lost money	5 years in 10
Worst year's rate of return	-2.5% (1994)

EFFICIENCY

Management expense/ $100 $1.61

STYLE

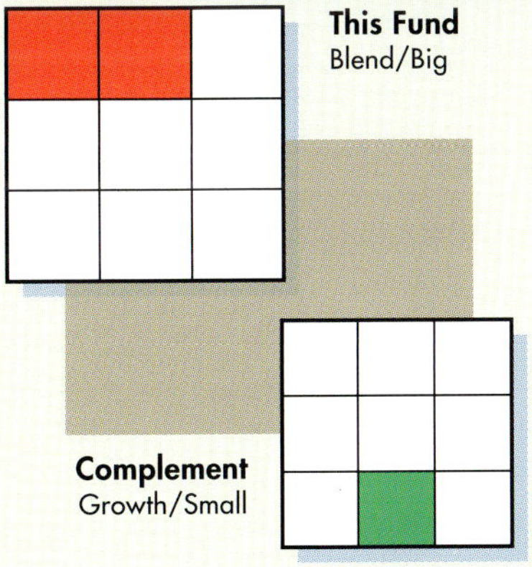

Lesley Beech can thank Fidelity, the Boston fund giant, for one of her wins this year. Fidelity's active lobbying on a mutual holding in a Gulf Canada preferred issue helped reinstate its dividend with arrears and prompted a huge credit rating upgrade.

But bigger wins were single-handed for Beech, like the Caldwell Partners preferreds she picked up for $5, which were recently fetching $12.50 after much stronger earnings. Stock selection is vital in a dividend fund.

The idea with this fund is to make a lot of dividend income – something few funds in the category actually do. Most of this fund's average 4% dividend payout comes from its 50% or so holdings of floating-rate preferreds. The floaters are liquid and have less interest-rate sensitivity than 'straight' preferreds – fixed dividend shares. Goodman & Co.'s bond whiz Norm Bengough adds interest-rate forecasting help to add value in this fund. His forecast these days is for rates to stay in a trading range. The fund's tax-advantaged payouts have generally been in line with GIC yields when compared on a tax-equivalent basis. But to get the tax benefits, the fund must be held outside an RRSP or RRIF account.

Even with astute interest rate calls and a few stock wins, this and all dividend funds struggle to overcome the annual expense burden. Dynamic Dividend's is below average at 1.61% – a positive for this solid fund.

MD GROWTH FUND

Templeton Management and Marvin & Palmer Associates

RRSP

RATING

CONSISTENCY

Performance Trend

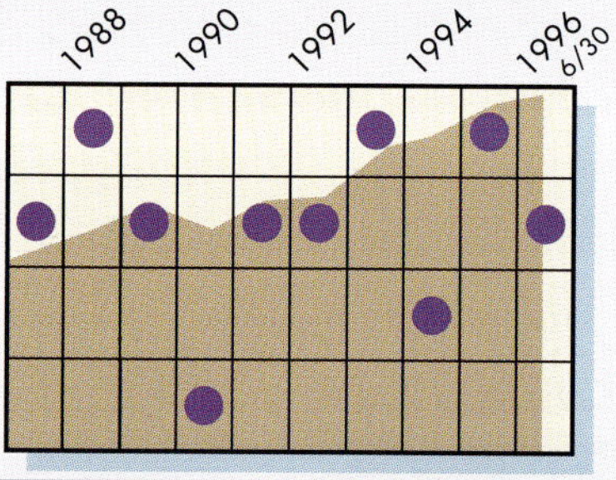

RISK

How often GICs performed better	4 years in 13
How often fund lost money	2 years in 13
Worst year's rate of return	-15.9% (1990)

EFFICIENCY

Management expense/ $100 $1.04

STYLE

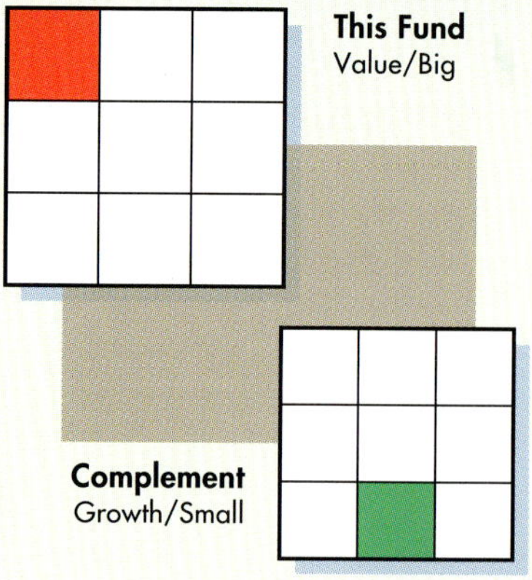

Medical school has finally paid off! Doctors and their families are able to buy this fund (essentially, it's a clone of the Templeton Growth Fund) for an annual expense ratio of just 1.04%, nearly a full percentage point cheaper than the rest of us. About 90% of the fund is managed by Templeton with a global mandate, and the balance goes to Marvin & Palmer – a firm with particular strength in emerging markets. The Templeton managers are selling stocks they've held since the beginning of time. It's been a year of change for the fund, as stock selections have matured, and price targets have been met. One of the groups being sold is banking, where gains averaged 50%. This is as good as things get for banks, say analysts on the fund, as loan loss provisions are nil, trading profits are at record levels, and interest rates have bottomed.

After profit-taking in the US, Hong Kong and the UK, the managers are buying European cyclical stocks in shipping and engineering, as well as forest products. The managers cite lots of attractive new names to buy now.

This is a core fund holding for any physician – its value style, broad diversification and efficient pricing structure make it a lay-up for long-term growth.

EQUITY-INTERNATIONAL

RRSP

SCEPTRE INTERNATIONAL FUND

Lennox McNeely (inception)/Sceptre

RATING

CONSISTENCY

Performance Trend

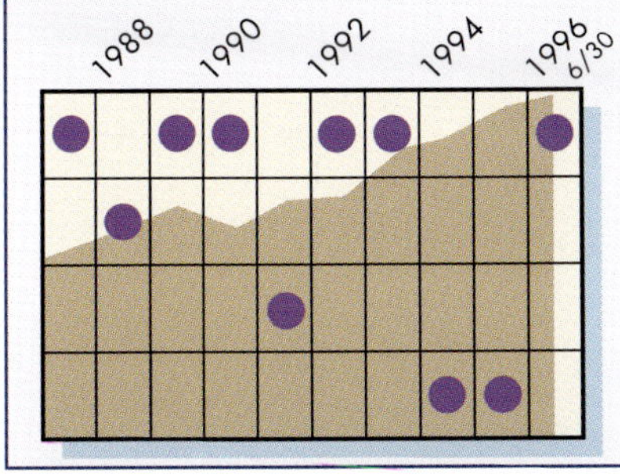

RISK

How often GICs performed better	4 years in 9
How often fund lost money	2 years in 9
Worst year's rate of return	-5.6% (1994)

EFFICIENCY

Management expense/ $100 $2.10

STYLE

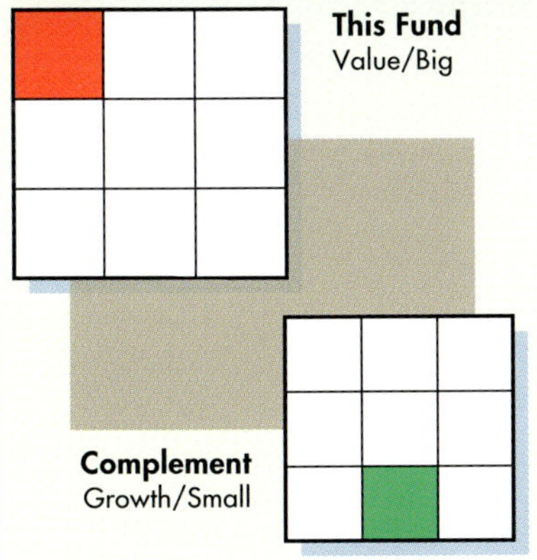

It's rare that a manager with a bearish outlook can excel when stock markets keep on climbing. But that's what Lennox McNeely manages to do with this special, under-appreciated fund. Though he's been dramatically underweight the US market as it has surged, he nonetheless continues to beat the Morgan Stanley World Index – by nearly 4 points in the first half of 1996, for example. But he's not the country-picking political whiz you'll find atop many global funds. He's just a stock picker. Sidekick Tariq Ahmad, their Asian manager, is responsible for fully 40% of this portfolio these days, because that much is invested in Asia and Japan.

This is a superb global choice for those bearish on the US or for those who already have a lot of Trimark Fund for example – which this one complements nicely. Interestingly, Sceptre funds are available from most brokers with a negotiable front-end load of up to 2%.

TRIMARK FUND
Robert Krembil, Richard Jenkins + team/Trimark

RRSP

RATING

★ ★ ★ ★

CONSISTENCY

Performance Trend

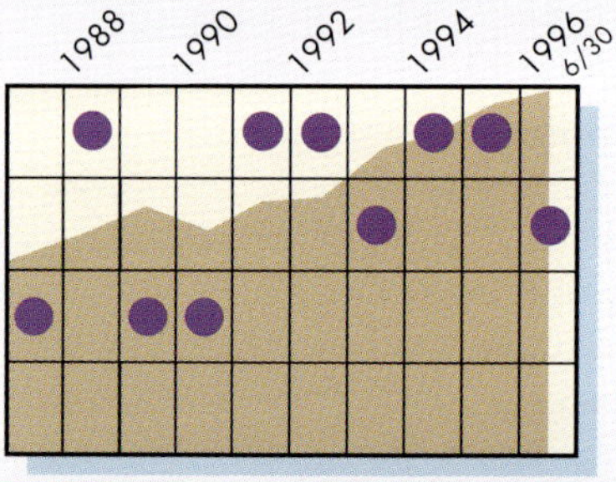

RISK

How often GICs performed better	3 years in 14
How often fund lost money	3 years in 14
Worst year's rate of return	-9.9% (1990)

EFFICIENCY

Management expense/ $100 $1.53

STYLE

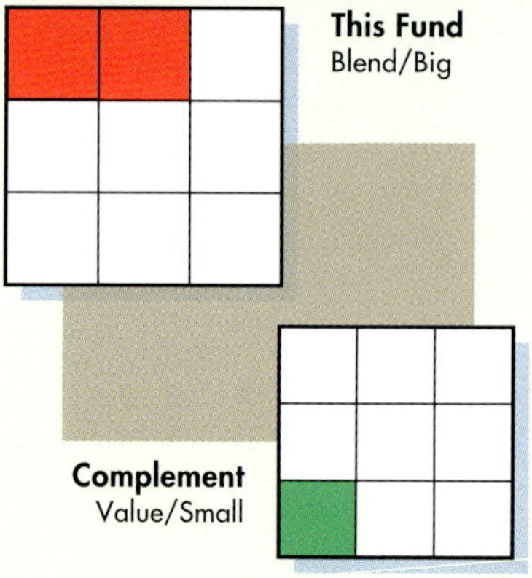

There are few money managers with as deep an understanding of technology as the team at Trimark. It's not that they load portfolios full of technology stocks. Rather, they can find businesses in any industry that are best at leveraging technology to improve quality, service, and price.

Trimark Fund is littered with scores of examples of companies that are becoming dominant in their industry, in part because they use technology better than their competitors. Trimark's understanding of technology helps them spot leaders in businesses as mundane as printing or shipping. While Trimark Fund isn't sensitive to interest rates or commodity prices, it would be sensitive to gyrations in the rich US equity market which makes up over 60% of the fund.

Are Trimark managers sweating the possibility of an end to the bull market? Not really. In fact, they'd likely appreciate the chance to add to their stock holdings during a pullback.

That's exactly when smart investors should be buying this low-cost, front-end load fund aggressively.

RRSP

TEMPLETON GROWTH FUND

Mark Holowesko (1988)/Templeton

RATING

★★★½

CONSISTENCY

Performance Trend

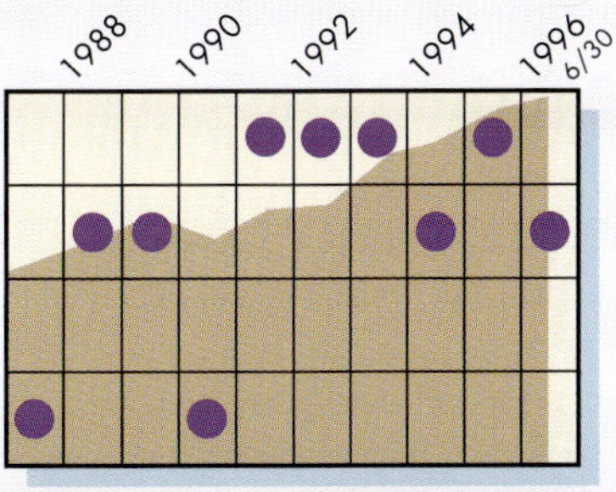

RISK

How often GICs performed better	4 years in 14
How often fund lost money	2 years in 14
Worst year's rate of return	-13.6% (1990)

EFFICIENCY

Management expense/ $100 $2.00

STYLE

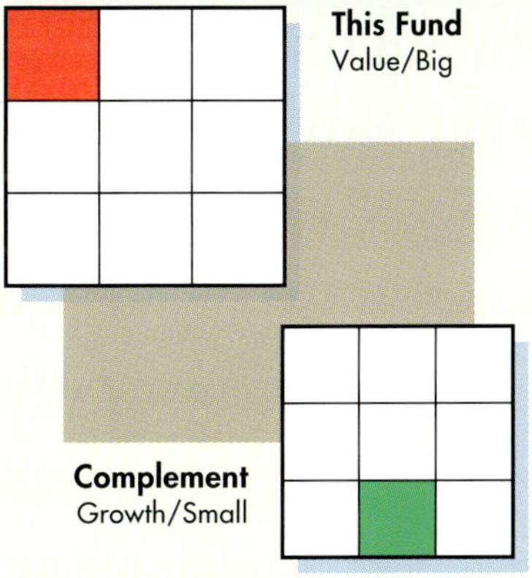

Farewell, old friend. Templeton Growth Fund is selling stocks it's held since the beginning of time. It's been a year of change for the fund, as stock selections have matured, and price targets have been met. One of the groups being sold is banking, where gains averaged 50%. This is as good as things get for banks, say analysts on the fund as loan-loss provisions are nil, trading profits are at record levels, and interest rates have bottomed.

After profit taking in the US, Hong Kong, and the UK, the managers are buying European cyclical stocks in shipping and engineering, as well as forest products. The managers cite lots of attractive new names to buy now.

Still, huge net unit sales have added to the cash from stock sales, and at writing the cash level sat at over 20%. That's rare for a Templeton fund, and is only an indication that even with attractive stocks available, they're not hasty at execution.

That cash could prove an opportunity or an obstacle. If markets weaken, the fund can buy aggressively. But if markets take a jump, the cash will act like an anchor – holding this fund back.

With 29 countries to choose from and a discipline to buy cheap, it's not surprising that the Templeton Growth Fund posts such dramatic long-term gains.

SAXON WORLD GROWTH FUND

Bob Tattersall (inception)/Howson Tattersall

RRSP

RATING

★★★½

CONSISTENCY

Performance Trend

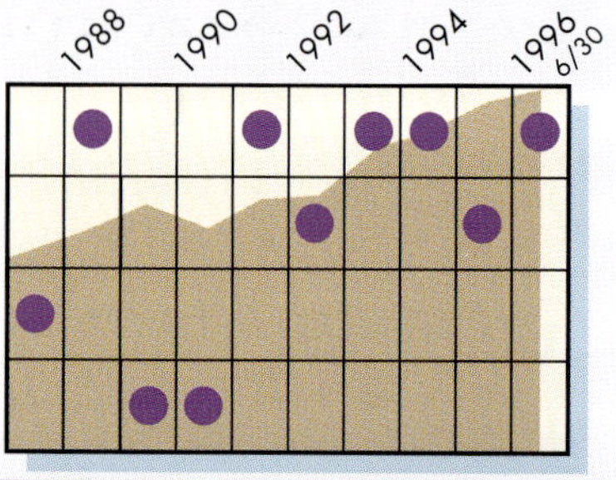

RISK

How often GICs performed better	2 years in 10
How often fund lost money	2 years in 10
Worst year's rate of return	-21.7% (1990)

EFFICIENCY

Management expense/ $100 $1.87

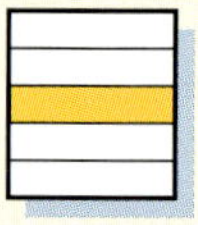

STYLE

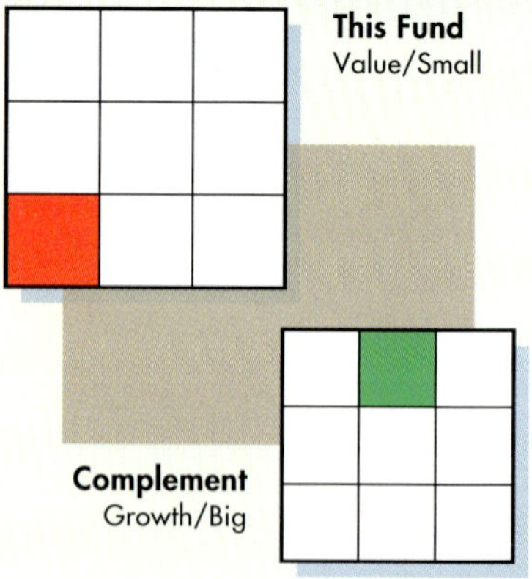

Here's a well kept secret: this teeny-tiny global fund practices the value-approach to investing almost as well as the legendary team at Templeton – but does so single-handedly. Can Bob Tattersall really stay on top of developments in so many markets? You bet. That's because he takes a page from the father of the value school of investing: he's really more accountant than market seer.

The approach doesn't always win and that's the only problem – if you can call it that – with value investors. Sure, they do better long-term, but there can be droughts. Tattersall buys statistically cheap stocks all over the world. Really cheap ones.

But he's not fussy about demanding some way out – seeing some change on the horizon that can turn a cheap stock around. His fate lies with the market. Eventually, he believes, fair market value is realized. He's had big wins in food and beverage stocks as well as some banks. Because he misses out on emerging markets and the occasional frenzies in commodities like gold or oil, he's been a counter-cyclical manager. Weak performance in down markets is the price investors pay to own this long-term gem.

EQUITY-INTERNATIONAL

RRSP

CUNDILL VALUE FUND

Peter Cundill (inception)/P. Cundill & Assoc.

RATING

CONSISTENCY

Performance Trend

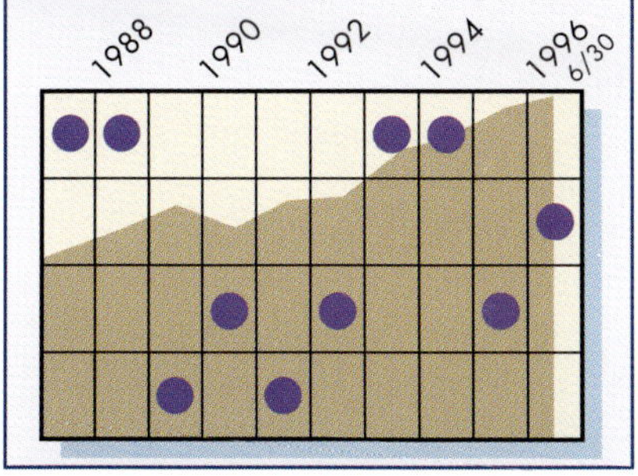

RISK

How often GICs performed better	5 years in 14
How often fund lost money	1 year in 14
Worst year's rate of return	-9.4% (1990)

EFFICIENCY

Management expense/ $100 $2.06

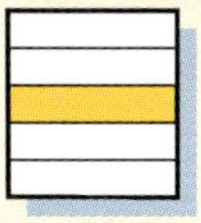

STYLE

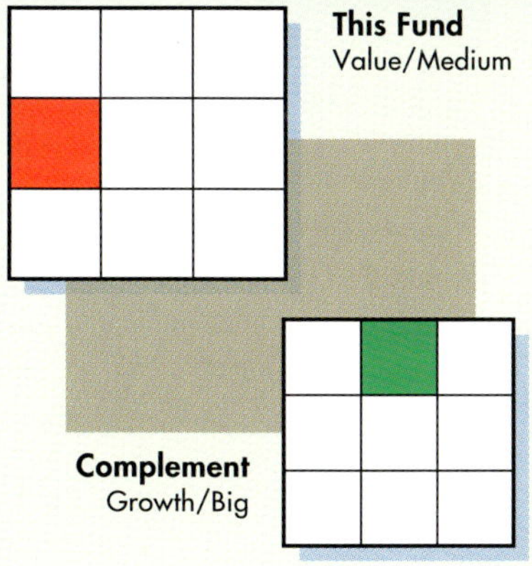

Unlike more conventional approaches to investing, the Cundill method is not based on top-down forecasting of the economy or corporate earnings. It does not rely on market timing, nor does it weight the portfolio by industry or country sector. The Cundill approach is the classic disciplined, patient, value style of management.

One of the fundamental tenets of value investing is that, eventually, undervalued securities will rise to reflect their fair value, and overvalued ones will decline. Peter Cundill attempts to buy $1 of value for 50 cents. To do this the Cundill approach identifies potential investments that meet the following criteria:

1. The price of the security must be less than half the book value,
2. The price must be less than half the former high and preferably at or near its all-time low,
3. Cash flow must be positive, even if earnings are negative.

Selling discipline is executed by liquidating half the position after it doubles, with the remainder being a free ride.

Currently, this approach indicates that the US market is overvalued. Of the 10,000 North American companies regularly screened, only 41 candidates were identified as undervalued. For this reason, the US component represents less than 12%, the lowest exposure in the fund's 21-year history. The current cash component exceeds 22%, illustrating a cautious approach.

TEMPLETON INTERNATIONAL STOCK FUND

Don Reed (inception)/Templeton

RRSP

RATING

CONSISTENCY

Performance Trend

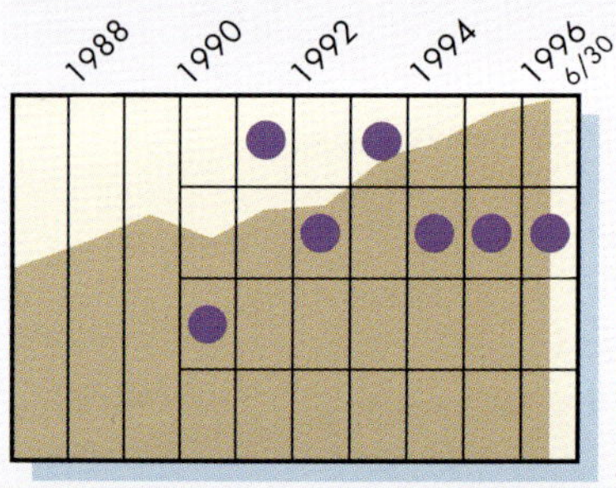

RISK

How often GICs performed better	2 years in 6
How often fund lost money	1 year in 6
Worst year's rate of return	-11.5% (1990)

EFFICIENCY

Management expense/ $100 $2.55

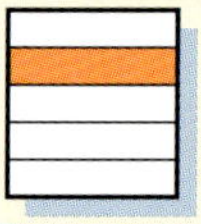

STYLE

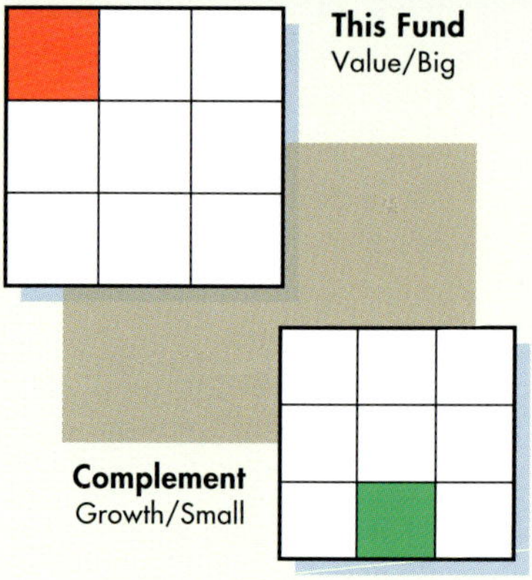

This is a truncated version of the Templeton Growth Fund so it should be expected to underperform the original. By mandate, Templeton International Stock can't buy US or Canadian stocks – an area the Templeton team thinks deserves nearly a third of its unconstrained Growth fund.

But this is a fund far better suited to investors who already have adequate North American exposure in their portfolio.

The fund is going through a year of change, as stock selections have matured, and price targets have been met. Some of the groups being sold are banking and insurance, where gains averaged 50%. This is as good as things get for banks, say analysts on the fund, as loan-loss provisions are nil, trading profits are at record levels, and interest rates have bottomed.

After profit-taking in Hong Kong and the UK, the managers are buying European cyclical stocks in shipping and engineering as well as forest products. The managers cite lots of attractive new names to buy now. Across-the-board attractiveness is how they describe developed nations' markets. The story for emerging markets looks just as good or better, they say.

With 31 analysts, 22 countries to choose from, and a discipline to buy cheap, it's not surprising that this fund posts such dramatic long-term gains – even without the help of the white-hot US market.

RRSP

CANADA LIFE US & INT'L EQUITY S34 FUND

Gary Kondrat + team/Canada Life

RATING

CONSISTENCY

Performance Trend

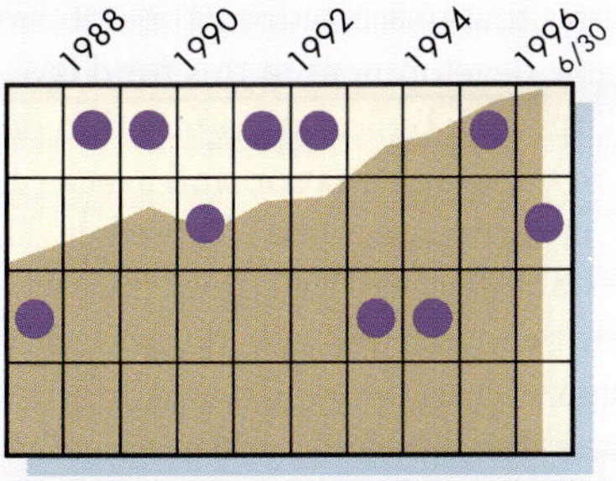

RISK

How often GICs performed better	3 years in 11
How often fund lost money	3 years in 11
Worst year's rate of return	-6.1% (1990)

EFFICIENCY

Management expense/ $100 $2.40

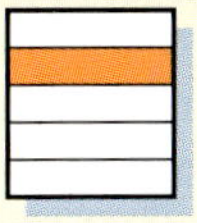

STYLE

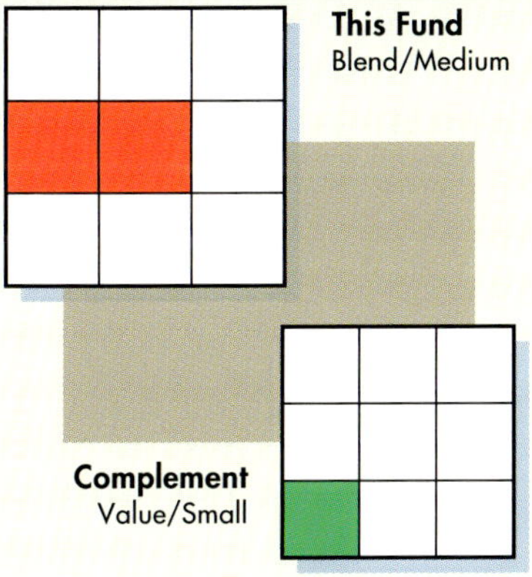

A changing of the guard is signalling some subtle changes for this fund, which has long been a standout. Part of its long-term success is attributable to a higher-than-most allocation to the US market. By policy, this fund is always overweight in the US at 40% to 60%. At writing it held 47% in the States.

The change involves a shift from a value approach under previous managers Lance Speck and others to a more growth-oriented style. Still, there is a value overlay. The result is fewer cyclicals and more blue chips.

The management team, which has been augmented lately, shortlists stocks first from a ranking of historical growth rates. Then they sort the fast-growing companies by relative priciness. The fund ends up with some 100 names, all trading at attractive prices relative to their own historic levels or to industry norms.

Typically, they will hold a stock for 4 years, so this fund should be ideal for taxable accounts. But don't rush out to buy it – even the managers sense that the current bull market is long in the tooth and so they postured the fund defensively in mid 1996. It should be mid 1997, when world growth synchronizes, that this fund takes off again.

NEW

BPI GLOBAL SMALL COMPANIES FUND

W. von Mueffling + E. Alexanderson (inception)/Lazard Frères

RRSP

RATING

★ ★ ★

CONSISTENCY

Performance Trend

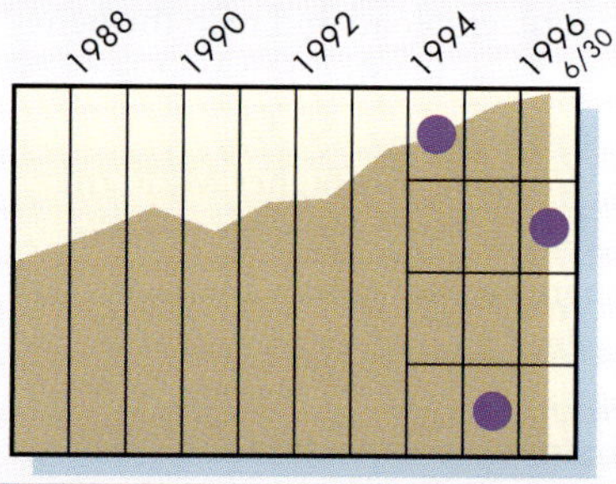

RISK

How often GICs performed better	1 year in 2
How often fund lost money	1 year in 2
Worst year's rate of return	-4.5% (1995)

EFFICIENCY

Management expense/ $100 $2.56

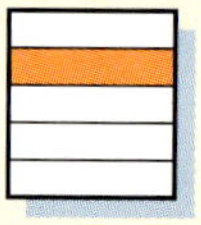

STYLE

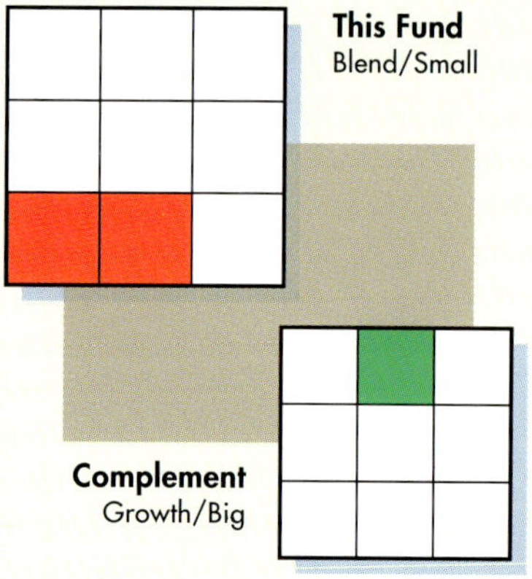

Better past performance, improved diversification, and a bigger opportunity set are just some of the reasons investors should consider a global small-cap fund. This one is an excellent choice because of its heavy European tilt, value bias, and focus on smaller small caps than, say, Templeton's comparable product.

Lazard's team uses quantitative screening to monitor valuations and financials of thousands of companies. Then they use bottom-up research to identify the best. They hold lots of names to diversify away company-specific risk. In this way, they are very similar to the Templeton approach. But an important difference between the two at the time of writing was Lazard's neutral stance on the US (evidenced by a typical 38% weight toward US small-cap stocks for this fund versus only half as much in the Templeton fund).

This fund is suitable for more than just aggressive investors. It can be a key part of a balanced global portfolio, even for a conservative growth investor.

RRSP

FONDS DESJARDINS INT'L EQUITY FUND

John Gilfoyle (1994)/Canagex

RATING

★ ★ ★

CONSISTENCY

Performance Trend

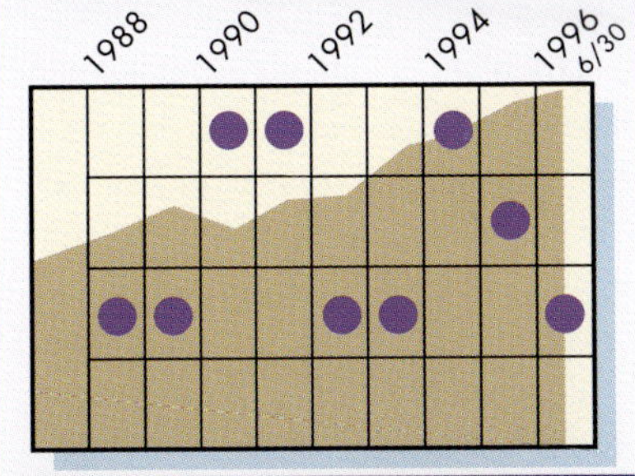

RISK

How often GICs performed better	4 years in 8
How often fund lost money	0 years in 8
Worst year's rate of return	1.2% (1990)

EFFICIENCY

Management expense/ $100 $2.37

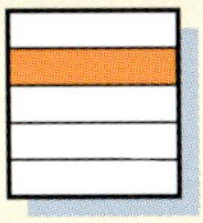

STYLE

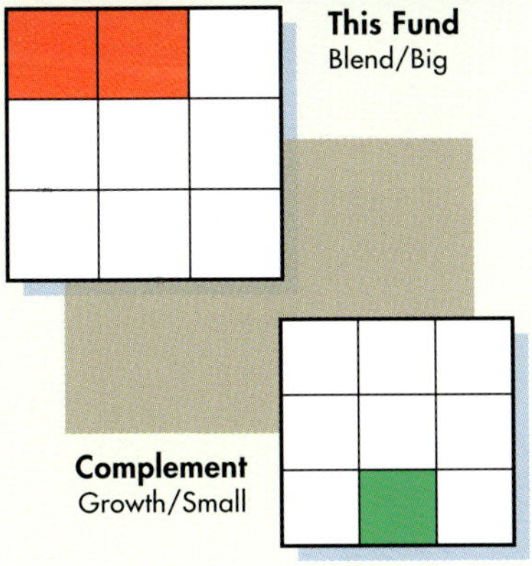

This fund is available only to Quebec residents. Its top-down approach to picking countries seldom disappoints. As an established markets-only fund, Gilfoyle has managed to avoid the emerging markets meltdown that affected some other global funds. Missing out on the emerging markets action was typical of this fund's conservative style – it misses out on both rallies and routs.

The fund is appropriate as a global fund for a bank customer who's a mutual fund novice. But, remember that this fund, like all global funds, will be adversely affected by a rise in the Canadian dollar.

NEW

BEUTEL GOODMAN INTERNATIONAL EQUITY FUND

RRSP

Gavin Ivory (inception)/Beutel Goodman

RATING

★ ★ ★

CONSISTENCY

Performance Trend

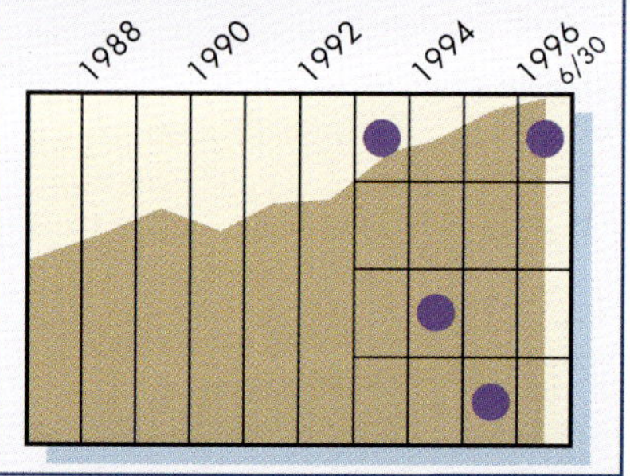

RISK

How often GICs performed better	2 years in 3
How often fund lost money	0 years in 3
Worst year's rate of return	0.9% (1994)

EFFICIENCY

Management expense/ $100 $2.60

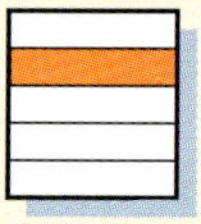

STYLE

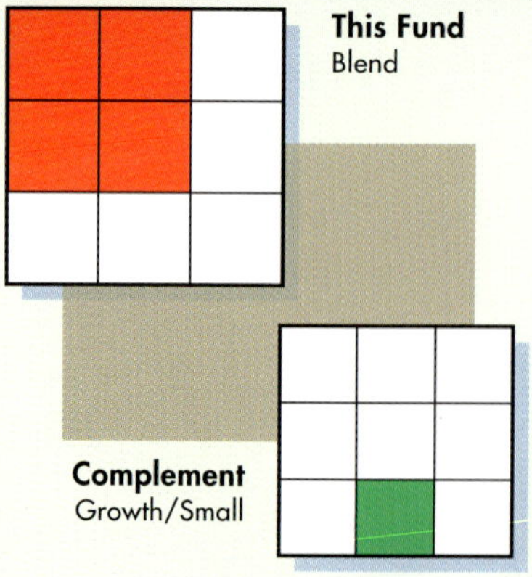

This fund is a nice complement for investors already holding plenty of the Trimark Fund, because it's a good performer with a non-North American mandate and is postured defensively today.

The fund is just old enough to make the *Top Funds* list and in its short history has both won and lost from its allocation to emerging markets (typically 15 to 20% of the fund).

The emerging markets exposure provides a nice diversification twist to this fund that's not found in most. And it may be a good time to be buying emerging markets, after they have been hammered for much of the last couple of years while chugging along with reform and continued growth. This is a bold fund, managed within tight constraints. Although nervous about the markets, Ivory remains 90% invested – the minimum allowed for this fund. The fund holds very few stocks (50 max), but is widely diversified by country (23 countries) – which means there's little diversification within markets.

The tilt toward statistically cheap stocks has led to an overweight position in service companies. Noticeably absent are tech, drugs, and other growth stocks. A rebound in emerging markets and a slowdown in established markets will put this fund on top again in 1997.

NEW

C.I. AMERICAN FUND

Bill Priest (inception)/BEA Associates

RRSP

RATING

★ ★ ★ ★ ★

CONSISTENCY

Performance Trend

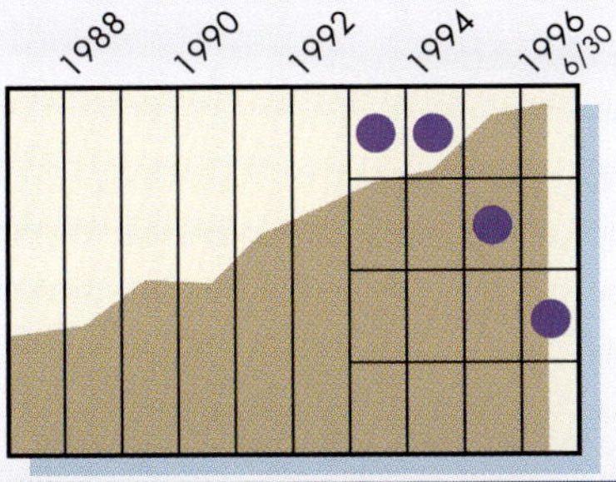

RISK

How often GICs performed better	0 years in 3
How often fund lost money	0 years in 3
Worst year's rate of return	8.1% (1994)

EFFICIENCY

Management expense/ $100 $2.49

STYLE

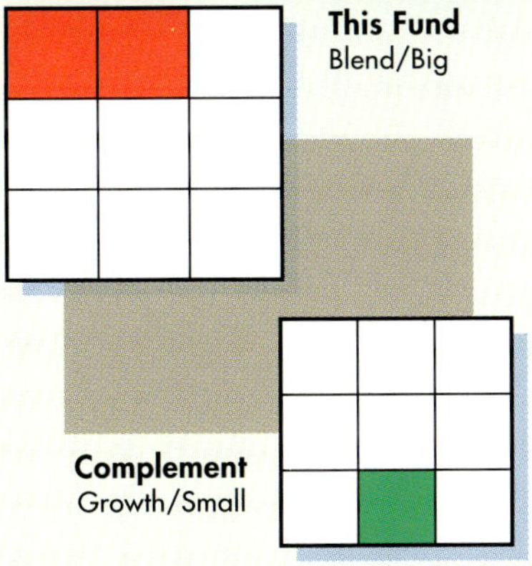

With just $120 million, this top-notch fund has been overlooked. And much of that has come from appreciation as the fund has doubled, and then some, since its inception less than 4 years ago. Much, but not all of the credit goes to a strong US market, but Priest has beaten it over time – even with an expense ratio of 2.49%.

His big-picture thinking involves two unmistakable, powerful, long-term trends. The first is restructurings. Corporations are engaging in global arbitrage in the labour market because 80% of the world's workforce works for wages that are one-thirtieth those of the developed nations. Priest looks for companies that will lead in the global competitiveness race.

The second major trend is toward 'global unit growth' by market leaders. Wages rise as emerging nations ramp up productivity, creating gigantic new markets for consumer products. C.I. American has profited from huge wins in consumer stocks Priest now considers fully-valued, like Coca-Cola, Gillette, and Duracell.

NEW

UNIVERSAL US EMERGING GROWTH FUND

James Broadfoot (inception)/Mackenzie Investment Mgmt.

RRSP

RATING

★★★★★

CONSISTENCY

Performance Trend

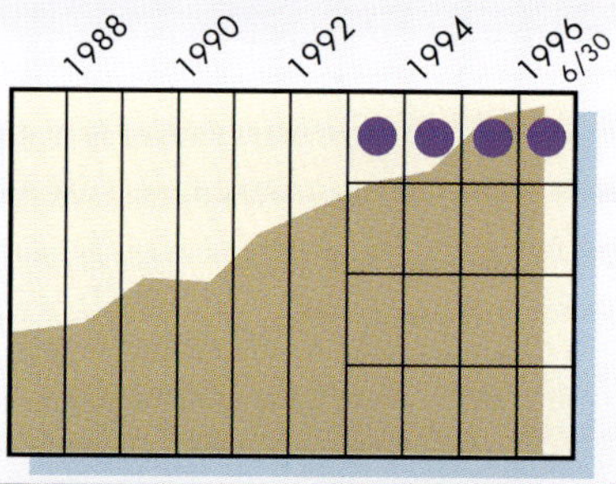

RISK

How often GICs performed better	1 year in 3
How often fund lost money	0 years in 3
Worst year's rate of return	7.2% (1994)

EFFICIENCY

Management expense/ $100 $2.46

STYLE

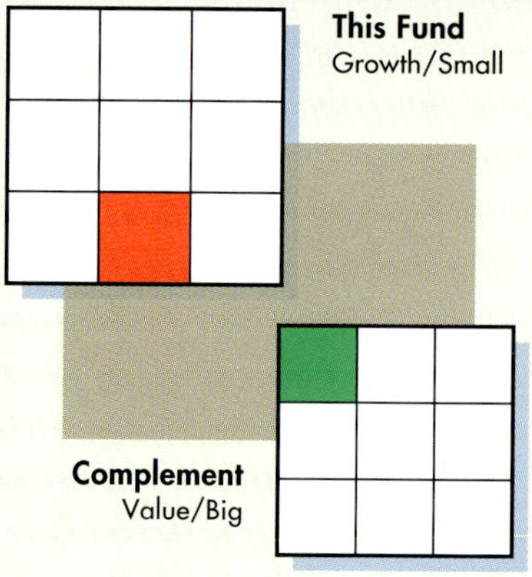

While almost all this Fund's holdings are listed on the NASDAQ, James Broadfoot's management philosophy of "sell first, ask questions later" has been a contributing factor to the fund's significant returns over the index. Broadfoot's intent is to identify stocks that have achieved strong earnings in sectors that can support a high rate of growth. In addition, he prefers to buy companies early in their product life cycle and in industries that are experiencing consolidation.

While Broadfoot keeps the portfolio well diversified, he currently favours both Internet and pharmaceutical stocks.

Concentrating on fertile, high-growth sectors has resulted in relatively high volatility for the fund. Yet it has maintained a high average monthly return.

The fund will pay a premium for high-growth companies and during sector weakness will build positions in stocks that maintain "bulletproof" earnings.

EQUITY-US

RRSP

FIDELITY GROWTH AMERICA FUND

Brad Lewis (inception)/Fidelity

RATING

★ ★ ★ ★ ★

CONSISTENCY

Performance Trend

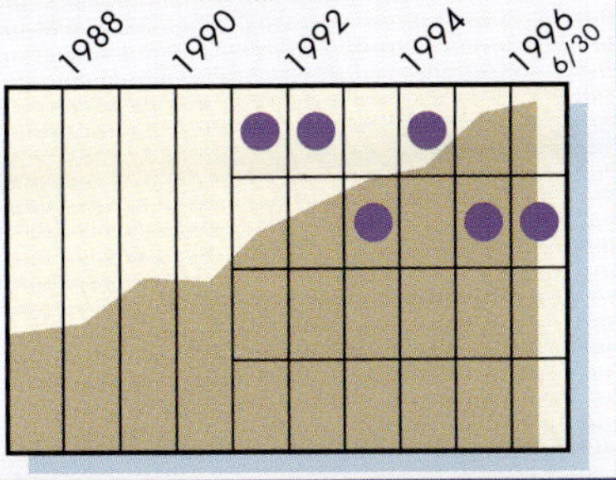

RISK

How often GICs performed better	1 year in 5
How often fund lost money	0 years in 5
Worst year's rate of return	6.2% (1994)

EFFICIENCY

Management expense/ $100 $2.40

STYLE

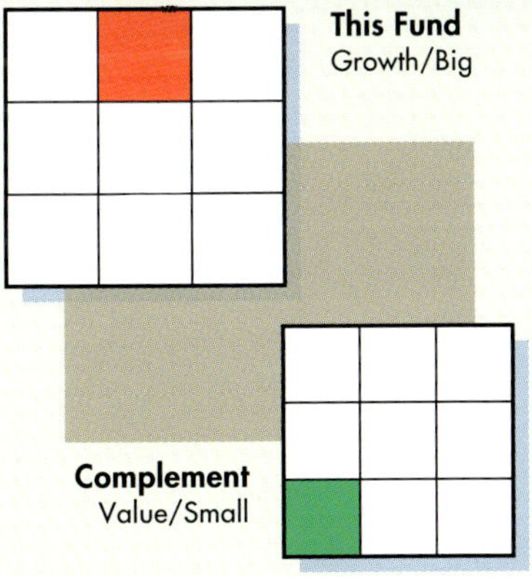

Fidelity Growth America Fund consistently achieves higher growth with lower P/E stocks. As opposed to the S&P 500's 13.7% growth rate with a 15.6 P/E ratio, Brad Lewis recently achieved a 17.8% growth rate with a P/E of only 14.7.

Lewis uses a computer-based screening process that searches 2000 stocks for favourable earnings momentum, corporate profitability, and valuation trends.

Lewis is not a trend-chaser. The fund had a 40% technology weighting in 1995, yet now maintains a much lower weighting. He feels that the technology sector still has some undervalued companies. The fund tries not to have cash on hand, but Lewis is an active trader with a 200% portfolio turnover. So with new purchases, he's recently built a large cash hoard.

The fund presently overweights financial sectors, with a focus on regional insurance and financial companies. Lewis would not be surprised at a sharp market downturn, but feels there are no foundations for a long-term bear market. He is confident that the market will sustain long-term growth, but investors should be prepared for some short-term volatility.

ALTAMIRA SELECT AMERICAN FUND

Ken Abrams (inception)/Wellington Management

RRSP

RATING

★ ★ ★ ★ ★

CONSISTENCY

Performance Trend

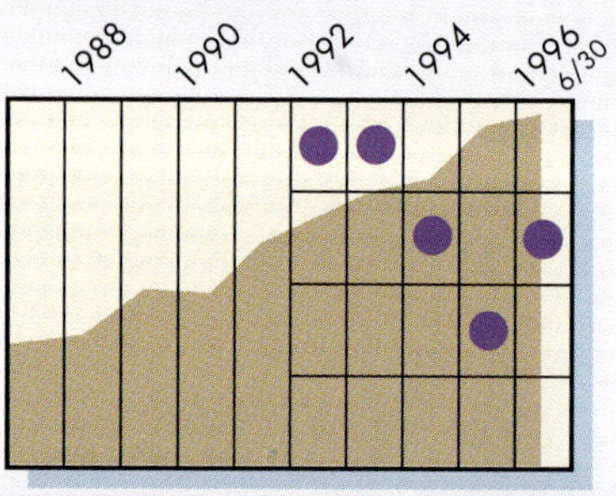

RISK

How often GICs performed better	1 year in 4
How often fund lost money	0 years in 4
Worst year's rate of return	2.1% (1994)

EFFICIENCY

Management expense/ $100 $2.32

STYLE

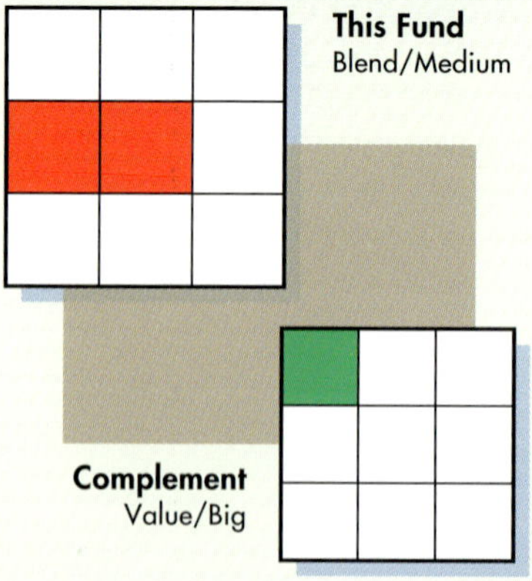

Every five years won't be as pretty as the past five, but from Ken Abrams's perspective, the future does look bright – well, except for computer hardware manufacturers. Though this fund has made a fortune in technology stocks, Abrams is decidedly bearish about some of technology's sub-sectors. Overall, his technology weighting by the third quarter of 1996 is half of what it was at the beginning of the year. In fact, it's now at its lowest level ever – about 12%. The market has been punishing high-flying growth stocks whose earnings come in even a touch below expectations, so Abrams has begun to pick stocks that can beat street expectations – every quarter.

There is little room for error in this fully invested fund – but with moderating US growth and inflation in check, capital markets are on a solid footing, says Abrams. He says his tilt toward smaller company shares will also help through 1997 because of their relatively low valuations today.

NEW

RRSP

HYPERION VALUE LINE US EQUITY FUND

John Moore (inception)/Value Line

RATING

★ ★ ★ ★

CONSISTENCY

Performance Trend

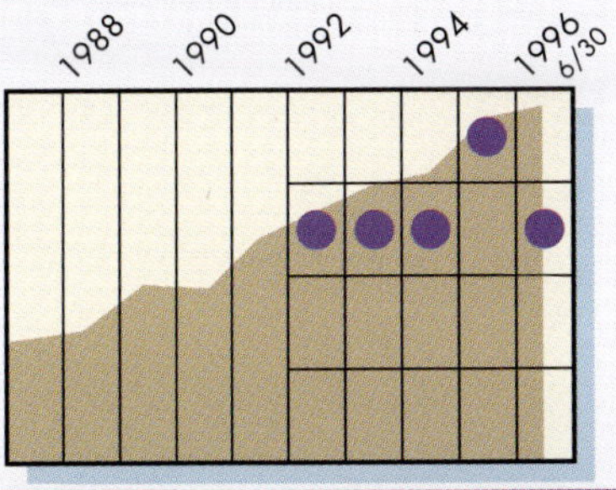

RISK

How often GICs performed better	1 year in 4
How often fund lost money	0 years in 4
Worst year's rate of return	0.6% (1994)

EFFICIENCY

Management expense/ $100 $3.01

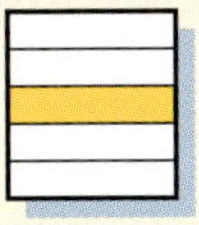

STYLE

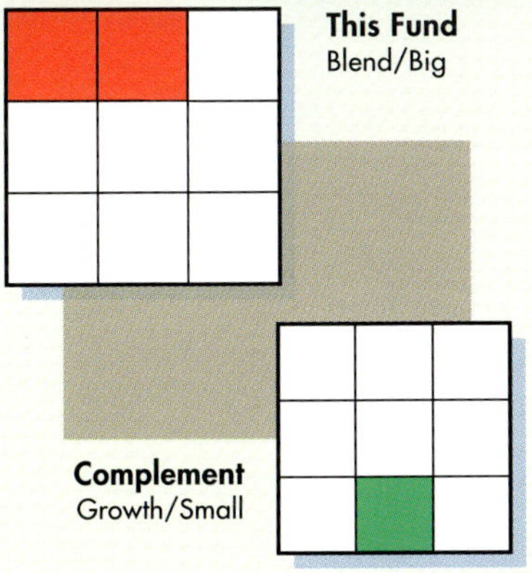

You'll get a remarkable mix of growth and value in this special fund. Value Line's approach has been so successful that academics offer it as proof that it must be possible to beat the US market. Their famous investment surveys chronicle the Value Line approach; good businesses, reasonable valuations, and timely purchases are the keys to success for this group.

While Moore works in a different area for Value Line (asset management), his approach is not much different. In this extended bull market, Moore is relying on established growth companies to deliver returns for Canadian investors. Even after paying its steep expenses every year, the fund has kept pace with the tough-to-beat S&P 500 Index, an impressive feat.

NEW

BEUTEL GOODMAN MONEY MARKET FUND

Bruce Corneil (1995)/Beutel Goodman

RRSP

RATING

★★★★★

CONSISTENCY

Performance Trend

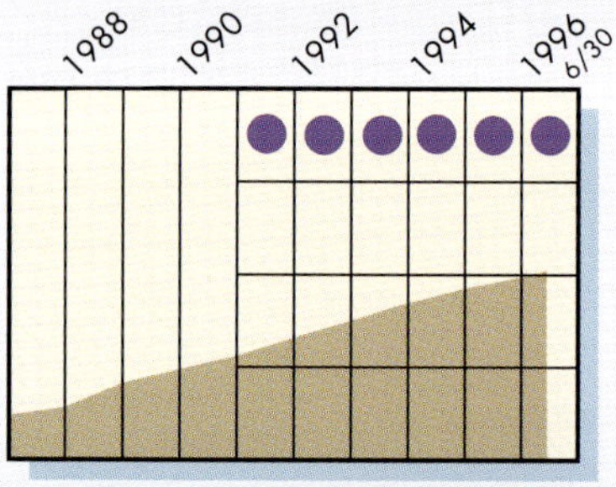

RISK

How often GICs performed better	3 years in 5
How often fund lost money	0 years in 5
Worst year's rate of return	4.8% (1994)

EFFICIENCY

Management expense/ $100 $0.59

STYLE

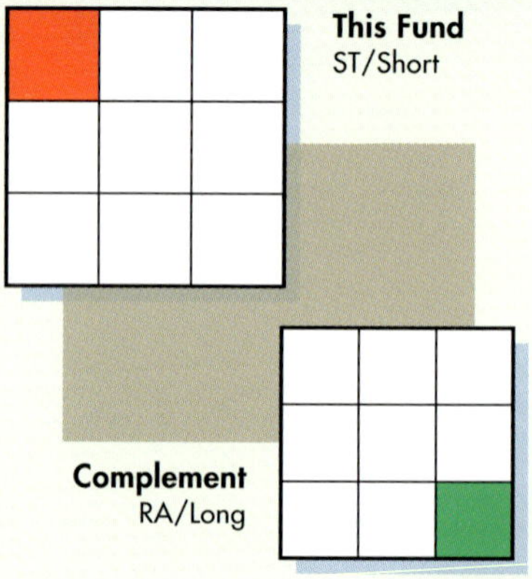

With a razor-thin management expense ratio of just 0.59%, this fund is already a half a percentage point out front of the pack every year. Add to that a little corporate paper, and it's easy to see why this fund is a leader.

NEW

RRSP

ICM SHORT TERM INVESTMENT FUND

George Kiddell (inception)/Integra Capital Management

RATING

★★★★★

CONSISTENCY

Performance Trend

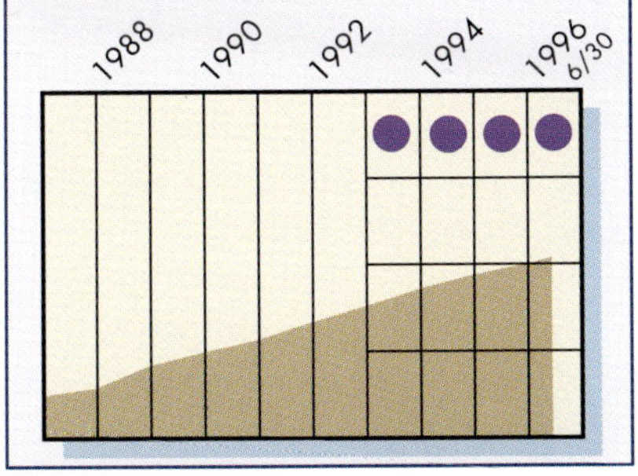

RISK

How often GICs performed better	2 years in 3
How often fund lost money	0 years in 3
Worst year's rate of return	5.5% (1994)

EFFICIENCY

Management expense/ $100 $1.00

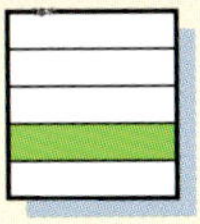

STYLE

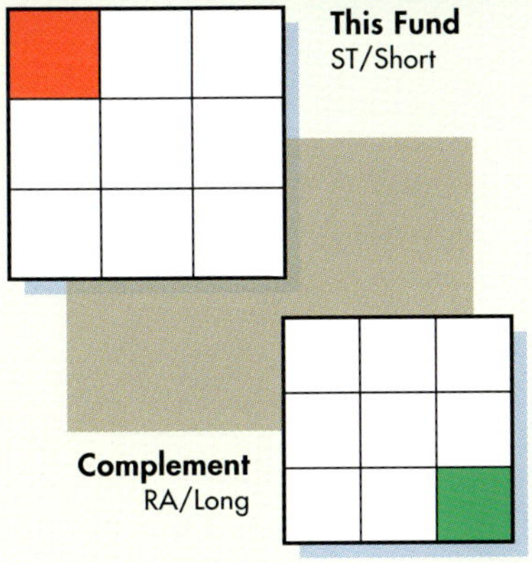

This fund was too new for inclusion in the *Top Funds* list last year. Since its debut in late 1992, it has outpaced its rivals consistently. Credit this to a substantial commitment of one-quarter of the fund to corporate paper, and tighter spreads for those corporate issues in comparison to governments. There's a $10,000 minimum for this fund, which also boasts an annual expense ratio that is just slightly lower than the group average of 1.07%.

NEW

ROYAL LIFE MONEY MARKET FUND

Peter Kotsopoulos/Royal Life

RRSP

RATING

★ ★ ★ ★ ★

CONSISTENCY

Performance Trend

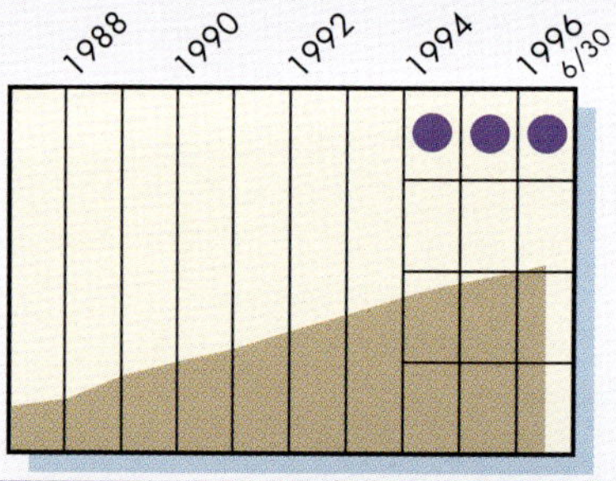

RISK

How often GICs performed better	2 years in 2
How often fund lost money	0 years in 2
Worst year's rate of return	5.2% (1994)

EFFICIENCY

Management expense/ $100 $1.00

STYLE

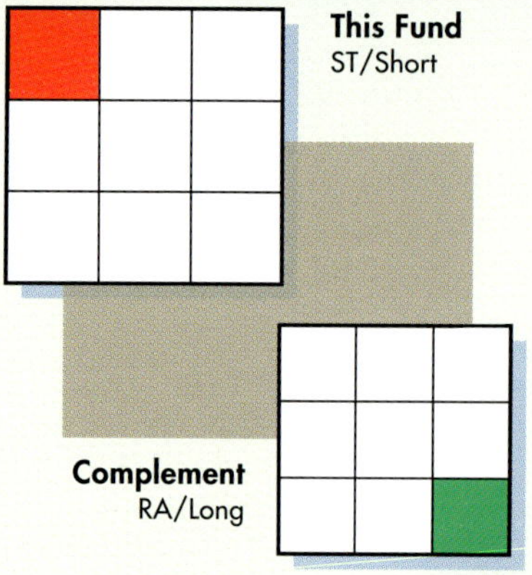

Just old enough to pass the three-year minimum track record hurdle for inclusion in *Top Funds*, this is a fund that beats its peers by taking on more credit risk. At writing, 19% of the fund was in Quebec issues and the remainder in corporates. That means more income volatility in tough times, and more upside otherwise. There's also a nice little currency hedge built into this fund, with a 10% holding in $US-pay paper. At 1%, the expense ratio is reasonable – which is key for any money market fund.

NEW

RRSP

HONGKONG BANK MORTGAGE FUND

Robert De Hart (inception)/M.K. Wong & Associates

RATING

★ ★ ★ ★ ★

CONSISTENCY

Performance Trend

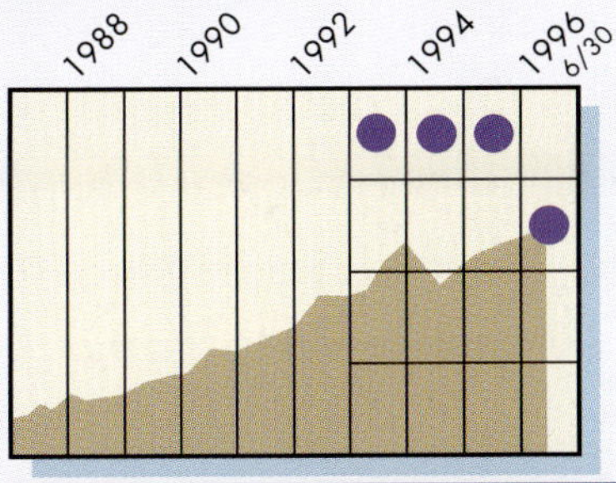

RISK

How often GICs performed better	1 year in 3
How often fund lost money	0 years in 3
Worst year's rate of return	3.6% (1994)

EFFICIENCY

Management expense/ $100 $1.76

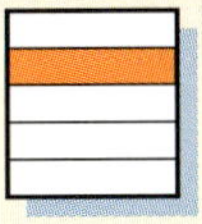

STYLE

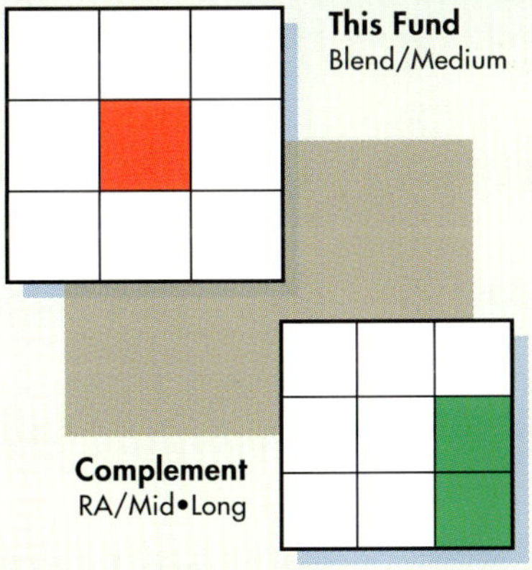

De Hart is a methodical researcher whose big-picture macroeconomic analysis leads him to firm views on where the economy – and interest rates – are going. This fund is just new enough to make the *Top Funds* list, but has had an impressive, if short, record.

He doesn't make big term bets for the fund, but does have to make calls on where rates are headed. Right now, that depends a great deal on where US rates go, and whether Canada can maintain such tight premiums off US debt securities.

While rates stay within a trading range, this fund has benefited from being fully invested. Cash drags down mortgage funds in this environment, so De Hart is keeping every penny working hard to overcome the 1.77% MER of this fund.

MORTGAGE

INVESNAT MORTGAGE FUND

Gilles Tremblay (inception)/Natcan Investment

RRSP

RATING

★★★★½

CONSISTENCY

Performance Trend

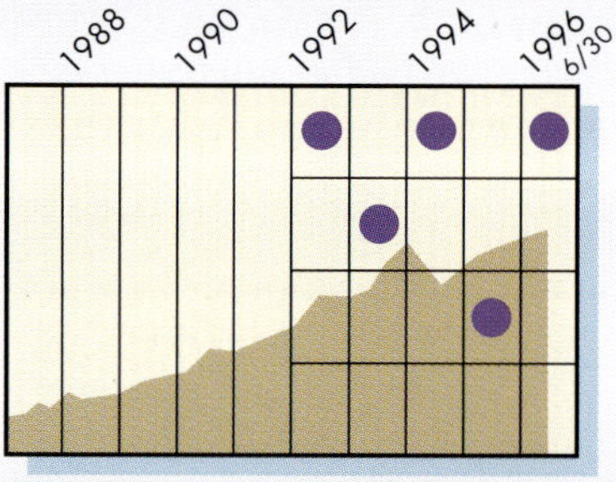

RISK

How often GICs performed better	1 year in 4
How often fund lost money	0 years in 4
Worst year's rate of return	1.7% (1994)

EFFICIENCY

Management expense/ $100 $1.53

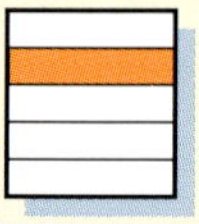

STYLE

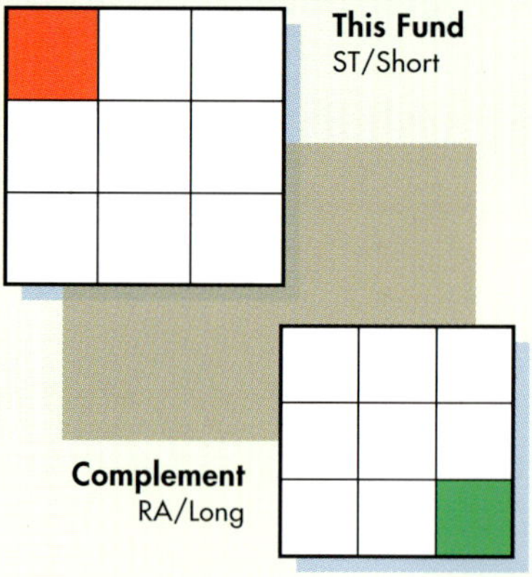

Here's an ultra-conservative mortgage fund for savers. It seldom dazzles, but pleases the National Bank clients for whom it's geared. Rather than swinging the portfolio around between longer- and shorter-term mortgages, Tremblay adds value by owning some with slightly longer maturities – and accordingly higher yields. About two-thirds of the mortgages in this fund come from the bank, with the rest being of the CMHC-insured variety. That means better liquidity, and fits with the mandate of this conservative fund.

NEW

RRSP

SCOTIA EXCELSIOR MORTGAGE FUND

Bruce Grantier/Scotia Investment Management

RATING

CONSISTENCY

Performance Trend

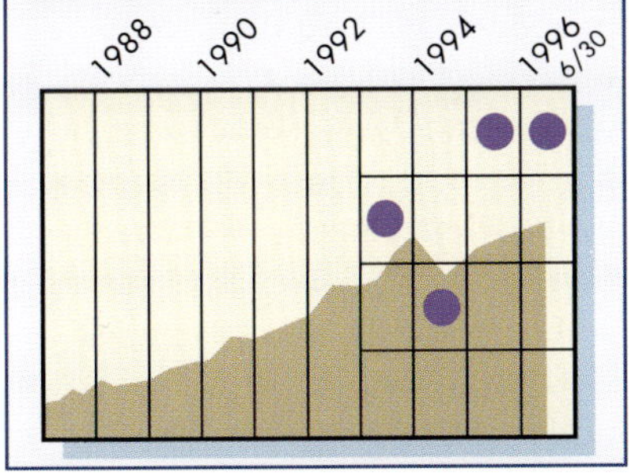

RISK

How often GICs performed better	1 year in 3
How often fund lost money	1 year in 3
Worst year's rate of return	-0.3% (1994)

EFFICIENCY

Management expense/ $100 $1.56

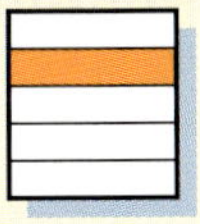

STYLE

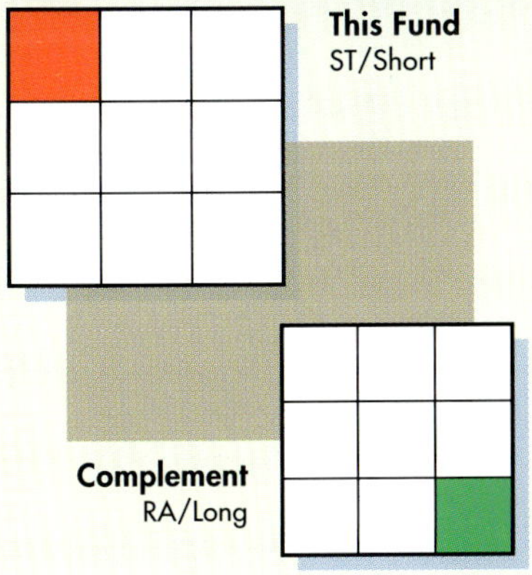

For savers, mortgage funds are an interesting alternative. This one invests in mortgages guaranteed by Scotiabank (about 50%) and the National Housing Administration (about 40%). The remainder sits in T-Bills. The bank guarantees the mortgages for principal and interest in exchange for a 0.25% annual fee from the fund.

This fund isn't a standout on most fronts; it doesn't vary term much but does, to some degree, vary cash levels to stick-handle interest-rate changes. With interest rates expected to trade in a tight range, this fund should continue to beat GICs.

ROYFUND MORTGAGE FUND

Barry Edwards + team (inception)/Royal Bank

RRSP

RATING

★ ★ ★ ★

CONSISTENCY

Performance Trend

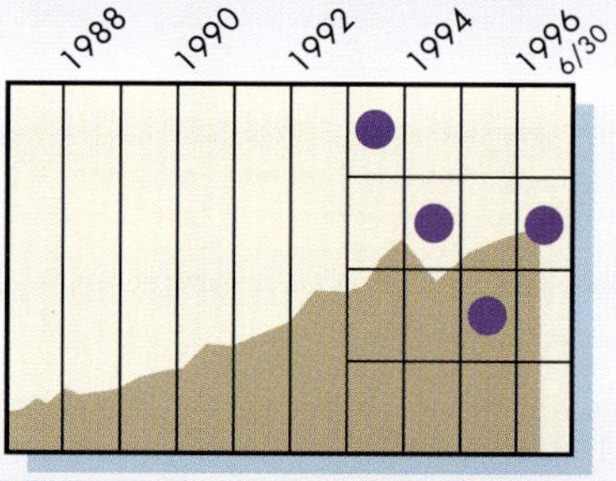

RISK

How often GICs performed better	1 year in 3
How often fund lost money	0 years in 3
Worst year's rate of return	1.0% (1994)

EFFICIENCY

Management expense/ $100 $1.81

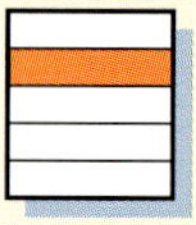

STYLE

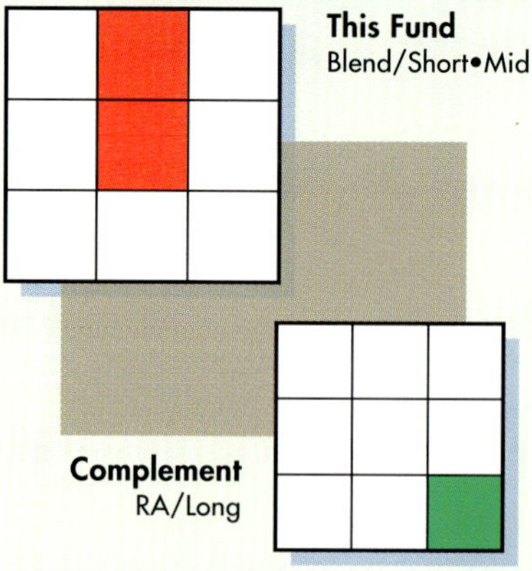

This Fund
Blend/Short•Mid

Complement
RA/Long

This is a fund for savers. The consistency with which it beats GICs has been impressive – about 2/3 of the time. It makes the *Top Funds* list partly because of its strong showing in a tough 1994 – it didn't lose money. As with most bank mortgage funds, it holds only residential mortgages bought from and guaranteed by its parent bank for both credit default and liquidity if necessary.

Edwards is moderately bullish now, with a bit heavier weighting in three- to five-year issues and a recent 80% allocation to mortgages. He's been bang-on in the first half of 1996 after underperforming in 1995. That's typical for this conservative fund – it excels in tough times but misses the party in good years.

MORTGAGE

RRSP

C.I. PACIFIC FUND

Shaun Chan (1990)/TCW Asia

RATING

★ ★ ★ ★ ★

CONSISTENCY

Performance Trend

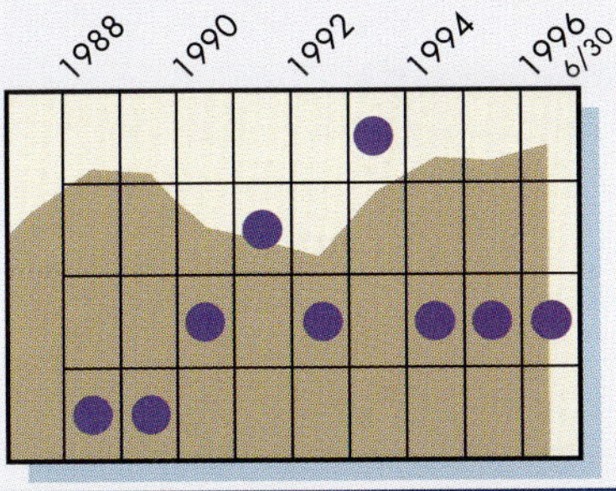

RISK

How often GICs performed better	6 years in 14
How often fund lost money	3 years in 14
Worst year's rate of return	-15.5% (1990)

EFFICIENCY

Management expense/ $100 $2.61

STYLE

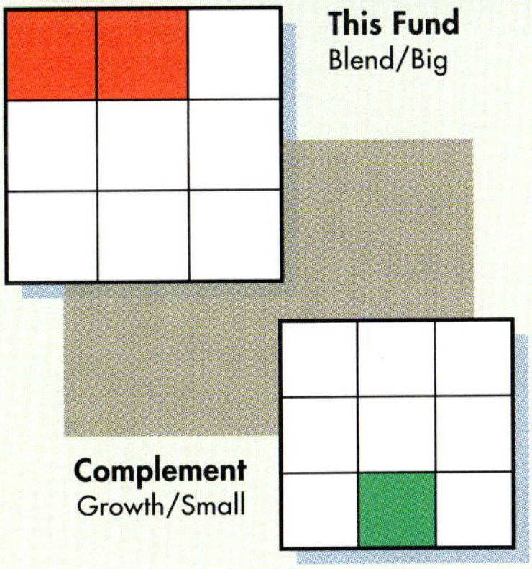

Shaun Chan is a big-picture thinker. He thinks Asia can be divided along two lines: the markets that are sensitive to US interest rates and the markets that are cyclicals-sensitive. He's confident that the latter group will lead the way this year.

The country decision vastly outweighs the stock decision in determining performance of an Asian fund. So Chan doesn't spend all his time on stock research. Rather he focuses on getting the country allocation right. That's not always easy in a region where the benchmark index design is flawed so as to overweight Japan.

Chan is never precisely right on the country mix. His appeal derives from the fact that he's never far wrong. He was early in cutting back Hong Kong holdings this year, only to watch the rally continue. And he was early buying back in to Malaysia before the worst was quite over. But he's been right in general since he took over this fund some 6 years ago.

As always, this fund benefits from broad diversification (including Japan) throughout a fast-growth region

INVESTORS PACIFIC INTERNATIONAL FUND

Jeremy Higgs/Carlson Investment Management

RRSP

RATING

★★★★½

CONSISTENCY

Performance Trend

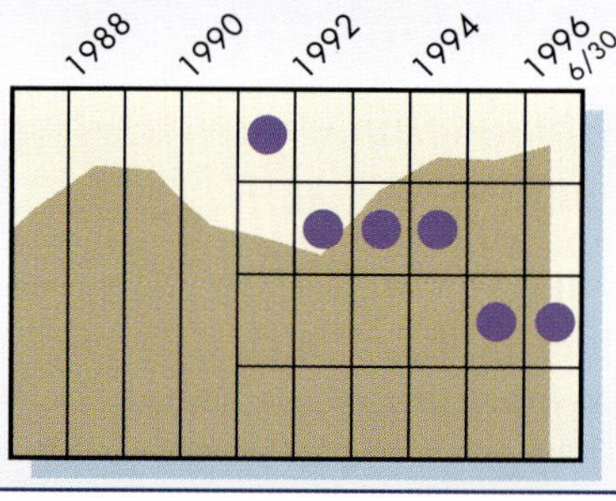

RISK

How often GICs performed better	2 years in 5
How often fund lost money	1 year in 5
Worst year's rate of return	-6.7% (1994)

EFFICIENCY

Management expense/ $100 $2.53

STYLE

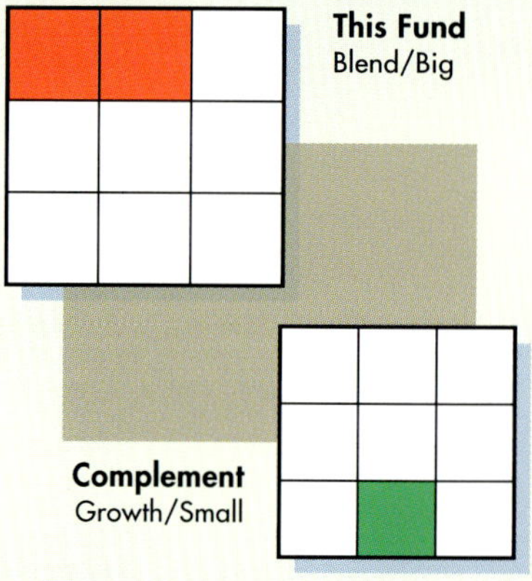

Here's an Asia *sans* Japan fund for the pragmatic investor. Higgs isn't a gunslinger making big predictions that Hong Kong will sink into the South China Sea. Nor is he so bullish that he'd load up the entire fund on Hong Kong. Compared to some Asian managers, he's downright meek.

As the biggest market in the group, Hong Kong is the big wild-card. The 1997 takeover by China has daunting economic implications – and explosive opportunities. Higgs feels there should be a degree of caution afforded to Hong Kong, but no more. He's a little underweight at the time of writing: 22% vs 28% for his benchmark.

The Asian growth story remains intact, though the markets have suffered since early 1994. High growth rates were trimmed only modestly by tighter monetary policies, which has helped lower inflation without killing growth – some feat. But the big-money foreign institutions that drove prices up in 1993 have since beaten a path to Wall Street, where gains have been huge. Their return is inevitable.

This is a low turnover, value style fund whose key characteristic is a lack of Japan. That means that investors should be sure to get some Japan exposure in their accounts elsewhere – both for diversification and growth reasons.

RRSP

FIDELITY FAR EAST FUND

K.C. Lee (inception)/Fidelity

RATING

★★★★½

CONSISTENCY

Performance Trend

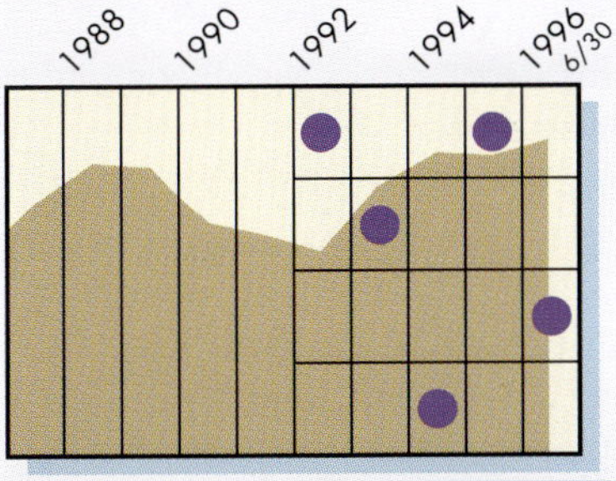

RISK

How often GICs performed better	1 year in 4
How often fund lost money	1 year in 4
Worst year's rate of return	-16.7% (1994)

EFFICIENCY

Management expense/ $100 $2.82

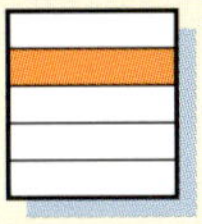

STYLE

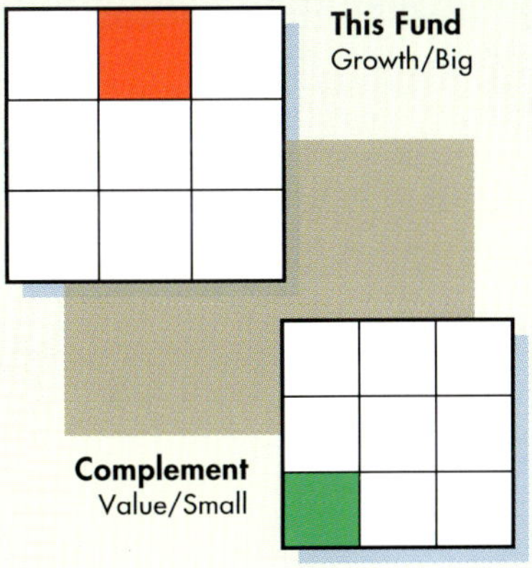

This Fund
Growth/Big

Complement
Value/Small

K.C. Lee has no concerns about Hong Kong in 1997. In fact, Lee believes that 1997 will not bring any surprises and, if anything, Hong Kong stocks will experience a spike, since the market generally reacts poorly to surprises that are negative in nature.

Lee feels that Hong Kong offers the best fundamental valuations and liquidity and will continue to weight it at about 55% of the fund's portfolio. Hong Kong's current economic climate is well suited to his blue-chip growth management style, as corporate earnings continue to improve.

Remaining overweight in Hong Kong has led to the fund's recent superior performance. Strong share appreciation in Malaysia and the Philippines has also played a key role. The Philippines portion of the fund did well in '96. During 1994, the fund remained heavily weighted in Hong Kong, which contributed to its weak performance that year.

Hong Kong is often regarded as a blue-chip market in that, due to its size, it is the first to lag and the first to rebound. Lee expects corporate earnings to increase over the next 12 months and form the foundation for an increase in share prices. He will continue to identify companies with high-quality and consistent earnings growth that are trading at a discount to their asset values.

AGF ASIAN GROWTH FUND A

David Chan + Stephen Way (inception)/AGF

RRSP

RATING

★ ★ ★ ★

CONSISTENCY

Performance Trend

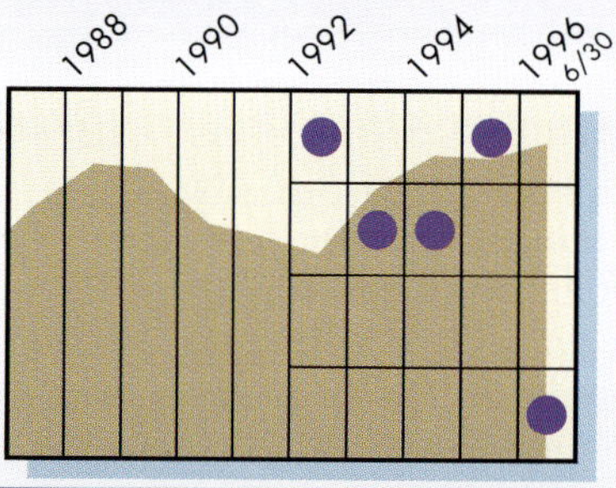

RISK

How often GICs performed better	1 year in 4
How often fund lost money	1 year in 4
Worst year's rate of return	-6.5% (1994)

EFFICIENCY

Management expense/ $100 $2.41

STYLE

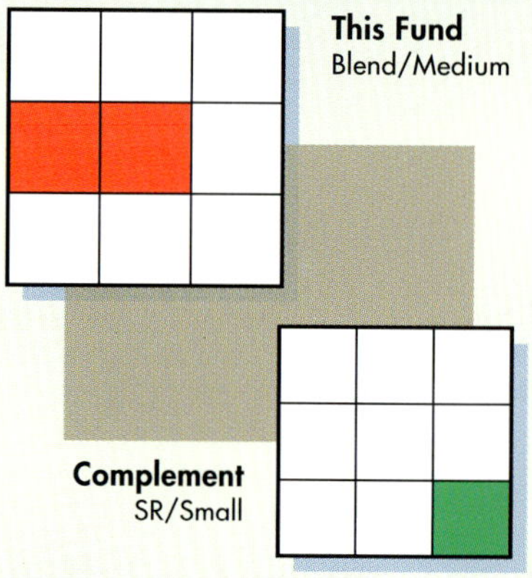

A year ago Nomura's David Chan liked the Hong Kong property developers, which were then trading at a 15% discount to net asset value. But things have since changed. Capital is so mobile today that lower US interest rates caused a rapid flow of funds into Asian stocks, erasing much of the discounts. For Chan, the geographic decision is most important. He's now modestly underweight in Hong Kong. In April, Singapore-based Chan left Nomura with most of his staff to work directly for AGF in Singapore.

Liquidity-driven Asian markets have strengthened since late 1995 on the heels of lower US interest rates and solid economic growth in the region. Those gains have erased much of the steep discounts enjoyed by stocks in the region, whose earnings gains continue at a 15%–18% clip.

The fund is overweight in markets with the highest earnings growth (Malaysia, Singapore and Indonesia), while underweight in those markets that have enjoyed the best gains (Hong Kong and Thailand). Better relations between Taiwan and China are easing military tension in the region.

This fund avoids Japan by policy, so investors must be sure to have Japanese exposure elsewhere.

NEW

HYPERION ASIAN FUND

RRSP

Duncan Mount (inception)/CEF Management Limited

RATING

★ ★ ★

CONSISTENCY

Performance Trend

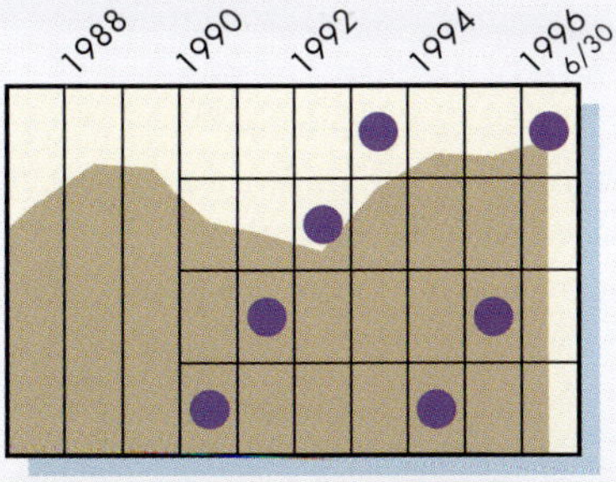

RISK

How often GICs performed better	3 years in 6
How often fund lost money	3 years in 6
Worst year's rate of return	-20.1% (1994)

EFFICIENCY

Management expense/ $100 $3.26

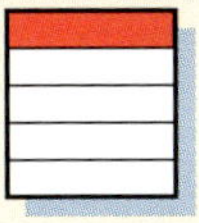

STYLE

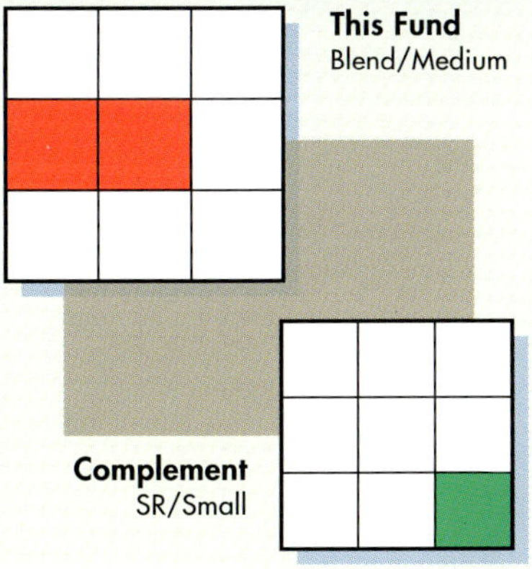

Being right about Hong Kong has, so far, separated the haves from the have-nots in Asian fund management. The large Hong Kong market makes up something like one-quarter of most Asian indexes and Asian funds. But with China's coming takeover in the summer of 1997, opinion is sharply divided on whether the market will soar or sink.

Mount, whose forte is getting the country allocation right, has so far bet that Hong Kong will be the positive beneficiary of the growth in trade and finance of the giant Chinese economy. And with its economic picture clearing these days, the benefit for Hong Kong can come sooner, rather than later.

The reverse is true in Japan, currently 16% of the fund. Its mature economy is being primed with low, low interest rates from the central bank. Again, Mount's timing has been bang on: After avoiding the Japanese market for 6 years (and missing a severe bear market) he bought back in early in 1996, just in time for the rally.

And so it is for an Asian fund. Get the country right and you're all set. But mistakes on country selection could be especially tough on investors in this fund – it typically buys larger positions in fewer markets, so it affords less diversification than its rivals. So far, adroit active management has paid off with steady grades in both rising and falling markets.

REGIONAL EQUITY-FAR EAST

NEW

AGF JAPAN FUND A

Stephen Way (AGF) + Masahito Imai (Nomura)

RRSP

RATING

★ ★ ★ ★ ★

CONSISTENCY

Performance Trend

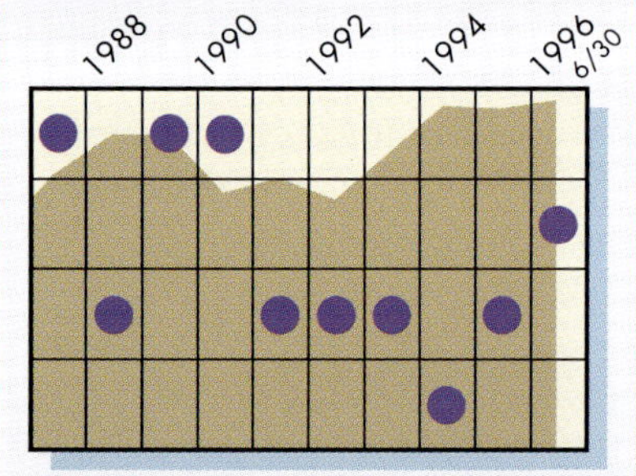

RISK

How often GICs performed better	6 years in 13
How often fund lost money	3 years in 13
Worst year's rate of return	-20.5% (1990)

EFFICIENCY

Management expense/ $100 $2.55

STYLE

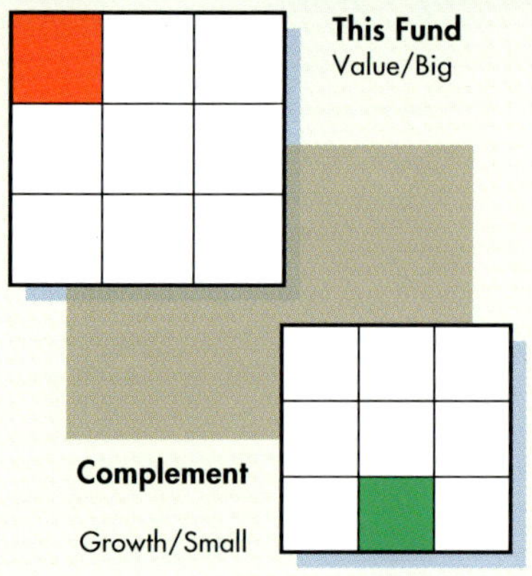

This is the only Japan-specific fund that made the *Top Funds* list this year.

It's been a gut-wrenching decade for Japanese investors, companies, and politicians. But for Japan's largest research firm, missing out on the yen's depreciation in 1995 was particularly tough. While the Nikkei index has rallied some 26% in the twelve months ended in Spring of 1996, this and other funds gave it all back.

A recent 30% hedge on the yen was begun in December of 1995, about five months too late. It's an important defensive move, and a costless one because short-term interest rates are so much higher in Canada. That very situation has lured many foreigners to the Japanese market, driving share prices up. Perhaps because of banking turmoil, there is little local institutional interest in stocks. The fund remains underweight in banks, which continue to be dogged by uncertainty over government bailout plans for agricultural mortgage cooperatives.

Still, the steep yield curve, weak yen, and strong recovery bode well for the market, which is cheaper today than the US in price/book-value terms.

The future lies in Nomura's bullishness on cyclical stocks. If the economy is on track, they'll fuel this important counter-cyclical fund.

NEW

RRSP

ROYAL EUROPEAN GROWTH FUND

Michael Levy (inception)/Bankers Trust

RATING

★ ★ ★ ★ ★

CONSISTENCY

Performance Trend

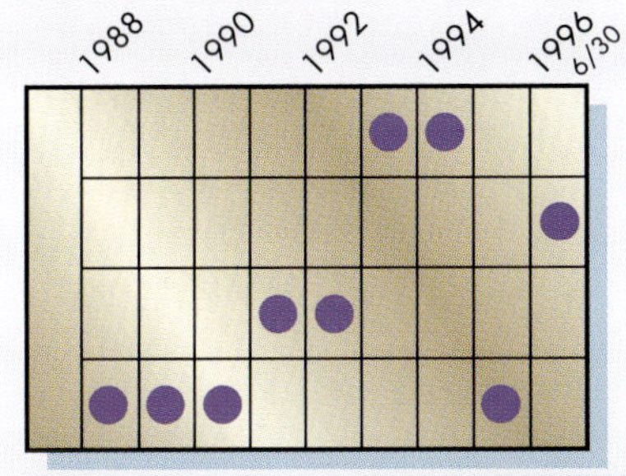

RISK

How often GICs performed better	4 years in 8
How often fund lost money	3 years in 8
Worst year's rate of return	-12.7% (1990)

EFFICIENCY

Management expense/ $100 $2.68

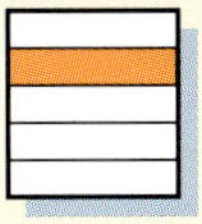

STYLE

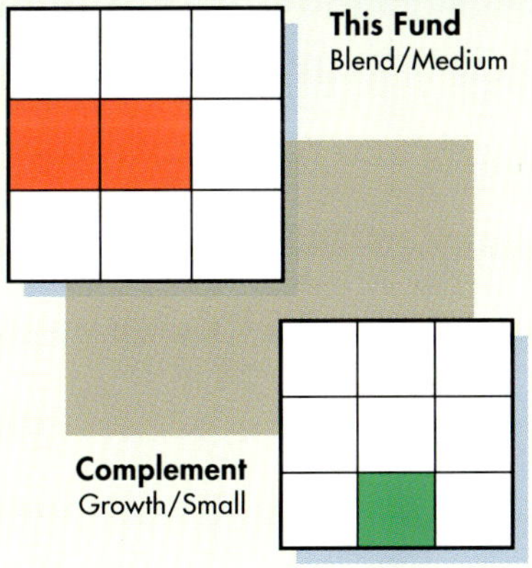

In a crowded field of also-rans, this bank fund stands out as being well-managed. Levy likes to diversify broadly by industry and country (though he sticks mostly to the established European equity markets). Within an industry, though, he makes relatively concentrated bets – that have paid off handsomely. As European economies emerge from recession, this fund is poised to move. It's fully invested and (at writing) had plenty of exposure to interest rate-sensitive and cyclical stocks.

FIDELITY EUROPEAN GROWTH FUND

Sally Walden (inception)/Fidelity

RRSP

RATING

★★★★½

CONSISTENCY

Performance Trend

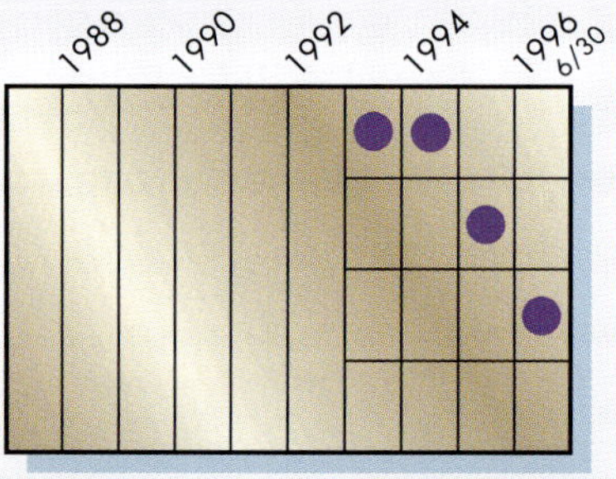

RISK

How often GICs performed better	0 years in 3
How often fund lost money	0 years in 3
Worst year's rate of return	10.1% [1994]

EFFICIENCY

Management expense/ $100 $2.82

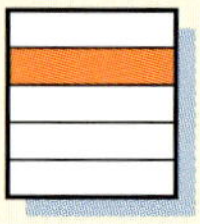

STYLE

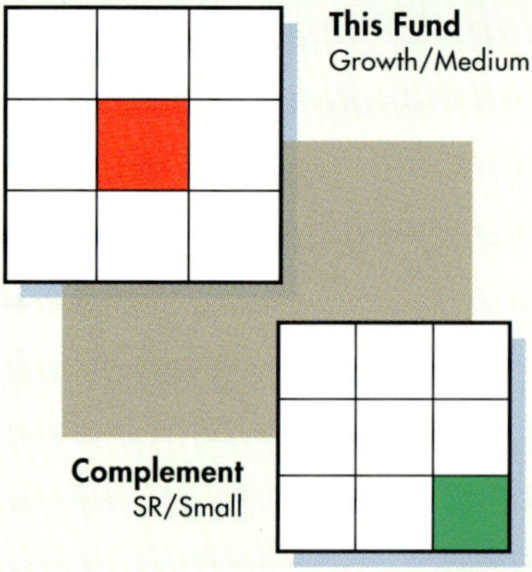

European inflation has turned downward lately – unfortunately, so have the markets. (The mad cow issue hasn't helped much either.)

In the UK, markets have been hurt by upcoming election-year politics. Overall, France has been down and Germany is in a recession, with no sign of improvement while its inflation creeps higher. Thankfully, Sally Walden has recognized that a European equity manager cannot perform well from a top-down approach.

Walden, a mid-size, bottom-up growth manager, has performed well due to stock selection. One of the biggest European market drivers has been the UK, where massive takeover activity has compressed the supply of equities in the market. As a result, British investors have a thirst for new issues. Walden has been successful in identifying smaller UK-based growth companies with strong balance sheets.

The fund has no predetermined country weightings. The manager identifies companies that have a clear focus on cash generation without heavy indebtedness. She chooses stocks based on company fundamentals and while she takes currency into consideration, it is not a driving force for investment decisions. Walden will continue to focus on cash-rich companies that benefit from deregulation and management restructuring.

HYPERION EUROPEAN FUND

RRSP

Bernadette Attard (inception)/Barings International

RATING

★★★½

CONSISTENCY

Performance Trend

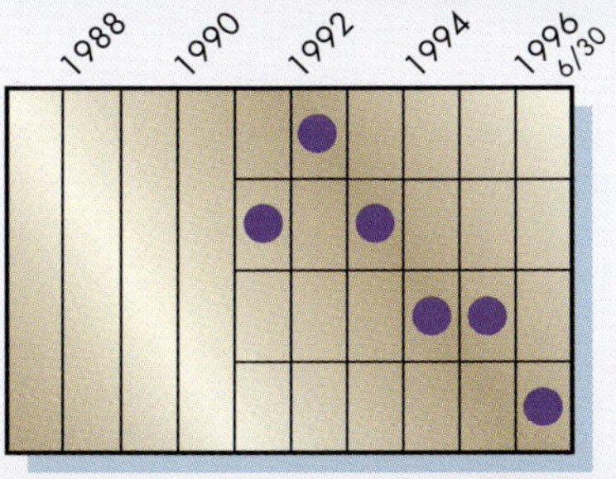

RISK

How often GICs performed better	3 years in 5
How often fund lost money	0 years in 5
Worst year's rate of return	3.0% (1994)

EFFICIENCY

Management expense/ $100 $3.03

STYLE

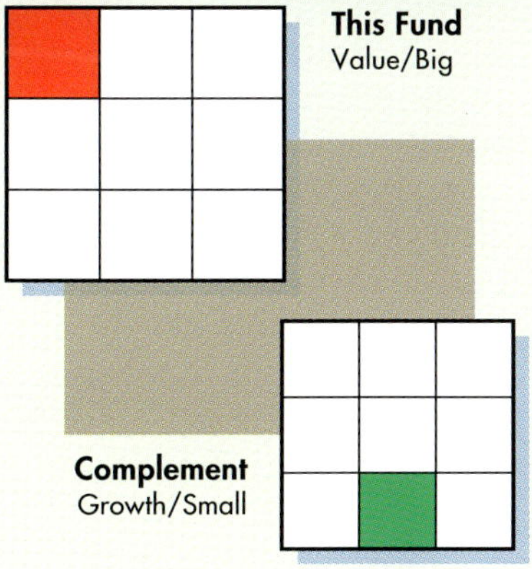

Though it's mostly invested in big companies lately, size doesn't really matter to Attard, whose top-down style of searching Europe for sustainable growth stocks selling at reasonable prices has served investors well. With interest rates still unreasonably high on the continent given the slow pace of the economy, this fund has not been helped by a recent focus on interest-sensitive blue-chip names. Going forward, though, this fund is poised to really move when European interest rates finally decouple and move justifiably lower.

At writing, the fund was fully invested and ready to move, signifying Attard's bullishness.

TEMPLETON EMERGING MARKETS FUND

Mark Mobius (inception)/Templeton

RRSP

RATING

★ ★ ★ ★ ★

CONSISTENCY

Performance Trend

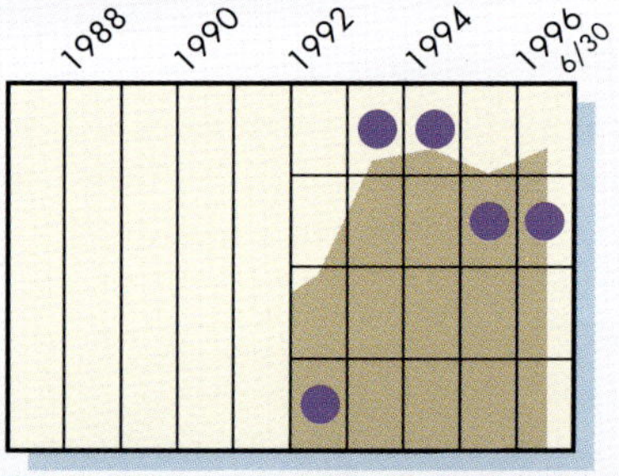

RISK

How often GICs performed better	3 years in 4
How often fund lost money	3 years in 4
Worst year's rate of return	-5.2% (1992)

EFFICIENCY

Management expense/ $100 $3.28

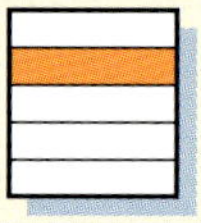

STYLE

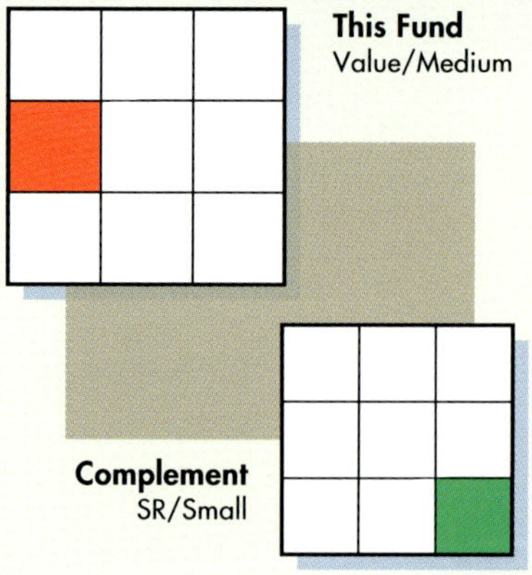

Spirits are high on Mark Mobius's emerging markets research team. The blow dealt to emerging markets, especially those in Latin America, by the 1994 Mexican peso devaluation has helped provide a two-year sale on stocks. All the while, reforms continue in Latin America. The region now makes up about one-fifth of the fund, and serves as a model for other regions in reducing inflation, trade barriers, and corruption.

Markets have been moving strongly since the Fall of 1995, but these value investors are still finding bargains everywhere. In Asia and Latin America, market sentiment has finally turned the corner after many fits and starts during 1995.

Stock selection, as always, is paramount at Templeton. But this fund owns mostly big-cap, proven companies in core industries like those helping to develop infrastructure. Banks, developers, and telecommunications companies account for nearly half the fund. One of the largest positions remains TelMex, the Mexican telephone monopoly that was timed so well just a year ago. TelMex had been sold because of price appreciation (not a market forecast) in the fall of 1994, just before the peso devaluation ripped the stock. Because it was again cheap, the shares were bought back after the meltdown.

The fund holds 28 countries at varying stages of development, offering important diversification for long-term investors.

RRSP

C.I. EMERGING MARKETS FUND

Emilio Bassini (inception)/BEA Associates

RATING

★ ★ ★ ★ ★

CONSISTENCY

Performance Trend

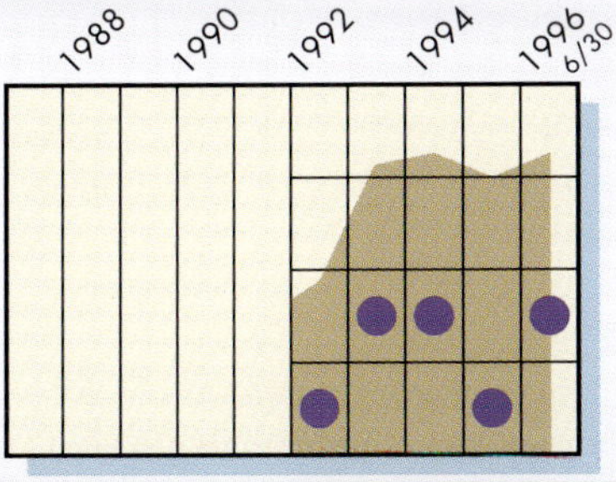

RISK

How often GICs performed better	2 years in 4
How often fund lost money	2 years in 4
Worst year's rate of return	-15.6% (1995)

EFFICIENCY

Management expense/ $100 $2.98

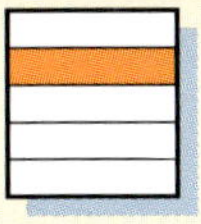

STYLE

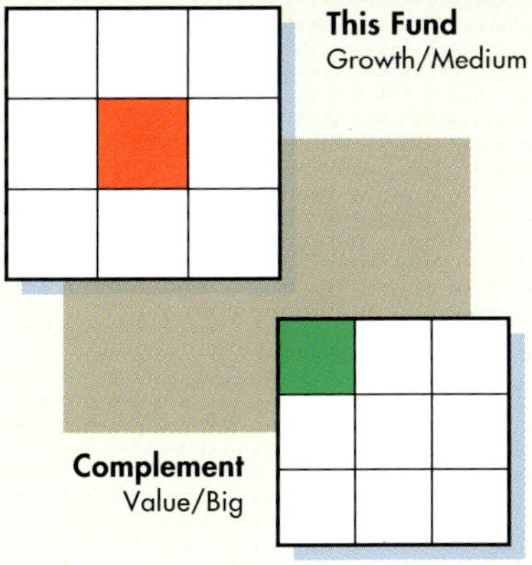

The quartile scores for this fund seem in contrast with its high overall rating. The rating is based on its average monthly rank (AMR), which has been high because in most months, this fund has been a leader. But in just a couple of terrible months (December 1994 and January 1995), this fund's calendar-year fate was sealed for two years. For a fund with better year-by-year ranks (but a lower AMR rating), consider Green Line Emerging Markets Fund.

BEA Associates use a top-down growth model for picking the right countries and stocks. For risk control, they hold 25 countries, with no one nation counting for more than 25%.

This fund has recovered substantially since being punished by manager Emilio Bassini's overweight position in Mexico as the massive peso devaluation rocked the market in December 1994. At the time, holding Mexico was an especially conservative move because its market reforms were the most advanced. Bassini's research strength has always been in the Latin world and as it prospered, so did the fund.

Now the geographic tilt is once again toward Latin America because of compelling valuations, a strong economic recovery, and continuing progress on reforms. But Asia's rebound has been hotter so far in 1996. If and when that changes, this fund should boom.

PRUDENTIAL NATURAL RESOURCE FUND

Jackee Pratt (1995)/Prudential Fund Management

RRSP

RATING

★★★★★

CONSISTENCY

Performance Trend

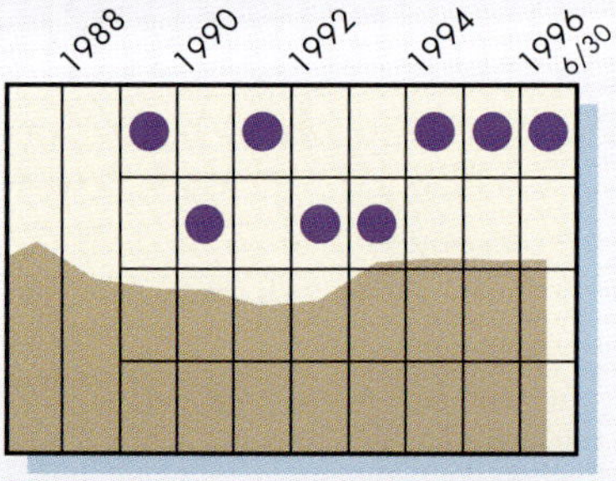

RISK

How often GICs performed better	3 years in 7
How often fund lost money	2 years in 7
Worst year's rate of return	-8.0% (1990)

EFFICIENCY

Management expense/ $100 $1.75

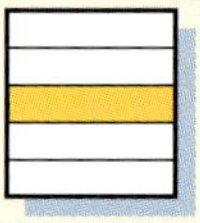

STYLE

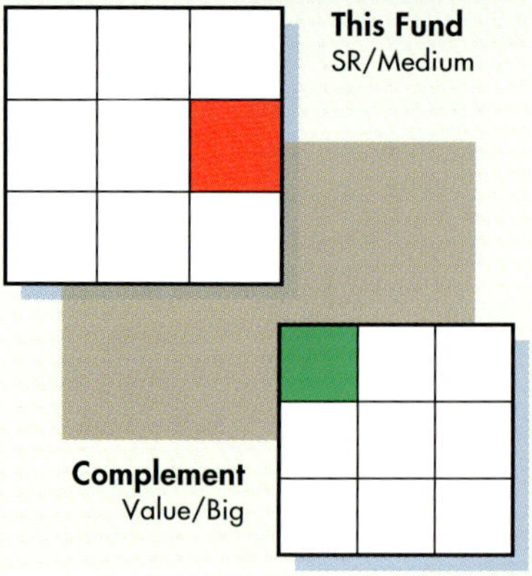

It's tough to inherit a hot fund from a star manager, and even tougher to decide on what to do with big winning positions in the fund. But all that hasn't fazed Jackee Pratt, who took over from departed star Veronika Hirsch. Pratt inherited 91 months of the 101-month history of this fund – the history that earned it a spot in these pages. But in her brief time at the helm she's beaten her benchmarks.

She blew out Diamond Fields Resources – a spectacular find of Hirsch's – after a near double while she held it, and, ultimately, a twentyfold increase to the fund. But she waxes enthusiastic about another hot inherited mining stock, Bre-X Resources, a position she's added to since taking over. This is a bigger-cap resource fund than most, and it employs a blend of value and growth approaches to pick sectors. For current holders of this fund, the advice is to stay, but new investors may want to wait for more confirmation that Pratt has staying power on the top of the charts.

NEW

BPI CANADIAN RESOURCE FUND

RRSP

Fred Dalley (1994)/BPI Capital Management

RATING

★★★★★

CONSISTENCY

Performance Trend

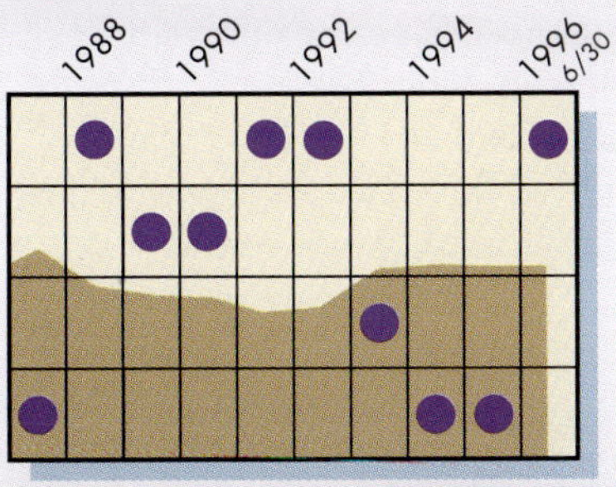

RISK

How often GICs performed better	6 years in 13
How often fund lost money	3 years in 13
Worst year's rate of return	-13.5% (1994)

EFFICIENCY

Management expense/ $100 $2.68

STYLE

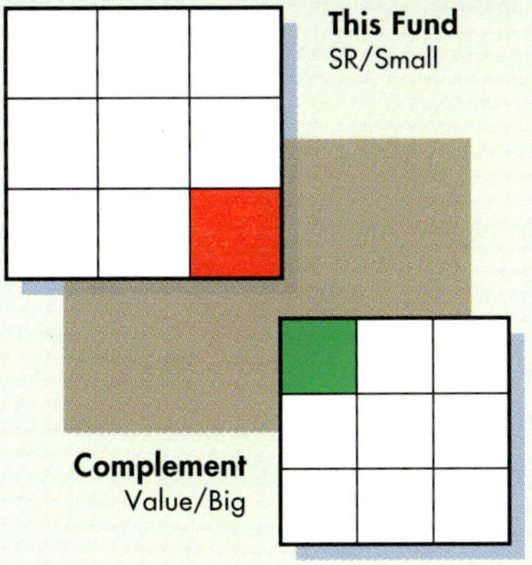

This is a high-octane, high-excitement play on the resource sector: it's not very diversified by group, it buys speculative mining stocks, it trades them heavily, and it makes heavy use of special warrants.

But the fund really does follow a true value discipline. In fact, that's why Dalley buys such small, obscure stocks – they're cheap. He trades so much because when the stocks reach full value, he pulls the trigger. It's tough to criticize or complement an aggressive fund like this; it offers a managed, diversified, leveraged way to play the mines that has never been available.

Its meteoric ascents, however, can be followed by punishing losses. Since 1992 this roller-coaster fund has doubled, then nearly halved, then doubled again. Still, the overall rank for this fund is high enough to put it near the very top of its group. Investors should recognize that if there were a risk continuum for the resource category of *Top Funds*, this would be the most aggressive, and Altamira Resource would today be the least. At time of writing, two-thirds of the fund was in gold and other mining stocks, with most of the remainder in oil and gas stocks. While bullish on gold, the management team welcomed the summer meltdown for gold stocks, as it took the excess air out of the balloon – and bruised this fund more than most.

ALTAMIRA RESOURCE FUND

David Taylor (March 1995)/Altamira Management

RRSP

RATING

CONSISTENCY

Performance Trend

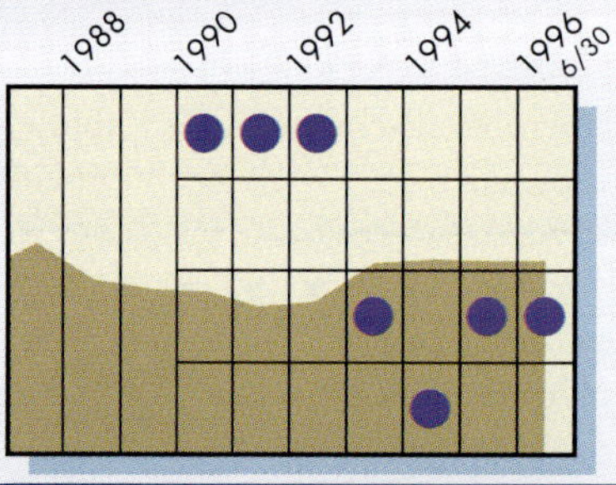

RISK

How often GICs performed better	3 years in 6
How often fund lost money	2 years in 6
Worst year's rate of return	-14.8% (1994)

EFFICIENCY

Management expense/ $100 $2.31

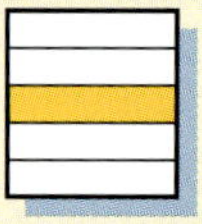

STYLE

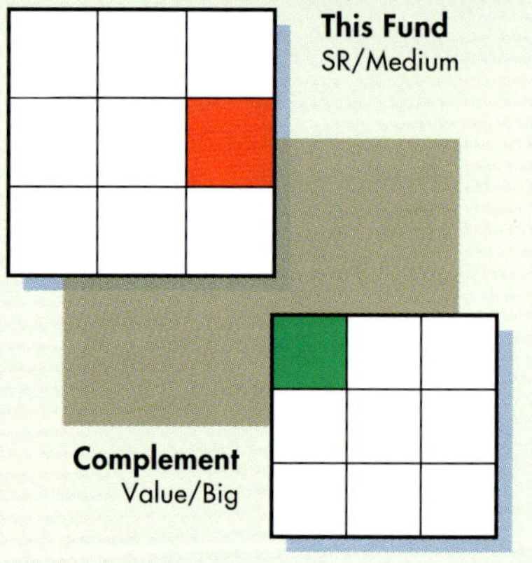

Under previous manager Norm LaMarche, this fund earned 170% in the two years ended December 1993, and investors piled in for more – driving assets all the way up to $1.3 billion. Then came punishing losses (the fund lost 22% in the 12 months ended January 1995). LaMarche moved on as assets tumbled to just one-third their prior peak.

So Altamira went on the hunt for a new and different manager, one who would complement the team's awesome skills at making good sector calls. In Dave Taylor they found a bottom-up guy, a real industry specialist who is more accountant than market seer. Rather than foretell the price of gas, he can find the company whose fundamentals argue that it should be the next takeover target – regardless of the price of the commodity.

Where previous manager Norm LaMarche made forecasts about commodity prices, then bought reams of companies poised to benefit, today's Altamira Resource is set to deliver more enduring satisfaction. Taylor is fiercely risk-averse. He cut the list of stocks held from 130 names to less than 50 to focus on the best. After all, true fundamental company analysis is time-consuming. Following too many names is dilutive. With the trimming came a focus on bigger companies and longer holding periods. The strategy will mute both the ups and downs for the fund, and should produce strong, stable returns over time.

RRSP

AGF CANADIAN RESOURCES FUND A

Bob Farquharson (inception)/AGF

RATING

CONSISTENCY

Performance Trend

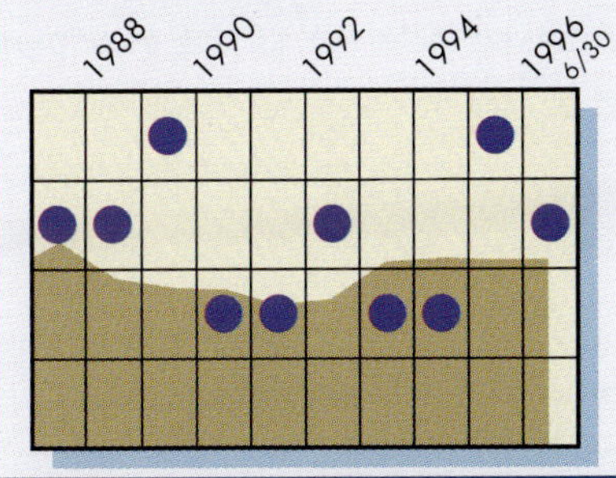

RISK

How often GICs performed better	6 years in 13
How often fund lost money	6 years in 13
Worst year's rate of return	-19.3% (1984)

EFFICIENCY

Management expense/ $100 $2.56

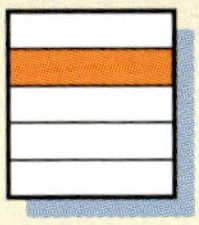

STYLE

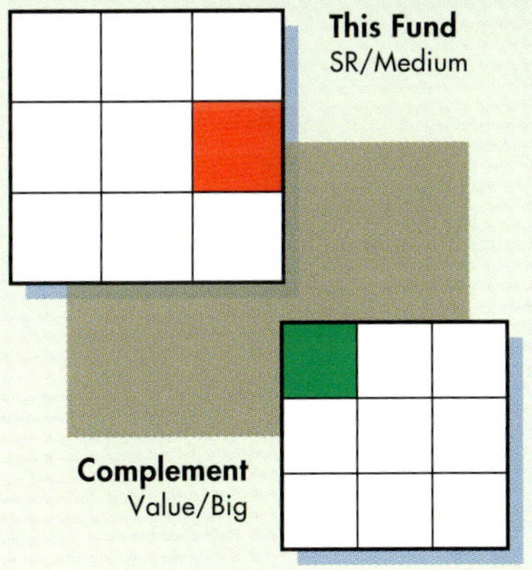

Recommending this fund now may seem odd; after all, even its manager thinks valuations are a bit rich for resource companies. And it's been a fund that tends to lose money after making a bundle.

But now, after a big advance in much of 1996 – and despite valuations – I'm convinced that the 'hedge' value of this fund is powerful, and that foreigners' new interest in our market could provide real growth at this stage in the economic cycle.

This hasn't really been a gold-heavy fund and the team didn't see the gold rally coming in the summer of 1995, when they bought precious metals stocks heavily. They were right on the money, as junior golds took off in the first four months of '96. Now they favour big-name, low-cost producers in a flight to quality.

Though it's lost money in 6 of the last 13 years, this fund isn't just for speculative investors. It's a nice complement to a balanced portfolio of Canadian and international stocks and bonds – because it tends to make money just when other assets are declining.

RESOURCE

ROYAL ENERGY FUND

Gordon Zive (1995)/Royal Bank

RRSP

RATING

CONSISTENCY

Performance Trend

Quartile rankings not meaningful because of lack of similar peers.

RISK

How often GICs performed better	6 years in 13
How often fund lost money	5 years in 13
Worst year's rate of return	-13.4% (1984)

EFFICIENCY

Management expense/ $100 $2.11

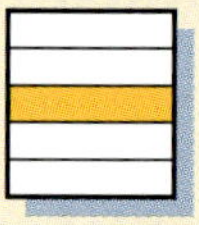

STYLE

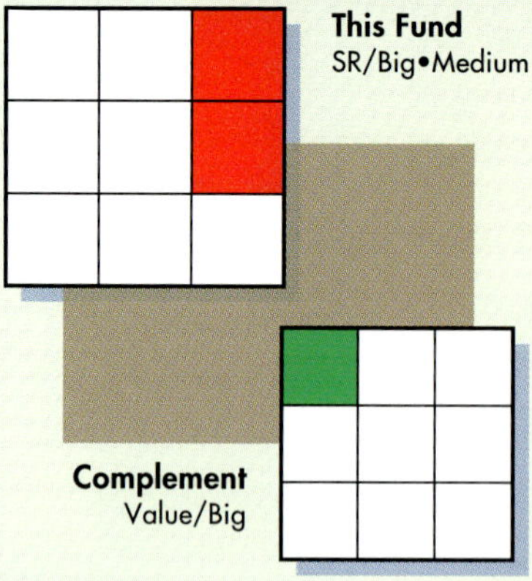

Ironically, my advice is not to buy this energy fund if you're extremely bullish on oil and gas prices.

That's because this is a fund filled with investments of such high calibre that it will miss out on part of the upside in frothy markets. Zive dosen't pretend to know where commodity prices are headed, and says he's never met anyone that consistently does.

What he does know is how to find good oil and gas businesses. Spotting them is like finding a good mutual fund; he looks for a great management track record, an honest established team, a strong growth rate, low exploration and development costs, and real financial strength. That leads to a list of (mostly pricey) highly regarded firms – usually in the bigger-cap area. Less than 1/4 of the fund is generally invested in juniors. But consistency wins the game for this big fund; it beats its peers over time and it beats the TSE oil and gas sub-index handsomely.

TOP FUNDS COMPANY OF THE YEAR:

TRIMARK MUTUAL FUNDS

Trimark's on a tear. The group placed second last year, but pulled ahead this year with seven Top Funds, more than any other company. These include:

- Trimark Canadian Fund
- Trimark Fund
- Trimark Income Growth Fund
- Trimark RSP Equity Fund
- Trimark Select Balanced Fund
- Trimark Select Canadian Growth Fund
- Trimark Select Growth Fund

This year, the runner-up spot is shared by **Altamira** (last year's winner) and **AGF**, both placing 6 funds on the list. Moving up from last year are **C.I.** and **Royal Bank**, with 5 funds, while **Phillips Hager & North** and **Templeton** placed 4 funds each. Companies placing 3 funds include **Beutel Goodman**, **Bissett**, **Dynamic**, **Fidelity**, **Hyperion**, and **Sceptre**. **ABC**, **BPI**, **Empire**, **Guardian**, **MD**, **Prudential**, and **Scotiabank** all placed 2 funds.

Trimark's remarkably consistent balanced and equity funds, both in Canada and abroad, earn high marks on my purely quantitative performance measurement system. But investors already know how strong Trimark's returns have been — they've added an average of $300 million to the family per month for more than a year — dwarfing all rivals. That asset growth has vaulted Trimark to its current #2 rank in assets with over $17 billion (behind **Investors Group**). Trimark's stock price has grown five-fold since its debut just a few years ago.

Trimark's investment approach is intuitively appealing: they don't try to predict the near-term movements of the stock market. Instead, they work hard finding businesses that have great products, are well-managed, and can grow. If anything, such businesses have become relatively cheaper as the North American bull market continues, so Trimark's style can more appropriately now be described as value, or a blend of value and growth. For more on their lead manager and founder Robert Krembil, see the *Top Funds Hall of Fame* (page 234).

Trimark's running a tighter ship all the time, with management expense ratios in their rear-load Select funds down to about 2.3% from nearly 2.6% on average in 1990.

Altogether, their Canadian equities under management total over $5 billion — more than 1% of the TSE. And while their girth is deterring some, I'm convinced that their low-turnover style and shortlist of target companies is poised to deliver impressively in the coming years. And manager turnover at the firm may actually have been a positive; the augmented team is arguably stonger functionally, bigger, and more experienced than before.

HOW TO BUILD A TOP FUNDS PORTFOLIO

I believe that the research findings presented in the *Top Funds* listings can be valuable to individual investors, but only if they are applied. Knowledge is **not** power; ***applied*** knowledge is.

So let's get started on building your *Top Funds* portfolio.

THE IMPORTANCE OF ASSET ALLOCATION

What is the most critical factor in successful mutual fund investing? Like many people, you may believe that it all depends on picking the "right" fund — the one with the best numbers. But as most fund managers know, consistently high returns do not depend on putting money into specific securities; rather, they depend on putting money into the right *types* of securities. The same rule applies to mutual fund investing: put your money into the right fund categories, and chances are you'll be further ahead in the long run.

The categories of funds you choose — and the weighting of each category relative to the portfolio as a whole — is known as asset allocation. And research has shown that it accounts for between 85% and 92% of total portfolio returns. (By contrast, the same research puts the contribution of security selection — that is, choice of specific investments — at only about 2%!)

Clearly, the overriding decision in the development of any investment portfolio is the mix of assets within it. Traditionally, however, individual investors have given the **least** consideration to this **most important** decision.

Conversely, the selection of individual components (securities) is of relatively little importance. Yet investors usually spend the most time and energy in making this **least significant** decision.

WHAT ASSET CATEGORIES SHOULD BE INCLUDED?

A well balanced portfolio should include the following:

Fixed-income investments, such as

- **Cash or cash equivalents** (CSBs, term deposits, Treasury bills) to provide liquidity for an emergency or an opportunity
- **Canadian bonds** for stability and high income
- **International bonds** for protection against Canadian interest-rate risk

Equity (stock) investments, such as

- **Canadian equities,** to participate in our growth via a number of world-class Canadian success stories
- **International equities,** to hedge the "Canada risk" and for the broadest possible range of investment choices
- **Real estate,** for inflation protection with tax benefits and income
- **Precious metals, including gold,** for protection from inflation and crisis
- **Oil and gas,** for inflation protection with tax benefits and income

WHAT'S THE RIGHT BALANCE FOR ME?

There is no "perfect" asset mix that's right for every investor. It will vary from person to person, depending on factors such as time horizon, investment objectives and risk tolerance.

Here are some super-simplified guidelines that will help you approximate the mix that's right for you:

1. Start with your age

The total percentage of your portfolio held in fixed-income investments (that is, cash and cash equivalents, as well as government and corporate bonds) should approximately match your age. So if you have a $100,000 portfolio and you are 40 years old, about $40,000 should be in fixed income. This is a very rough rule of thumb, but without a questionnaire or interview, this is the best way for you to start on your own.

2. Assess your risk tolerance

Imagine a scale ranging from 1 to 10, where a "1" represents the most pathologically cautious, nervous type of investor — the sort of person who keeps their money under the mattress because they're certain the banks will collapse. A "10" is (or would like to be) a professional gambler.

Which number are you? My experience is that everyone has an intuitive sense of where they fall on the scale.

3. Adjust your fixed-income percentage

Here we combine the previous two factors: age and risk tolerance.

If your risk tolerance is in the middle of the scale at "5," then make no adjustment to the fixed-income component of your portfolio based on your age.

For every number **higher** than 5, reduce the fixed-income component by 5%. For example, if you are 40 years old and rate yourself a "7" on the risk tolerance scale, reduce your fixed-income component by 10% — in this case, from 40% to 30%.

For every number **lower** than 5, add 5% to the fixed-income component. For example, if you are 40 years old and rate yourself a "2" on the risk tolerance scale, **increase** your fixed-income component by 15% — in this case, from 40% to 55%.

Notice that the effect of these guidelines is to increase the conservative component of our portfolio as we age and become less aggressive.

Top Funds Close Up

What about Asset Allocation Funds?

While there are several asset allocation funds available now in Canada, as well as at least two asset allocation services (which switch among several funds), none of these can be personalized to meet **your** unique needs.

While these asset allocation funds are making important tactical bets to trim risk and boost returns, they've not been able to outperform most balanced funds. So, I believe that you should develop a portfolio mix specifically designed to meet your time horizon and investment personality.

WHAT ABOUT THE OTHER ASSET WEIGHTINGS?

Again, this will vary from person to person. But let's continue with the example of our 40-year-old investor who ranks a "5" on the risk-tolerance scale.

For this individual, a reasonable balance might look like this:

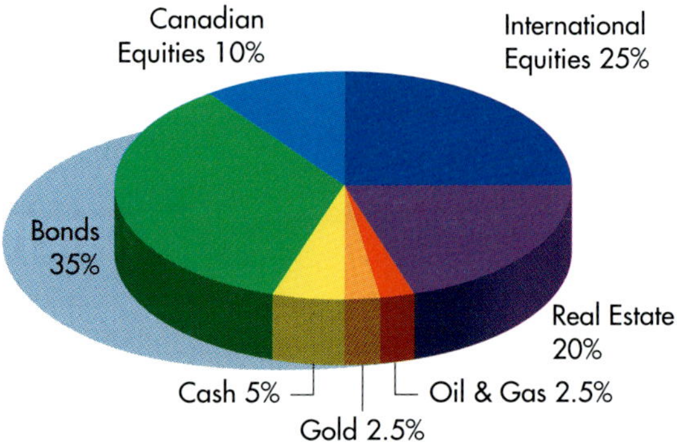

RETURNS BY ASSET TYPE

Year	Cash	Bonds	Canadian Equities	International Equities	Real Estate	Oil & Gas	Gold	Balanced Portfolio
Asset Allocation	5%	35%	10%	25%	20%	2.50%	2.50%	100%
1979	12	-3	45	14	13	82	91	15
1980	13	7	30	33	23	46	43	21
1981	18	4	-10	-5	26	-29	-38	4
1982	14	35	6	21	1	-14	39	20
1983	9	12	36	25	7	19	-2	16
1984	11	15	-2	16	12	-19	-20	11
1985	10	21	25	40	10	11	33	24
1986	9	15	9	29	13	-2	29	17
1987	8	4	6	5	14	18	17	7
1988	9	10	11	10	17	-8	-28	10
1989	12	13	21	21	20	25	5	17
1990	13	8	-15	-12	5	-10	1	0
1991	9	22	12	22	0	-9	-12	14
1992	7	10	-1	6	-6	23	2	5
1993	6	18	33	22	-4	68	83	18
1994	5	-4	0	10	2	-12	-3	1
1995	8	21	15	26	5	13	-17	17
Average	10	12	13	17	9	12	13	13
Variation high to low	13	39	60	52	32	111	129	24
# of years of positive rates	17	15	13	15	15	9	10	17
# of years of negative rates	0	2	4	2	2	8	7	0

Courtesy of the Equion Group
Sources
Cash 91 day Canada T-bill **Bonds** Scotia McLeod Universe Bond Index prior to 1985 - Scotia McLeod Long Bond Index **Cdn. Equities** TSE 300 Return Index
Int'l Equities 50% Morgan Stanley World Total Return Index, 50% S&P 500
Real Estate Russell Property Index prior to 1990 - Morguard Property Index
Oil & Gas AGF Canadian Resource Fund **Gold** Gold Trust Mutual Fund

How do we know that this balance will work? Well, history is on our side, as you'll see — just study the table shown at left. It outlines the portfolio that's been developed for our 40-year-old investor. As you'll see, it shows that a balanced portfolio has offered a number of major advantages over this period.

The bottom line for the balanced portfolio is that it can provide **above-average returns** with **reduced risk**, and offer **preferred tax treatment** at the same time. (See pages 172–174 for more on tax-advantaged mutual fund investing.) My experience is that investors who can obtain all three of these advantages are very happy indeed.

Clearly, there's a lot to be said for developing the right balance among asset categories.

THE IMPORTANCE OF DIVERSIFICATION

A Nobel Prize was awarded for research related to investments. The prizewinning conclusion: it's better not to put "all your eggs in one basket"!

Sounds simple, and it is. But what does it mean for individuals and why is it so important?

We've already discussed the concept of a balanced portfolio — where that balance is achieved by weighting your holdings across various asset categories. There are other ways to diversify, some of which were discussed earlier in the book.

DIVERSIFICATION TYPE	EXAMPLES
Geography	Canada, US, Pacific Rim, Latin America
Investment Style	value, growth
Investment Objective	growth, income
Management Team	Altamira, Mackenzie, Templeton, Trimark

As our portfolio becomes appropriately balanced, it becomes more diversified, and there are major advantages to this diversification.

The accompanying chart shows how diversifying across asset categories helps to reduce risk. Notice that with one asset category in a portfolio (that is, "all your eggs in one basket"), the risk (measured by standard deviation) is about 15%. With each additional asset category, the risk declines, so that with representation in eight asset categories (and there really aren't many more) it's cut almost in half to 9%.

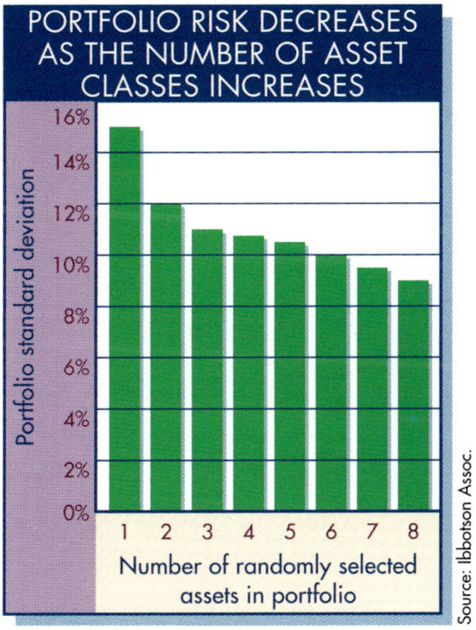

Similarly, when dealing with stocks only, unsystematic risk is substantially reduced by going from owning one stock to owning 128 (although research shows that after 50 stocks are in a portfolio, subsequent additions reduce risk only minimally).

Top Funds Close Up

Can you be overdiversified?

My rule on diversification is this: Don't buy two things that do the same thing. That is, you don't need three small-cap Canadian equity value funds. They're just too similar. If you're going to buy three Canadian equity funds you should get three of legitimately different styles. I would argue that such a strategy could lower the risk to your portfolio through diversification. In his introduction to *Bogle on Mutual Funds,* Paul Samuelson shows that returns by underdiversified managers are lower. And Morningstar has proven that such managers do have higher risk. Those are two arguments that overdiversification is a myth. So the real enemy is over-duplication!

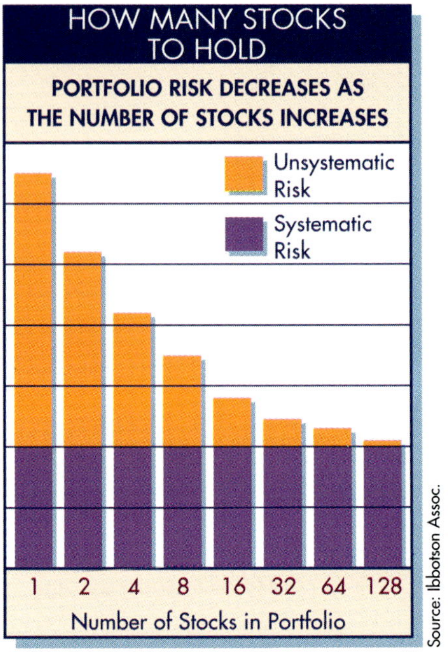

Essentially, diversification is a conservative strategy which acknowledges that we will not always be right in our selection of securities, geographic location, or manager. By not overweighting our position in any one of these, the negative impact of being wrong is reduced. Once we acknowledge that we will not be right all the time, we are able to adjust our thinking to achieve more consistent (if less spectacular) growth and avoid big (and potentially) devastating losses.

A FUND FAMILY APPROACH TO INVESTING

Good fund families have all or most of these characteristics:

- broad choice of consistent funds
- reasonable expenses
- easy availability (i.e., not available only through the Sled-Dog Owners Association of Baffin Island)
- good administration/service/communication
- deep stable of talented analysts on staff or on contract
- sufficient resources to hire the best, promote their funds and keep from being acquired (when your fund company gets bought, the new owners often get their own team in, even if they're not always better)

Let's explore the merit of the fund family approach to investing.

Try to pick a great family (or a couple of them if you've got lots of dough).

A family that's strong all around — great stock funds in Canada and abroad, and great bond and specialty funds. Since few fund families actually possess all these attributes here's a subjective listing of all the major fund families and best/worst characteristics of each. Decide which are best for you by leaning towards those that are strong in areas you favour:

	Strength	**Weakness**
Templeton	International equities	Domestic stocks & bonds
AGF 20/20	Bonds, specialty/ regional funds	Loss of star manager Veronika Hirsch
Mackenzie	Broad selection, STAR program	Few standout funds
Investors	Asia (Carlson), training	No unbiased intermediary
Trimark	North America, balanced	Very sensitive to rich US market
MD	International	Domestic equities
Bank funds	TD, Royal & Canada Trust	Bank of Montreal

BUILDING YOUR PERSONALIZED PORTFOLIO

Now we get down to the business of portfolio construction. Here I'll provide two specific examples as a guide — although I emphasize that, for your own personal needs, you should seek assistance from an experienced, professional financial advisor. It's too big and important a decision to be making without some experienced professional help.

Earlier, I identified two key factors that you can use in deciding the right allocation between the two major asset categories of equities and fixed income: your **age** and **risk tolerance**, identified on a scale from 1 to 10.

Use the table below to calculate how much of your portfolio should be in fixed-income investments and how much should be in equities.

MODIFYING THE "AGE RULE"

Percentage variation to the Fixed-Income/Equity Split

Investment Split \ Risk Tolerance (1-10)	1	2	3	4	5	6	7	8	9	10
Fixed Income	+20	+15	+10	+5	age	-5	-10	-15	-20	-25
Equity	-20	-15	-10	-5	only	+5	+10	+15	+20	+25

Fund Fact

The Myth of Managed Money

It sounds so prestigious — a discretionary money manager taking care of your substantial portfolio. Trouble is, if you go to the manager for advice, you're unlikely to be advised to diversify by manager and by style. You see, a segregated account where you actually own the securities (100 shares of Coca-Cola, for example) is different from owning a pool (like a mutual fund) but only slightly. And for the give-up in terms of flexibility (you need big dollars to go segregated with one manager), you sacrifice so much — because you probably can't afford to get other complementary managers.

So let's look at two people of different ages and risk tolerance, and see what type of mix would be right for them. While the overall mix might not change much in different economic conditions, I might alter specific fund recommendations to reflect different geographic weighting, bond maturities, or investment styles. The specific funds recommended reflect my views at August 1996, and may change over time.

EXAMPLE #1

Steven is 45 years old with a portfolio valued at $300,000; he's fairly aggressive with a risk-tolerance rating of 8 on a scale of 10.

The Process

Using the model, Steven's asset split will be approximately 30% fixed income and 70% equities. We start with his age to get an initial 45% fixed-income component and adjust it according to his risk-tolerance assessment (8). Here, the risk value is three above the median value of five, so we reduce his fixed-income split by 15% (3 × 5%), to 30%. That leaves equities at 70%.

Now that we have worked out the relative proportions of fixed-income and equity investments for Steven's portfolio, we need to select specific types of investments for each category. To simplify this process, refer to the "decision trees" for each category.

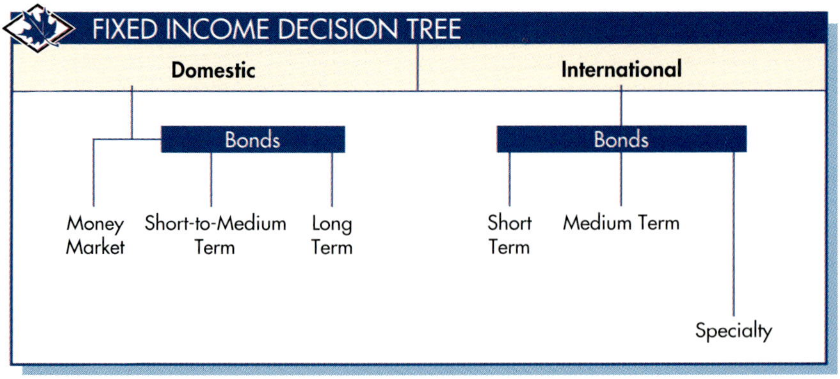

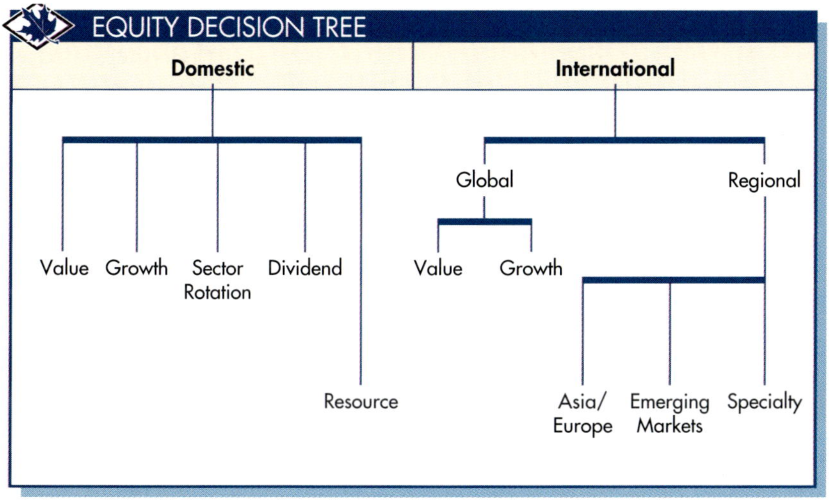

EQUITY DECISION TREE

Take a look now at the Fixed Income Decision Tree. The process is simple: we go to the top left branch and allocate $10,000. Then we keep moving to the right, allocating $10,000 at each branch until we run out of money. Once we've reached the rightmost branch — assuming more money remains to be allocated — we go down to the next level of the tree.

The same procedure is used for both the Fixed Income and Equity Decision Trees — work across and down the branches, investing approximately $10,000 at each level until we run out of money. (By the way, $10,000 is just a suggested minimum per fund; you should allocate enough to have evenly-sized positions.) The decision trees simply represent a prioritization tool. Start with basics, then get specialty funds. The decision tree isn't meant to be taken too literally — there's no need to follow slavishly every branch.

Fixed Income ($100,000)

Let's start with the fixed-income component, where we have $100,000 to place. We begin always on the left (more conservative) branch and allocate as follows:

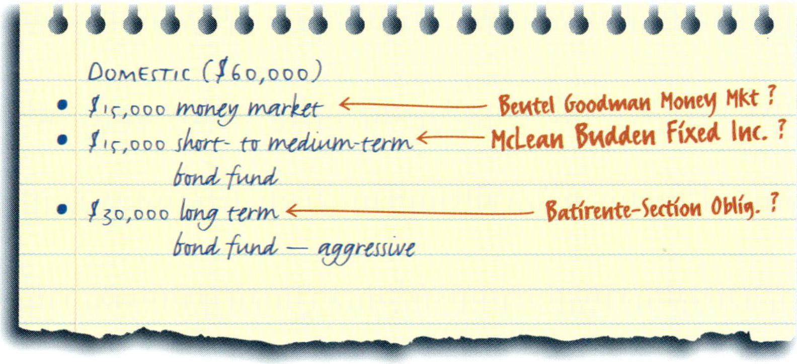

As a general rule, I suggest about two-thirds of bonds be Canadian and one-third foreign: $60,000 invested as outlined above meets the Canadian goal. (In this example, we have sufficient funds to invest $15,000 under each heading.) The remaining $40,000 fixed income would go to:

INTERNATIONAL ($40,000)

- $30,000 medium-term bond fund hedged ← Global Strategy World Bond ?
- $10,000 specialty bond fund in emerging markets ← Fidelity Emerging Markets Bond ?

Note the diversification achieved with domestic and international positions as well as maturities of different terms. Note also that international bond funds do not tend to hold long-term bonds (foreign governments seldom issue 30-year debt like Canada does), so we go from medium-term to specialty funds.

This more aggressive selection recognizes the investor's relatively high tolerance for risk.

Equity $200,000

We now move to the equity component where we have $200,000 to position and the proposal looks like this:

DOMESTIC ($70,000)

- $20,000 value, small cap ← Sceptre Equity Growth ?
- $10,000 growth, small cap ← Bissett Small Cap ?
- $10,000 sector rotation small cap ← BPI Cdn. Small Cos ?
- $10,000 precious metals ← Dynamic Precious Metals ?
- $10,000 energy (oil and gas) ← Royal Energy ?
- $10,000 preferred dividend ← PH&N Dividend ?

FOREIGN ($130,000)

- $30,000 global value ← Templeton International Stock Fund ?
- $20,000 global growth ← Trimark Fund ?
- $20,000 regional, Asia ← C.I. Pacific ?
- $40,000 regional, Europe ← Royal European Growth ?
- $20,000 single-country ← AGF Japan ?

Because of the nature of the investor, we'll pass on the more conservative value, large-cap fund.

Note the balance geographically as well as among styles of managers.

This portfolio is a non-registered account and has $170,000 in foreign content. If it were registered, we could hold $60,000 in foreign content and would adjust as follows:

- delete $20,000 from international fixed income and add to Canadian fixed income,
- retain $40,000 foreign equity: $10,000 global value; $20,000 global growth; $10,000 regional growth,
- reposition $90,000 foreign equity to domestic equity, with similar style allocation.

EXAMPLE #2

Ellen is 70 years old with a portfolio of $200,000 and a self-assessed "6" on the risk-tolerance scale.

• *The Process*

Ellen's asset split will be approximately 65% fixed income and 35% equities. We start with her age to get an initial 70% fixed-income component and adjust it according to her risk-tolerance assessment (6). Here, the risk value is one above the median value of five, so we reduce her fixed-income split by 5%, to 65%. That leaves equities at 35%.

We then go to the appropriate decision trees for the fixed-income and equity components (pages 153 and 159) and work across and down the branches, usually investing approximately $10,000 at each level until we run out of money.

• *Fixed Income ($130,000)*

Again we go to the decision tree, generally working left to right under each major heading, investing a minimum of $10,000 per fund.

In this case, there is enough money — at $10,000 per fund — to cover all headings, so we go back and allocate additional amounts in a somewhat subjective fashion, attempting to match the allocation as closely as possible to the individual's needs and aggressiveness.

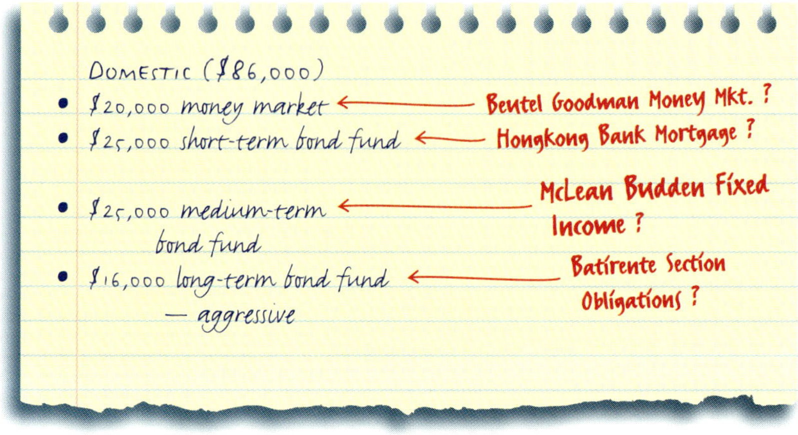

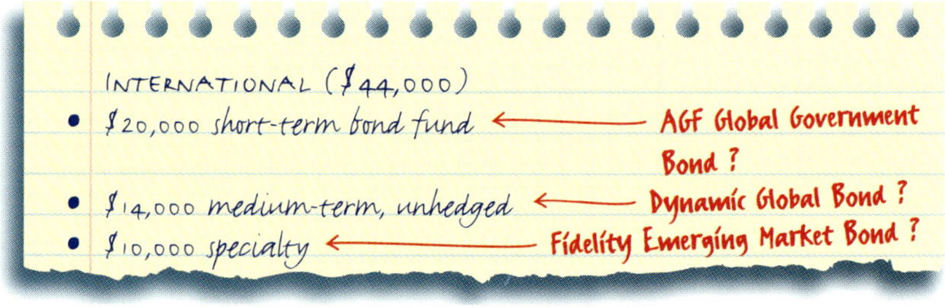

• *Equity ($70,000)*

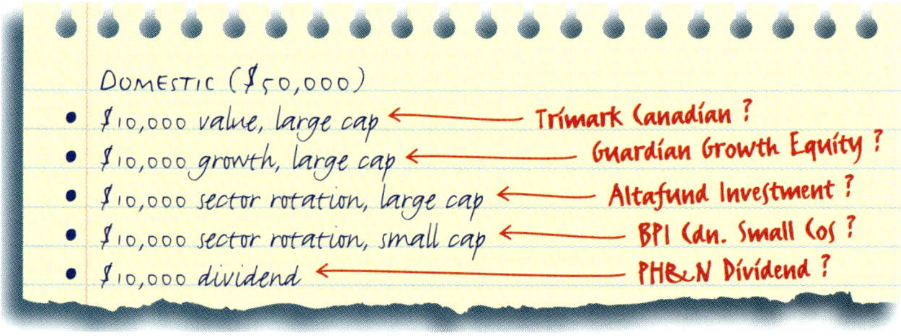

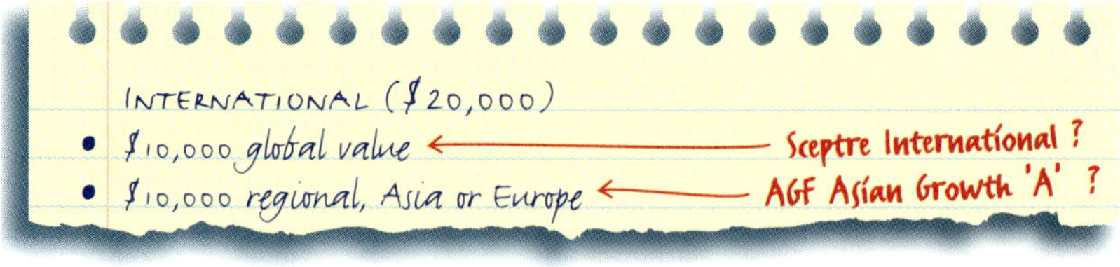

If this were a fully registered plan, we'd have $40,000 available for foreign content ($200,000 × 20%) and would adjust it as follows:

- reduce international fixed income to $20,000 by holding only $10,000 short-term and $10,000 medium-term,
- roll other $24,000 into Canadian fixed income,
- equity portion would be unchanged.

Using our rules of thumb for allocating resources among the asset categories, and using the *Top Funds* listings, you can construct a portfolio for virtually any situation.

MUTUAL FUND CHECKUP

Is your fund portfolio a mess? Many are. Many investors acquire funds like groceries; they buy whatever strikes their fancy at that moment. They end up with too many funds, too much paperwork, and no real plan. Here's a quiz to identify whether you're making some of the more common mistakes:

- ***Is your asset allocation off-balance?***

This is by far the most important determinant of how you do over time, so don't ignore it. Some investors hope that great funds in a random mix will help them prosper. But even owning great funds (in the wrong asset categories) could sink you. Achieving a balanced portfolio is critical to reducing risk and making more money. Use the simple "Age Rule" guide on page 153 or an asset-allocation questionnaire such as Mackenzie's STAR, Bank of Montreal's MatchMaker, or Midland Walwyn's COMPASS to determine your optimal asset allocation. Rejig within the same families you already own to achieve a more appropriate mix if necessary.

Top Funds Close Up

Bond funds — an idea whose time has gone?

Most bond funds are well managed and have made money for their investors. But with today's low interest rates, their expenses are looking disproportionately high against the returns you're likely to get. As a result, if you're willing to forgo the convenience of funds, you should be able to get a slightly higher yield by buying and holding bonds yourself.

It's not that bond fund returns are awful — they're not. But a large proportion of their gains were made in periods when interest rates were falling from double-digit levels.

But MERs can really cut into investors' returns in a year like this, when the average Canadian bond fund's gross yield is less than 8%.

To be fair, bond funds do provide convenience, diversification, and liquidity. Specialty bond funds would be impossible to duplicate on your own.

In order to set up a properly diversified portfolio, you should wait until you have about $25,000 to invest before buying directly.

In short, if you want long-term income from your bonds rather than short-term trading gains, you might as well buy them directly. Otherwise, you're paying a premium price for what is basically just a commodity product.

Templeton Growth Fund is a classic example of a buy-and-hold fund. A $10,000 investment in this fund in November 1954 — with no subsequent contributions or withdrawals — was worth over $3.7 million in 1996. You could have been Rip Van Winkle and slept for 40 years and done very well with Templeton Growth.

But even if your interest is to "buy and hold," I'm generally not comfortable ignoring the investment completely. So to monitor, I suggest you look for changes in the fund's management or for changes to its investment philosophy and, of course, continue to be aware of its performance compared to others in its category.

The buy-and-hold strategy isn't as exciting as some others, but if you can find a true "buy and hold" fund, you'll be a happy investor.

THE "BOB AND WEAVE" STRATEGY

This approach is quite the opposite of "buy and hold" and "dollar cost averaging." It's based on a belief that we, as individuals, can anticipate certain trends, developments, or events, and can "bob and weave," or switch among funds and asset categories to take advantage of them.

Most fund companies now allow you to switch from one of their funds to another — generally at no cost, although a fund's prospectus often provides for a fee of up to 2%. Some of the no-load funds charge an administration fee each time you do so after a certain number of "free" switches.

Now it's true that certain asset categories tend to do better at different times in the economic cycle. For example, when interest rates are falling, government bonds will tend to do well; when interest rates are low, equities will likely do well; and, when rates are rising, a cash-type investment may perform best.

But I believe very strongly that you should hold a balanced portfolio. So I urge that the "bob and weave" approach not be taken too far. Sure, there could be strategic times to rebalance; but those who attempt to be "market timers" do not consistently come out on top. It's a risky strategy and one that I urge be used with caution — probably as part of ongoing discussions with your financial advisor.

THE ASSET ALLOCATION STRATEGY

The asset allocation approach is a much more disciplined and more effective strategy than the "bob and weave." In this strategy, the overall mix between fixed income and equities is determined by your age and aggressiveness as an investor. (For more about asset allocation, see pages 151–154.) Then the specific components of the portfolio are selected and "plugged in" to the overall framework.

Remember, the research shows very clearly that the overall mix between equities and fixed income is **the single most important investment decision.** All other variables, including market timing, are of very little importance.

Of course, it will be necessary to rebalance your portfolio from time to time, particularly if one asset category has done extremely well in the past year. If it has, it may have grown to a larger-than-appropriate percentage of the portfolio.

Another reason to adjust your portfolio may be advancing age. I believe that as you age (and all other things being equal), the relative weighting of fixed-income assets in your portfolio should grow. As well, some investors become more (or less) aggressive over the years — for a whole variety of reasons — and this change must be reflected in the overall holdings.

Finally, as indicated above, certain economic conditions lend themselves to shifts in the weighting of certain asset categories that may not otherwise be appropriate.

The main point here is that changes made to a balanced portfolio should be the result of a well-considered set of plans and have little to do with an attempt to time the market — which is more a part of the "bob and weave" approach.

THE LEVERAGING STRATEGY

This is an aggressive strategy with great upside potential — as well as some significant risk. The theory is to use other people's money — usually a bank loan — adding it to yours and investing the entire amount. What you owe remains constant, or may be reduced by monthly payments, while the overall investment grows in value.

Let's assume you take $20,000 of your own money and borrow another $80,000 to make a $100,000 investment. Let's assume your investment grows by 20% to $120,000. You still owe $80,000, so you "own" $40,000 of the investment. Although the value of the portfolio grew by only 20%, your "stake" actually doubled from $20,000 to $40,000 — a 100% increase!

It can get even better. Assuming you borrowed the money to invest **outside** your RRSP, the interest you pay the bank to finance the loan will be tax deductible. (Interest on RRSP loans is no longer deductible.) And assuming that you selected investments that generate tax-advantaged dividends or capital gains, your after-tax returns will be better still. (Even though the $100,000 capital gains exemption has been abolished, capital gains are still taxed at only 75% of the amount charged on, say, interest income.)

So far, we've seen only the rosy side of leveraging. But there's another side that must be considered. Let's assume our $100,000 **declines** in value by 20% to $80,000. That represents the entire amount of your contribution to the total investment. So your original $20,000 will have been wiped out — for a pretty frightening loss of 100%!

Given the potential dangers inherent in leveraging strategies, I suggest that you adhere to the following guidelines:

- Borrow to a maximum of one-third of the total investment.
- Be sure cash flow will allow ongoing loan payments; don't expect to pay the loan back from profits.
- Try to avoid "securing" the loan with other assets, especially your home; unsecured loans are widely available at slightly higher rates.

THE INCOME-SPLITTING STRATEGY

For those who want to reduce their income tax burden, income splitting is very effective.

This simple strategy attempts to take a portion of the earnings attributed to a high-income earner, and place it in the hands of the lower-income spouse. By doing so, many thousands of tax dollars can be saved annually.

Take a look at the chart below.

SAVE TAXES THROUGH INCOME SPLITTING

THE USUAL SITUATION

	Jim	Peggy
Annual Retirement Income	$100,000	$0.00
Marginal Tax Rate	53.19%	0.00%
Tax Liability	$40,509	$0.00

THE INCOME SPLITTING STRATEGY

	Jim	Peggy*
Annual Retirement Income	$60,000	$40,000
Marginal Tax Rate	50.05%	41.86%
Tax Liability	$19,377	$10,688
Total Tax Liability	$30,065	

Tax Savings: $10,443 after-tax per year

* Basic personal exemption only

In most cases, as shown in the first example, retirement income is concentrated (if not placed exclusively) in the hands of the higher-income earner. By creating and contributing to a spousal RRSP over a number of years, Jim has achieved the same level of retirement income, but it is more evenly split between Jim and Peggy, as the second example shows.

Notice that in the first example, the tax bill is over $40,000, but that in the income-splitting example, the combined tax bill is just over $30,000. This has been achieved by moving Jim to a lower tax bracket so he pays only about $20,000 in tax instead of $40,000. Peggy now pays tax too, but at a lower rate, so she pays about $10,000.

That's an after-tax saving of over $10,000 per year! By repeating the scene over and over again, Jim and Peggy can likely save well over $100,000 in taxes over 10 years.

THE TAX-EFFICIENT STRATEGY

Tax-Efficient/Inefficient Portfolio

Examine the tax-**inefficient** portfolio. Notice that the bonds are held outside the RRSP and are therefore fully taxed. The stocks held in an equity fund are inside the RRSP and therefore tax-free. Because the bonds are taxed, the after-tax return is 11.25%.

Now look at the tax-**efficient** portfolio and notice that now, the bonds are held inside the RRSP and therefore tax-free. The equities are held outside the RRSP and even though they are subject to tax, capital gains or dividends are taxed more favourably than interest generated by fixed-income vehicles. The after-tax return in this situation is 12.2%, and while that 1% may not sound like a lot, it becomes very significant as it compounds over the years.

The message is that, where possible, hold assets which are fully taxed (fixed income) inside the RRSP and more favourably taxed assets (equities) **outside** the RRSP.

TAX-INEFFICIENT PORTFOLIO

ASSET CLASS	RRSP	NON-RRSP	TOTAL
Bonds ($100,000 @ 15%)	0	$15,000	$15,000
Stocks ($100,000 @ 15%)	$15,000	0	$15,000
Taxes payable (@ 50%)	0	-$7,500	-$7,500
Total	$15,000	$7,500	$22,500
After-tax return: $22,500/$200,000 = 11.25%			

TAX-EFFICIENT PORTFOLIO

ASSET CLASS	RRSP	NON-RRSP	TOTAL
Bonds ($100,000 @ 15%)	$15,000	0	$15,000
Stocks ($100,000 @ 15%)	0	$15,000	$15,000
Taxes payable (@ 50%)	0	$5,625	$5,625
Total	$15,000	$9,375	$24,375
After-tax return: $24,375/$200,000 = 12.2%			

FIND YOUR OWN PERSONAL "MONEY COACH"

You are **forced** to play the "money game" from the time you begin to earn a living until you die, and many of us will play it for 40, 50, 60 years or more. Don't you agree that when you're going to play a game for that length of time, it makes sense to be able to play it as well as possible? There are rules to the game and there are strategies you can use to play more effectively and successfully.

In this game, it's important to know who your teammates are and who's the "opposition." Revenue Canada makes the rules, interprets the rules, and enforces the rules of the game — Revenue Canada is not on your "team."

To learn the rules and the strategies of the money game, you need a "money coach" to work with you over the long term, and more and more people are coming to this conclusion.

If, like many others, you are too busy to take the time to learn all the rules and strategies, or if you don't have the interest, the ability or the inclination to learn them, then you need to find expert advice.

It's true that books like this one can provide some useful assistance, but your personal situation is unlikely to be covered in any book. You really need an individual to coach you, over the long term, in all aspects of your financial life. It's my heartfelt belief that an experienced professional advisor can help you save thousands of dollars in taxes over time and can increase the value of your portfolio over what you can do yourself by many thousands of dollars.

Why would you not use the expertise of someone who can help you achieve those results? Well, more and more people are recognizing the advantages of seeking a "money coach." But where do you look to find one?

Some people use a bank manager, but their expertise is generally limited to loans or mortgages. Accountants are often thought to be good money coaches and no doubt many are. Again, I'd suggest you look for someone with a broader overview. Tax considerations are significant, but there are many others that need to be taken into account in creating an overall financial strategy. Lawyers are often relied upon for general financial and investment advice, but they are not trained in investment theory and may have no expertise in the area of asset allocation or in personal taxation.

I recommend you seek out someone whose professional career is completely focused on providing expert, pertinent, and timely financial advice.

WHAT QUALIFICATIONS SHOULD YOUR MONEY COACH HOLD?

Generally, someone in the field will have at least completed the Investment Funds course which (along with being registered by the appropriate

Securities Commission) allows one to sell mutual funds to the public. The Canadian Securities Course (along with the appropriate registration) allows one to sell a full range of securities (including stocks and bonds as well as mutual funds). Stockbrokers have all completed the Canadian Securities Course.

But those are minimum qualifications — both prerequisites for anyone registered to sell securities. You should also look for an advisor who has completed (or is enrolled in) the Professional Financial Planner program. It's offered by the Canadian Securities Institute as part of their ongoing educational programs and covers many pertinent topics such as taxation, personal financial planning, asset management, estate planning, etc.

Some people take advanced programs offered by the Canadian Securities Institute, including the FCSI designation (Fellow of the Canadian Securities Institute) or the new Certified Investment Manager (CIM) designation.

Any of these programs ensure that your advisor has a commitment to ongoing professional development, which will likely be beneficial to you.

As well, you should probably expect that your advisor would be a member of the Canadian Institute of Financial Planners and adhere to its Code of Ethics.

HOW DO YOU FIND THE RIGHT ADVISOR?

Many advisors provide an ongoing series of educational seminars which are intended to provide up-to-the-moment information on trends in the economy, which funds are "hot," methods of tax reduction, and so on. You may find it worthwhile to attend some of these and get a sense of whether you could work with that individual.

TOP TEN PICKS FOR MUTUAL FUND INVESTORS

Here's my subjective listing of the "best of the best" for mutual fund investors.

1. TOP MUTUAL FUND WEB SITE

http://www.fundlib.com (The Fund Library)

Provides superb customization, links, news, chat groups, and data you can download. There is no other site with as much to offer the Canadian fund investor.

2. TOP NEW FUND COMPANY

GT Global

While their funds are still a little too new to pass the *Top Funds* screens, their debut has been awesome. Diverse specialty funds and talented management make GT a must-own new fund company. My favourite fund: GT Global Health Care.

3. TOP FUND NEWSLETTER

Gordon Pape's Mutual Fund Update

It's cheap, unbiased and well-written. It leaves the others in the dust.

4. TOP BANK FUND FAMILY

Royal Mutual Funds

They placed five funds on the *Top Funds* list this year, including stock, bond, and foreign funds.

5. TOP SOFTWARE PROGRAM FOR FUND KEENERS

PalTrak for Windows

You get way, way more than performance numbers. You can see inside the portfolios and get style and tax information on the funds. One-month free trial: $30.

6. TOP EVENT FOR FUND INVESTORS

The Financial Forum

Booths, brokers, managers, and free stuff. Don't miss it — starting February 1, 1997 in Toronto and February 14 in Vancouver.

7. TOP MONTHLY FUND SURVEY

The Globe and Mail's Report on Mutual Funds

Finally, a source for year-by-year returns! No more distortive compounding.

8. TOP MARKET CALL

K.C. Lee – Fidelity Far East Fund

K.C. went way overweight on Hong Kong in late 1994 when others were fleeing. He made a killing while some were predicting the death of the Hong Kong market.

9. TOP FUND COMPANY TURNAROUND

Global Strategy Financial

After a thumping in the area of global bonds, they've retooled with an awesome lineup of foreign managers for their multi-advisor funds.

10. TOP MUTUAL FUND STATEMENT

Trimark Mutual Funds

You see what you put in, what you made, and what you're worth. It's easy to follow.

THE MONSTER FUND TABLES

In this section, you'll find information on the over 1200 funds available in Canada, in alphabetical order. My *Top Funds* selections are highlighted — you'll find more detailed information in the *Top Funds* full-page reviews.

THE FUND TABLES LEGEND

Information in each fund is presented in a standardized format. Here's a key to the elements in each column:

Fund #. This number has no bearing on fund rankings and is simply a numerical identifier for each fund *(see FundMates)*.

Rating. 1 to 5 stars. Corresponds to the overall AMR score of the fund — how it's done compared to similar funds over time. Technically, it corresponds to the ranking its performance has achieved, on average, over its full history of months. The more stars the better. I have included star ratings even for rookies, though you should treat new funds' short records with caution.

Type. This code identifies the fund category, as follows:

Asia	Regional Equity–Asia & Pacific
Balan	Balanced–Canadian
Bond	Bond–Canadian
CdnEq	Equity–Canadian Large-Cap
CdnSm	Equity–Canadian Small-Cap
Div	Equity–Canadian Dividend
Emerg	Regional Equity–Emerging Markets
Europe	Regional Equity–Europe
Gold	Resource–Precious Metals
InBal	Balanced–International

InBond	Bond–International
Index	Market Index
InEq	Equity–International
InMon	Money Market–International
Japan	Regional Equity–Japan
Labor	Labour-sponsored Venture Capital
Latin	Regional Equity–Latin America
Money	Money Market–Canadian
Mortge	Mortgage
OilGas	Resource–Oil & Gas
USEq	Equity–US

CONSISTENCY

Performance trend. These bars represent the relative performance of a fund through the past 15 calendar years. That's a far better way to look at returns than the silly compound return numbers — which get distorted by one blockbuster year. A bar at the top represents better performance over that calendar year than three quarters of all similar funds (we call this 'top quartile' — it's good). A bar at the bottom represents worse performance than three quarters of all similar funds. You get the picture: The more consistently high the bars, the better.

Performance in up markets. For the first time ever in Canada, you'll see how each fund did in bull markets separately from how it's fared in bear, or declining, markets. So if you're bullish, pick a fund that scores well in up markets (A is the best score possible, D is the worst). Each letter grade (A through D) represents one quartile. So a Canadian equity fund's score of 'B' for up markets means that overall, through the past four bull markets on the TSE (or the portion of them that this fund existed), it has earned a second-quartile rank. That's better than half its competitors, but not as good as one-quarter of the crowd. Everything's customized by category, too. So a bear market in Canadian stocks is defined as a loss (peak to trough) of more than 10% in the TSE 300 Total Return Index. For, say, Global Bond funds, I use the Salomon Brothers World Government Bond Index as a benchmark. No matter what category, this rule always applies: for stocks, a bear market is a slide of more than 10%. For bonds, it's a decline of 5% or more.

RISK

Performance in down markets. If you're nervous about where the markets are headed, pick a fund that has done well in down markets (A is the best score possible, D is the worst). Each letter grade (A through D) represents one quartile. So a Canadian equity fund's score of 'B' for down markets means that overall, through previous bear markets on the TSE (or the portion of them that this fund existed), it has earned a second-quartile rank. That's better than half its competitors, but not as good as one-quarter of the crowd. (*See Performance in up markets* for more information.)

GICs better. This column tells you how often (as a % of the fund's existence) the monthly return for this fund has fallen below the monthly return on a 5-year GIC.

Worst 12-month stretch. This is a great peek into how bad it's been at its worst in a particular fund. Of all the possible 12-month stretches one could create with a particular fund, this is the worst period. The ending date of that drought is followed by the rate of return. This is more significant for older funds, but nonetheless provides a clue as to the possible downside of a particular fund.

EFFICIENCY

MER. This is the total annual expense burden of the fund, shown as the dollar amount charged by the fund for every $100 of assets managed. The coloured dot beside the expenses signifies how this compares to other funds in its category. A green dot signifies that the fund is cheap — its expenses are in the lowest quintile of similar funds. An orange dot means expenses are average, and red tells us that expenses that are in the highest quintile — higher than 80% of all similar funds. Colours are the same as those used for the Top Funds Efficiency measure.

FIT

This special feature allows readers to help build their portfolios by offering special insight as to which funds go best with which. This proprietary system is courtesy of Midland Walwyn. It uses past performance trends to identify the most similar, and conversely, the most complementary fund for any given fund in Canada. Technically, it is a returns-based style analyzer using trailing three-year covariance analysis.

FundMate: most similar. Among all funds in its category, the fund whose number appears here is the most similar to the fund you're looking up. It's a great substitute if you're unable to buy the fund in question; for example, because you're stuck in another fund family. The most similar fund to any given holding would be a terrible diversifier — it would be so similar that it wouldn't allow for any risk reduction.

FundMate: best complement. This column shows you how to diversify properly. It identifies, within the category, the fund that is most different (or complementary) to the one in question. To some degree, its returns zig while your fund's may zag. So it offers a great way to reduce risk. The fund is identified only by its number, so you'll find it easily — and be able to look up more detail on its stand-alone past performance.

N/A. Either not applicable (e.g., fund too new) or data not available.

Fund #	Rating	Fund name	Type	CONSISTENCY: Performance trend 82 83 84 85 86 87 88 89 90 91 92 93 94 95 June 96	RISK: Up mkt	RISK: Down mkt	RISK: GICs better	RISK: Worst 12-mo. end	RISK: Worst 12-mo. chnge	EFFICIENCY: MER	FIT: FundMate # sim.	FIT: FundMate # comp.
1	★★	20/20 Asia Pacific Fund	Asia		C	D	53%	02/95	–0.18%	$2.67	238	1014
2	★★★	20/20 Canadian Growth Fund	CdnEq		D	C	52%	01/93	–9.37%	$2.57	411	154
3	★★★	20/20 Cdn Tactical Asset Allocation	Balan		D	B	46%	01/95	–9.69%	$2.50	660	393
4	★★★★½	20/20 Dividend Fund	Div		A	C	47%	09/90	–7.24%	$1.98	321	1183
5	★★★	20/20 European Asset Allocation	InBal		C	A	50%	01/95	–5.49%	$2.62	N/A	N/A
6	★	20/20 Foreign RSP Bond Fund	InBond		D	B	62%	09/94	–7.13%	$2.02	N/A	N/A
7	★★½	20/20 Income Fund	Bond		D	B	50%	01/95	–0.10%	$1.98	1124	389
8	★	20/20 India Fund	Emerg		D	D	68%	11/95	–0.49%	$3.49	N/A	N/A
9	★★★	20/20 International Value Fund	InEq		B	C	48%	02/95	–5.14%	$2.89	1172	978
10	★★★	20/20 Latin America	Latin		D	D	57%	12/95	–0.29%	$3.22	N/A	N/A
11	★★½	20/20 Managed Futures Value Fund	Sector		N/A	N/A	38%	05/96	0.19%	$3.00	N/A	N/A
12	★★★★½	20/20 Money Market Fund	Money		N/A	N/A	79%	12/94	4.18%	$1.05	193	498
13	★	20/20 Multimanager Emerging Markets	Emerg		D	D	58%	11/95	–0.25%	$3.50	N/A	N/A
14	★★★★★	20/20 RSP Aggr. Smaller Companies	CdnSm	N/A	N/A	N/A	25%	N/A	N/A	$2.00	N/A	N/A
15	★★★★½	20/20 RSP Aggressive Equity	CdnSm		N/A	N/A	37%	01/95	–0.18%	$2.51	N/A	N/A
16	★★★	20/20 RSP Int'l Equity Allocation	InEq		N/A	N/A	44%	01/95	–8.13%	$2.52	N/A	N/A
17	★★★★★	20/20 US Short-Term High Yield	InMon		N/A	N/A	48%	12/95	–1.10%	$2.49	N/A	N/A
18	★★½	20/20 World Bond Fund	InBond		C	B	56%	09/94	–9.67%	$1.99	644	455
19	★★★	20/20 World Fund	InBal		D	C	55%	09/90	–0.20%	$2.60	1155	642
20	★★	ABC American-Value Fund	USEq	N/A	N/A	N/A	100%	N/A	N/A	$2.00	N/A	N/A
21	★★★½	ABC Fully-Managed Fund	Balan		A	A	46%	01/95	–6.47%	$2.00	396	393
22	★★★★★	ABC Fundamental Value Fund	CdnEq		C	A	43%	01/95	–8.11%	$2.00	60	154
23	★	Admax American Select Growth Fund	USEq		N/A	N/A	64%	06/96	–6.03%	$2.60	758	311
24	★	Admax Asset Allocation Fund	Balan		D	A	47%	01/95	–4.26%	$2.54	1045	393
25	★★	Admax Canadian Performance Fund	CdnEq		A	D	52%	01/95	–0.13%	$2.67	38	154

Fund #	Rating	Fund name	Type	Up mkt	Down mkt	GICs better	Worst 12-mo. end	Worst 12-mo. chnge	MER	FundMate # sim.	FundMate # comp.
				RISK					**EFFICIENCY**	**FIT**	
26	★	Admax Canadian Select Growth Fund	CdnEq	D	C	57%	01/93	–0.05%	$2.63	806	N/A
27	★	Admax Cash Performance Fund	Money	N/A	N/A	95%	04/94	3.04%	$1.16	446	498
28	★★★★★	Admax Global Health Sciences Fund	Sector	N/A	N/A	36%	10/94	1.24%	$7.83	1227	869
29	★★★	AGF American Growth Fund Ltd. 'A'	USEq	B	D	48%	08/88	–0.22%	$2.37	882	310
30	★★★	AGF American Growth Fund Ltd. 'B'	USEq	N/A	N/A	38%	06/96	0.17%	$2.85	N/A	N/A
31	★★★	AGF American Growth Fund Ltd. 'C'	USEq	N/A	N/A	38%	06/96	0.17%	$2.84	N/A	N/A
32	★★★★	AGF Asian Growth Fund Limited 'A'	Asia	A	A	50%	01/95	–0.11%	$2.41	675	1015
33	★★½	AGF Asian Growth Fund Limited 'B'	Asia	N/A	N/A	67%	10/95	–6.53%	$2.87	N/A	N/A
34	★★½	AGF Asian Growth Fund Limited 'C'	Asia	N/A	N/A	67%	10/95	–6.27%	$2.83	N/A	N/A
35	★★★	AGF Canadian Bond Fund 'A'	Bond	C	C	48%	01/95	–0.11%	$1.40	314	389
36	★★★	AGF Canadian Bond Fund 'B'	Bond	N/A	N/A	43%	05/96	7.68%	$1.90	N/A	N/A
37	★★★	AGF Canadian Bond Fund 'C'	Bond	N/A	N/A	43%	05/96	7.74%	$1.90	N/A	N/A
38	★★★	AGF Canadian Equity Fund 'A'	CdnEq	B	C	45%	06/82	–0.31%	$2.81	900	154
39	★★★	AGF Canadian Equity Fund 'B'	CdnEq	N/A	N/A	43%	10/95	1.65%	$3.30	N/A	N/A
40	★★★	AGF Canadian Equity Fund 'C'	CdnEq	N/A	N/A	43%	10/95	1.92%	$3.17	N/A	N/A
41	★★★½	AGF Canadian Resources Fund 'A'	OilGas	B	D	46%	06/82	–0.52%	$2.56	115	505
42	★★★	AGF Canadian Resources Fund 'B'	OilGas	N/A	N/A	28%	12/95	0.13%	$3.06	N/A	N/A
43	★★★	AGF Canadian Resources Fund 'C'	OilGas	N/A	N/A	28%	12/95	0.13%	$2.99	N/A	N/A
44	★★	AGF China Focus Fund Ltd. 'A'	Asia	D	C	62%	10/95	–0.12%	$2.99	N/A	N/A
45	★	AGF China Focus Fund Ltd. 'B'	Asia	D	C	62%	10/95	–0.13%	$3.50	N/A	N/A
46	★	AGF China Focus Fund Ltd. 'C'	Asia	N/A	N/A	57%	10/95	–0.13%	$3.48	N/A	N/A
47	★★★★★	AGF European Growth Fund Ltd. 'A'	Europe	N/A	N/A	46%	10/95	3.48%	$2.79	N/A	N/A
48	★★★★★	AGF European Growth Fund Ltd. 'B'	Europe	N/A	N/A	46%	10/95	2.90%	$3.33	N/A	N/A
49	★★½	AGF European Growth Fund Ltd. 'C'	Europe	N/A	N/A	43%	10/95	2.78%	$3.31	N/A	N/A
50	★★★★½	AGF Germany Class 'A'	Europe	N/A	N/A	39%	12/95	0.13%	$2.36	N/A	N/A

				CONSISTENCY	RISK					EFFICIENCY	FIT	
Fund #	Rating	Fund name	Type	Performance trend 82 83 84 85 86 87 88 89 90 91 92 93 94 95 June 96	Up mkt	Down mkt	GICs better	Worst 12-mo. end	Worst 12-mo. chnge	MER	FundMate # sim.	FundMate # comp.
51	★★★	AGF Germany Class 'C'	Europe		N/A	N/A	39%	12/95	0.13%	$2.42	N/A	N/A
52	★★★★★	AGF Germany Class 'M'	Europe		N/A	N/A	39%	12/95	0.15%	$1.36	N/A	N/A
53	★★★	AGF Germany Class 'B'	Europe		N/A	N/A	39%	12/95	0.13%	$2.49	N/A	N/A
54	★★★★★	AGF Global Government Bond Fund 'A'	InBond		B	B	47%	03/89	–6.93%	$1.28	1061	455
55	★★★½	AGF Global Government Bond Fund 'B'	InBond		B	C	38%	05/96	4.17%	$1.78	N/A	N/A
56	★★★½	AGF Global Government Bond Fund 'C'	InBond		B	C	33%	05/96	4.04%	$1.76	N/A	N/A
57	★★★½	AGF Growth & Income Fund 'A'	Balan		A	A	44%	06/82	–0.22%	$2.00	178	393
58	★★★	AGF Growth & Income Fund 'B'	Balan		N/A	N/A	38%	09/95	5.57%	$2.50	N/A	N/A
59	★★★	AGF Growth & Income Fund 'C'	Balan		N/A	N/A	43%	09/95	5.35%	$2.50	N/A	N/A
60	★★★½	AGF Growth Equity Fund Ltd. 'A'	CdnEq		C	B	42%	06/82	–0.50%	$2.44	379	154
61	★★★½	AGF Growth Equity Fund Ltd. 'B'	CdnEq		N/A	N/A	33%	10/95	–3.24%	$2.94	N/A	N/A
62	★★★½	AGF Growth Equity Fund Ltd. 'C'	CdnEq		N/A	N/A	33%	10/95	–2.70%	$2.92	N/A	N/A
63	★★★	AGF High Income Fund 'A'	Div		C	C	48%	01/95	–3.50%	$1.43	730	1183
64	★½	AGF High Income Fund 'B'	Div		N/A	N/A	33%	09/95	8.46%	$1.94	N/A	N/A
65	★½	AGF High Income Fund 'C'	Div		N/A	N/A	33%	09/95	0.08%	$1.93	N/A	N/A
66	★★½	AGF Int'l Short Term Income 'A'	Money		N/A	N/A	57%	03/96	0.04%	$2.85	N/A	N/A
67	★★★½	AGF Int'l Short Term Income 'B'	Money		N/A	N/A	57%	03/96	3.18%	$3.04	N/A	N/A
68	★★½	AGF Int'l Short Term Income 'C'	Money		N/A	N/A	62%	03/96	3.26%	$3.60	N/A	N/A
69	★★★★★	AGF Japan Fund Ltd.'A'	Japan		B	C	48%	07/82	–0.26%	$2.55	739	1032
70	★★★	AGF Japan Fund Ltd.'B'	Japan		B	D	57%	10/95	–0.20%	$3.05	N/A	N/A
71	★★½	AGF Japan Fund Ltd.'C'	Japan		B	D	57%	10/95	–0.20%	$3.06	N/A	N/A
72	★★★★★	AGF Money Market Account 'A'	Money		N/A	N/A	67%	04/94	3.57%	$0.91	328	498
73	★	AGF Money Market Account 'B'	Money		N/A	N/A	95%	06/96	4.47%	$1.41	N/A	N/A
74	★	AGF Money Market Account 'C'	Money		N/A	N/A	86%	06/96	5.03%	$0.91	N/A	N/A
75	★★	AGF Resource Capital Fund 'P'	OilGas		N/A	N/A	50%	10/95	–0.21%	$3.27	N/A	N/A

				CONSISTENCY	RISK					EFFICIENCY	FIT	
Fund #	Rating	Fund name	Type	Performance trend 82 83 84 85 86 87 88 89 90 91 92 93 94 95 June 96	Up mkt	Down mkt	GICs better	Worst 12-mo. end	Worst 12-mo. chnge	MER	FundMate # sim.	FundMate # comp.
76	★★★½	AGF Special Fund Ltd. 'A'	USEq		B	D	47%	05/82	–0.18%	¡$2.38	1232	310
77	★★	AGF Special Fund Ltd. 'B'	USEq		N/A	N/A	38%	06/96	0.13%	$2.87	N/A	N/A
78	★★	AGF Special Fund Ltd. 'C'	USEq		N/A	N/A	38%	06/96	0.13%	$2.83	N/A	N/A
79	★½	AGF Strategic Income Fund 'A'	Money		N/A	N/A	57%	10/90	–0.18%	$1.79	1217	502
80	★★★★	AGF Strategic Income Fund 'B'	Money		N/A	N/A	48%	06/96	1.54%	$2.30	N/A	N/A
81	★★★★½	AGF Strategic Income Fund 'C'	Money		N/A	N/A	52%	06/96	1.69%	$2.29	N/A	N/A
82	★★★★★	AGF US Dollar Money Market ($US)	InMon		N/A	N/A	100%	03/94	2.58%	$0.84	331	118
83	★★	AGF US Income Fund 'A'	InBond		D	C	60%	09/94	–8.37%	$1.92	54	455
84	★	AGF US Income Fund 'B'	InBond		D	C	57%	06/96	1.47%	$2.44	N/A	N/A
85	★	AGF US Income Fund 'C'	InBond		D	C	62%	06/96	1.08%	$2.38	N/A	N/A
86	★	AGF World Equity 'A'	InEq		N/A	N/A	54%	06/96	8.99%	$2.00	N/A	N/A
87	★	AGF World Equity 'B'	InEq		N/A	N/A	62%	06/96	8.49%	$2.50	N/A	N/A
88	★	AGF World Equity 'C'	InEq		N/A	N/A	62%	06/96	8.49%	$2.50	N/A	N/A
89	★★★½	AIC Advantage Fund	CdnEq		A	D	45%	09/90	–0.26%	$2.70	750	883
90	★★★★★	AIC Diversified Canada Fund	CdnEq		N/A	N/A	18%	06/96	0.33%	$2.75	N/A	N/A
91	★★	AIC Emerging Markets Fund	Emerg		D	C	71%	11/95	–0.23%	$2.75	N/A	N/A
92	★	AIC Money Market Fund	Money		N/A	N/A	87%	06/96	5.20%	$1.00	N/A	N/A
93	★★★	AIC Value Fund	USEq		A	D	42%	11/94	–7.16%	$2.75	134	310
94	★	AIC World Equity Fund	InEq		N/A	N/A	53%	12/94	–6.97%	$2.75	N/A	N/A
95	★★½	All-Canadian CapitalFund	CdnEq		C	A	46%	07/88	–0.13%	$2.00	96	154
96	★★½	All-Canadian Compound	CdnEq		C	A	45%	07/88	–0.13%	$0.00	95	883
97	★★	All-Canadian ConsumerFund	CdnEq		D	A	53%	01/93	–0.98%	$1.95	96	154
98	★★★	All-Canadian Resources Corporation	OilGas		D	A	52%	01/91	–0.36%	$2.01	394	1029
99	★★★★½	Altafund Investment Corp.	CdnEq		A	A	39%	01/95	–0.13%	$2.38	806	312
100	★★½	Altamira Asia Pacific Fund	Asia		D	D	57%	12/95	–0.17%	$2.38	1016	1015

				CONSISTENCY		RISK				EFFICIENCY	FIT	
Fund #	Rating	Fund name	Type	Performance trend 82 83 84 85 86 87 88 89 90 91 92 93 94 95 June 96	Up mkt	Down mkt	GICs better	Worst 12-mo. end	Worst 12-mo. chnge	MER	FundMate # sim.	FundMate # comp.
101	★★	Altamira Balanced Fund	Balan		D	D	49%	08/88	–0.20%	$2.00	807	393
102	★★★	Altamira Bond Fund	Bond		A	D	45%	01/95	–0.10%	$1.31	805	389
103	★★★	Altamira Capital Growth Fund	CdnEq		C	A	46%	05/88	–0.17%	$2.02	879	154
104	★★★★½	Altamira Dividend Fund	Div		N/A	N/A	38%	10/95	0.13%	$1.64	N/A	N/A
105	★★★★★	Altamira Equity Fund	CdnEq		A	A	38%	01/95	–7.56%	$2.31	806	154
106	★★★	Altamira European Equity Fund	Europe		N/A	N/A	41%	04/95	1.02%	$2.41	N/A	N/A
107	★★★	Altamira Global Bond Fund	InBond		B	D	53%	09/94	–5.65%	$1.83	N/A	N/A
108	★★★	Altamira Global Discovery Fund	Emerg		B	C	48%	10/95	–0.20%	$3.13	N/A	N/A
109	★★	Altamira Global Diversified Fund	InEq		D	C	50%	08/88	–0.28%	$2.00	495	254
110	★★★★★	Altamira Growth & Income Fund	Balan		D	A	40%	10/95	–9.04%	$1.41	1045	393
111	★★★½	Altamira Income Fund	Bond		B	B	49%	01/95	–9.06%	$1.00	805	389
112	★★★★★	Altamira Japanese Opportunity Fund	Japan		A	A	52%	10/95	–0.18%	$2.38	N/A	N/A
113	★★½	Altamira North American Recovery	CdnEq		D	A	41%	01/95	–0.11%	$2.31	N/A	N/A
114	★★★★★	Altamira Prec. and Strategic Metal	Gold		D	A	24%	10/95	0.11%	$2.32	N/A	N/A
115	★★★½	Altamira Resource Fund	OilGas		C	C	33%	01/95	–0.22%	$2.31	478	505
116	★★★★★	Altamira Science & Technology Fund	Sector		N/A	N/A	30%	N/A	N/A	$2.37	N/A	N/A
117	★★★★★	Altamira Select American Fund	USEq		N/A	N/A	38%	01/95	–3.24%	$2.32	198	310
118	★★★★★	Altamira Short Term Global Income	InMon		N/A	N/A	47%	10/95	–1.56%	$1.22	726	1224
119	★★½	Altamira Short Term Gov't Bond Fund	Bond		N/A	N/A	33%	05/96	7.31%	$1.33	N/A	N/A
120	★½	Altamira Spec. High Yield Bond	Bond		N/A	N/A	60%	N/A	N/A	$1.91	N/A	N/A
121	★★★	Altamira Special Growth Fund	CdnSm		B	D	48%	01/95	–0.26%	$1.82	634	979
122	★★★½	Altamira US Larger Company Fund	USEq		N/A	N/A	44%	01/95	–1.76%	$2.36	N/A	N/A
123	★★½	AMI Private Capital Equity	CdnEq		B	B	50%	10/90	–0.20%	$1.75	1138	154
124	★★★	AMI Private Capital Income	Bond		C	C	47%	01/95	–7.45%	$1.25	898	389
125	★★★★★	AMI Private Capital Money Market	Money		N/A	N/A	71%	06/94	4.38%	$0.75	721	498

				CONSISTENCY	RISK					EFFICIENCY	FIT	
Fund #	Rating	Fund name	Type	Performance trend 82 83 84 85 86 87 88 89 90 91 92 93 94 95 June 96	Up mkt	Down mkt	GICs better	Worst 12-mo. end	Worst 12-mo. chnge	MER	FundMate # sim.	FundMate # comp.
126	★★½	AMI Private Capital Optimix	Balan		B	C	49%	01/95	–8.40%	$1.75	985	393
127	★★★	APEX Asian Pacific Fund	Asia		B	C	62%	01/95	–0.16%	$1.88	N/A	N/A
128	★½	APEX Balanced Allocation Fund	Balan		D	A	47%	01/95	–0.07%	$2.00	N/A	N/A
129	★★★	APEX Equity Growth Fund	CdnEq		B	A	47%	01/95	–0.13%	$1.98	N/A	N/A
130	★	APEX Fixed Income Fund	Bond		D	B	50%	01/95	–6.79%	$1.74	N/A	N/A
131	★★★	APEX Money Market Fund	Money		N/A	N/A	90%	01/95	0.05%	$0.75	N/A	N/A
132	★	APEX Mortgage Fund	Mrtge		N/A	N/A	61%	03/96	5.79%	$1.74	N/A	N/A
133	★★	Associate Investors Ltd.	CdnEq		D	B	100%	05/78	–1.00%	$2.28	286	883
134	★★	Atlas Amer. Large Cap Growth Fund	USEq		C	C	46%	08/88	–0.21%	$2.68	849	310
135	★½	Atlas Amer. Large Cap Value Fund	USEq		N/A	N/A	55%	10/95	3.60%	$2.68	N/A	N/A
136	★★★★★	Atlas American Advantage Fund	InBal		N/A	N/A	30%	06/96	0.19%	$2.68	N/A	N/A
137	★	Atlas American Emerging Value Fund	USEq		N/A	N/A	50%	06/96	3.96%	$2.68	N/A	N/A
138	★★½	Atlas American Money Market ($US)	InMon		N/A	N/A	100%	01/94	2.10%	$1.18	1063	118
139	★★	Atlas American Opportunity Fund	USEq		N/A	N/A	30%	10/95	0.11%	$2.68	N/A	N/A
140	★★	Atlas Canadian Balanced Fund	Balan		A	B	58%	10/90	–6.56%	$2.30	1140	393
141	★★½	Atlas Canadian Bond Fund	Bond		B	B	45%	01/95	–6.48%	$1.97	517	389
142	★½	Atlas Canadian Diversified Fund	Balan		N/A	N/A	65%	10/95	3.43%	$2.34	N/A	N/A
143	★★★★★	Atlas Canadian Emerging Growth Fund	CdnSm		N/A	N/A	25%	10/95	0.21%	$2.45	N/A	N/A
144	★	Atlas Canadian Emerging Value Fund	CdnSm		N/A	N/A	35%	10/95	–4.12%	$2.74	N/A	N/A
145	★★½	Atlas Canadian High Yield Bond Fund	Bond		N/A	N/A	35%	06/96	0.10%	$1.92	N/A	N/A
146	★★½	Atlas Canadian Large Cap Growth	CdnEq		B	B	54%	08/88	–0.16%	$2.53	123	154
147	★	Atlas Canadian Large Cap Value Fund	CdnEq		N/A	N/A	55%	10/95	4.30%	$2.73	N/A	N/A
148	★★★	Atlas Canadian Money Market Fund	Money		N/A	N/A	79%	04/94	3.64%	$1.12	1049	498
149	★	Atlas Canadian T-Bill Fund	Money		N/A	N/A	77%	05/94	3.39%	$1.29	710	498
150	★★½	Atlas Global Equity Fund	InEq		C	B	51%	06/91	–7.31%	$2.73	1172	254

				CONSISTENCY	RISK					EFFICIENCY	FIT	
Fund #	Rating	Fund name	Type	Up mkt	Down mkt	GICs better	Worst 12-mo. end	Worst 12-mo. chnge	MER	FundMate # sim.	FundMate # comp.
151	★★★★½	Atlas Managed Futures Fund ($US)	InMon	N/A	N/A	50%	03/96	–3.14%	$12.85	N/A	N/A
152	★★★	Atlas NAFTA Fund	USEq	N/A	N/A	47%	01/95	–0.13%	$2.73	N/A	N/A
153	★★★	Batirente - Sec. Marché Monétaire	Money	N/A	N/A	69%	04/94	0.04%	$1.61	973	502
154	★½	Batirente - Section Actions	CdnEq	D	D	53%	02/94	–1.03%	$1.61	1167	1185
155	★★★	Batirente - Section Diversifiée	Balan	A	D	43%	01/95	–6.55%	$1.61	707	393
156	★★★★½	Batirente - Section Obligations	Bond	A	B	40%	01/95	–6.20%	$1.61	1136	389
157	★★★	Beutel Goodman American Equity	USEq	N/A	N/A	38%	01/95	–4.28%	$2.70	698	310
158	★★½	Beutel Goodman Balanced Fund	Balan	B	A	44%	01/95	–6.37%	$2.20	836	393
159	★★	Beutel Goodman Canadian Equity	CdnEq	B	A	50%	01/93	–8.57%	$2.26	1138	154
160	★★★½	Beutel Goodman Income Fund	Bond	C	D	41%	01/95	–0.10%	$1.32	898	389
161	★★★	Beutel Goodman International Equity	InEq	N/A	N/A	42%	02/95	–0.14%	$2.60	1173	755
162	★★★★★	Beutel Goodman Money Market Fund	Money	N/A	N/A	71%	06/94	4.57%	$0.59	1058	498
163	★★★★½	Beutel Goodman Private Balanced	Balan	A	A	41%	01/95	–3.02%	$2.20	171	393
164	★★	Beutel Goodman Small Cap Fund	CdnSm	N/A	N/A	35%	06/96	0.25%	$2.50	N/A	N/A
165	★★½	Bissett American Equity Fund	USEq	B	C	48%	08/88	–0.22%	$1.50	882	310
166	★★★	Bissett Bond Fund	Bond	A	A	47%	01/95	–6.23%	$0.75	1084	389
167	★★★½	Bissett Canadian Equity Fund	CdnEq	A	B	43%	08/88	–0.15%	$1.35	146	154
168	★★★	Bissett Dividend Income Fund	Div	A	A	51%	01/93	–0.99%	$1.50	321	1183
169	★★★★★	Bissett Money Market Fund	Money	N/A	N/A	76%	07/94	4.39%	$0.50	867	247
170	★★★★★	Bissett Multinational Growth Fund	InEq	N/A	N/A	26%	08/95	0.11%	$1.50	N/A	N/A
171	★★★★½	Bissett Retirement Fund	Balan	A	A	39%	01/95	–0.05%	$0.36	268	393
172	★★★★★	Bissett Small Cap Fund	CdnSm	B	A	42%	01/95	–0.16%	$2.00	1028	897
173	★★★	BNP (Canada) Bond Fund	Bond	B	C	40%	01/95	–8.69%	$1.74	1151	389
174	★	BNP (Canada) Canadian Money Market	Money	N/A	N/A	95%	04/94	3.61%	$1.36	725	498
175	★★	BNP (Canada) Equity Fund	CdnEq	B	C	42%	01/95	–6.98%	$2.42	482	154

				CONSISTENCY			RISK				EFFICIENCY	FIT	
Fund #	Rating	Fund name	Type	Performance trend 82 83 84 85 86 87 88 89 90 91 92 93 94 95 June 96	Up mkt	Down mkt	GICs better	Worst 12-mo. end	Worst 12-mo. chnge	MER	FundMate # sim.	FundMate # comp.
176	★★★	BPI American Equity Value Fund	USEq		C	A	51%	10/90	–0.05%	$2.63	165	310
177	★★★	BPI American Small Companies Fund	USEq		A	A	47%	09/88	–0.28%	$2.99	198	310
178	★★	BPI Canadian Balanced Fund	Balan		D	B	50%	01/95	–0.12%	$2.72	569	393
179	★	BPI Canadian Bond Fund	Bond		D	D	51%	01/95	–9.50%	$1.51	911	389
180	★★★	BPI Canadian Equity Value Fund	CdnEq		B	B	52%	01/95	–0.15%	$2.74	806	154
181	★★★★★	BPI Canadian Opportunities RSP Fund	CdnEq		N/A	N/A	9%	N/A	N/A	$2.50	N/A	N/A
182	★★★★★	BPI Canadian Resource Fund Inc.	OilGas		A	D	48%	06/82	–0.34%	$2.68	115	505
183	★★★	BPI Canadian Small Companies Fund	CdnSm		A	C	50%	10/90	–0.22%	$2.50	839	754
184	★★	BPI Emerging Markets Fund	Sector		N/A	N/A	58%	05/95	–6.89%	$2.71	N/A	N/A
185	★★★	BPI Global Balanced RSP Fund	InBal		C	A	55%	04/90	–0.02%	$2.51	1222	642
186	★★★	BPI Global Equity Fund	InEq		C	B	48%	08/88	–0.23%	$2.79	1173	978
187	★★★½	BPI Global Opportunities Fund	InEq		N/A	N/A	43%	06/96	0.16%	$2.50	N/A	N/A
188	★★★★½	BPI Global RSP Bond Fund	InBond		A	A	36%	06/96	0.11%	$1.50	N/A	N/A
189	★★★	BPI Global Small Companies Fund	InEq		N/A	N/A	45%	10/95	–5.60%	$2.56	1173	254
190	★★★	BPI Income Fund	Div		A	A	52%	10/90	–4.42%	$1.23	862	1183
191	★★★	BPI International Equity Fund	InEq		C	B	45%	08/95	–9.23%	$2.66	325	958
192	★★	BPI N.A. Balanced RSP Fund	InBal		A	D	51%	01/95	–0.12%	$2.88	1222	642
193	★★★★★	BPI T-Bill Fund	Money		N/A	N/A	70%	05/94	3.83%	$0.65	1051	498
194	★★★★★	BPI US Money Market ($US)	InMon	N/A	N/A	N/A	100%	N/A	N/A	$0.65	N/A	N/A
195	★★★★★	Bullock American Fund 'A'	USEq		N/A	N/A	35%	10/95	0.22%	$2.31	N/A	N/A
196	★★★★★	Bullock American Fund 'B'	USEq		N/A	N/A	35%	10/95	0.22%	$2.56	N/A	N/A
197	★★★½	Bullock American Fund 'C'	USEq		N/A	N/A	35%	10/95	0.22%	$2.82	N/A	N/A
198	★★★	Bullock American Fund 'D'	USEq		A	A	46%	09/88	–0.32%	$2.26	521	310
199	★★★½	Bullock Asian Dynasty 'A'	Asia		B	B	53%	01/95	–0.14%	$2.33	N/A	N/A
200	★★★	Bullock Asian Dynasty 'B'	Asia		B	B	53%	01/95	–0.15%	$2.58	N/A	N/A

Fund #	Rating	Fund name	Type	Up mkt	Down mkt	GICs better	Worst 12-mo. end	Worst 12-mo. chnge	MER	FundMate # sim.	FundMate # comp.
201	★★★	Bullock Asian Dynasty 'C'	Asia	B	B	53%	01/95	–0.15%	$2.83	N/A	N/A
202	★★	Bullock Asset Strategy Fund 'A'	Balan	N/A	N/A	40%	10/95	5.97%	$2.32	N/A	N/A
203	★★	Bullock Asset Strategy Fund 'B'	Balan	N/A	N/A	40%	10/95	5.81%	$2.57	N/A	N/A
204	★	Bullock Asset Strategy Fund 'C'	Balan	N/A	N/A	40%	10/95	5.34%	$2.82	N/A	N/A
205	★★	Bullock Asset Strategy Fund 'D'	Balan	C	C	55%	07/93	–1.00%	$2.25	748	393
206	★★★★★	Bullock Emerging Markets 'A'	Emerg	A	A	50%	02/95	–0.27%	$2.33	N/A	N/A
207	★★★★★	Bullock Emerging Markets 'B'	Emerg	A	A	50%	02/95	–0.27%	$2.58	N/A	N/A
208	★★★★★	Bullock Emerging Markets 'C'	Emerg	A	A	50%	02/95	–0.27%	$2.83	N/A	N/A
209	★★★★★	Bullock European Enterprise 'A'	Europe	N/A	N/A	25%	02/96	0.26%	$2.30	N/A	N/A
210	★★★★★	Bullock European Enterprise 'B'	Europe	N/A	N/A	25%	02/96	0.26%	$2.56	N/A	N/A
211	★★★★★	Bullock European Enterprise 'C'	Europe	N/A	N/A	31%	02/96	0.25%	$2.80	N/A	N/A
212	★★★	Bullock Global Bond 'A'	InBond	C	D	60%	06/96	–1.60%	$2.03	N/A	N/A
213	★★½	Bullock Global Bond 'B'	InBond	D	D	60%	06/96	–1.91%	$2.29	N/A	N/A
214	★★	Bullock Global Bond 'C'	InBond	D	D	60%	06/96	–2.18%	$2.53	N/A	N/A
215	★★	Bullock Growth Fund 'A'	CdnSm	N/A	N/A	30%	10/95	6.00%	$2.34	N/A	N/A
216	★★	Bullock Growth Fund 'B'	CdnSm	N/A	N/A	30%	10/95	5.76%	$2.58	N/A	N/A
217	★★	Bullock Growth Fund 'C'	CdnSm	N/A	N/A	30%	10/95	5.43%	$2.83	N/A	N/A
218	★★★	Bullock Growth Fund 'D'	CdnSm	C	B	45%	06/82	–0.46%	$2.28	907	897
219	★★★	Bullock Optimax USA. Fund 'A'	USEq	N/A	N/A	40%	12/94	1.71%	$2.33	N/A	N/A
220	★★½	Bullock Optimax USA. Fund 'B'	USEq	N/A	N/A	40%	12/94	1.43%	$2.59	N/A	N/A
221	★★½	Bullock Optimax USA. Fund 'C'	USEq	N/A	N/A	40%	12/94	1.26%	$2.83	N/A	N/A
222	★★★★★	C.I. American Fund	USEq	N/A	N/A	31%	01/95	6.25%	$2.49	239	310
223	★★★★★	C.I. American RSP Fund	USEq	N/A	N/A	29%	N/A	N/A	$2.48	N/A	N/A
224	★★★½	C.I. Canadian Balanced	Balan	B	A	44%	01/95	–4.72%	$2.35	399	393
225	★★★	C.I. Canadian Bond Fund	Bond	A	A	46%	01/95	–4.88%	$1.65	400	389

				CONSISTENCY	RISK					EFFICIENCY	FIT	
Fund #	Rating	Fund name	Type	Performance trend 82 83 84 85 86 87 88 89 90 91 92 93 94 95 June 96	Up mkt	Down mkt	GICs better	Worst 12-mo. end	Worst 12-mo. chnge	MER	FundMate # sim.	FundMate # comp.
276	★★	Canada Trust Everest Emerging Mkts.	Emerg		C	B	53%	05/96	4.67%	$4.00	N/A	N/A
277	★★	Canada Trust Everest EuroGrowth	Europe		N/A	N/A	48%	01/95	–0.16%	$2.29	N/A	N/A
278	★★½	Canada Trust Everest Int'l Bond	InBond		B	C	50%	05/96	3.02%	$2.43	N/A	N/A
279	★★★	Canada Trust Everest Int'l Equity	InEq		D	A	44%	02/95	–0.13%	$2.91	519	958
280	★★½	Canada Trust Everest Money Market	Money		N/A	N/A	68%	04/94	3.43%	$1.12	328	498
281	★★★½	Canada Trust Everest Mortgage Fund	Mrtge		N/A	N/A	44%	05/81	–1.53%	$1.61	1088	345
282	★★½	Canada Trust Everest North American	InEq		D	C	46%	06/82	–0.28%	$2.35	1172	978
283	★★★	Canada Trust Everest Special Equity	CdnSm		C	D	46%	07/88	–0.25%	$2.19	319	979
284	★★★	Canada Trust Everest Stock Fund	CdnEq		D	D	48%	01/95	–0.12%	$1.86	828	N/A
285	★★	Canada Trust Everest US Equity	USEq		N/A	N/A	41%	09/94	–4.68%	$2.28	882	310
286	★★	Canadian Investment Fund	CdnEq		B	C	48%	06/82	–0.23%	$2.28	1138	N/A
287	★★★★★	Canadian Medical Discoveries Fund	Labor		N/A	N/A	75%	02/96	9.50%	$5.00	N/A	N/A
288	★★	Canadian Protected Fund	CdnEq		D	A	63%	08/94	–5.15%	$2.40	180	1185
289	★★★★★	Capital Alliance Ventures Inc.	Labor		N/A	N/A	75%	03/96	9.18%	$4.00	N/A	N/A
290	★★★★★	Capstone Cash Management Fund	Money		N/A	N/A	57%	06/94	3.62%	$0.60	485	498
291	★★★	Capstone Int. Investment Trust	InEq		A	B	51%	09/90	–0.10%	$2.14	270	978
292	★★★	Capstone Investment Trust	Balan		B	A	52%	08/88	–0.17%	$2.14	660	393
293	★★★	Cassels Blaikie American Fund ($US)	USEq		D	A	47%	06/84	–0.28%	$1.24	679	310
294	★★★	Cassels Blaikie Canadian Fund	CdnEq		B	D	45%	01/95	–4.36%	$1.16	286	883
295	★★★	CCPE Diversified Growth Fund R	CdnEq		B	D	50%	01/95	–4.87%	$1.35	315	N/A
296	★★½	CCPE Fixed Income Fund	Bond		A	A	46%	01/95	–0.06%	$1.35	857	389
297	★★½	CCPE Global Equity	InEq		N/A	N/A	53%	03/96	0.14%	$1.75	N/A	N/A
298	★★½	CCPE Growth Fund R	CdnEq		A	B	50%	10/90	–0.13%	$1.35	422	N/A
299	★	CCPE Money Market Fund	Money		N/A	N/A	88%	06/96	5.59%	$0.75	N/A	N/A
300	★★	CCPE US Equity	USEq		N/A	N/A	35%	06/96	0.10%	$1.75	N/A	N/A

				CONSISTENCY	RISK					EFFICIENCY	FIT	
Fund #	Rating	Fund name	Type	Performance trend 82 83 84 85 86 87 88 89 90 91 92 93 94 95 June 96	Up mkt	Down mkt	GICs better	Worst 12-mo. end	Worst 12-mo. chnge	MER	FundMate # sim.	FundMate # comp.
301	★★	CDA Aggressive Equity Fund	CdnSm		N/A	N/A	52%	03/95	–0.15%	$1.00	N/A	N/A
302	★★★	CDA Balanced Fund	Balan		C	B	45%	06/82	–0.23%	$0.92	522	393
303	★★★	CDA Bond and Mortgage Fund	Bond		A	A	47%	01/95	–5.59%	$0.86	434	389
304	★★★	CDA Common Stock Fund	CdnEq		D	C	46%	06/82	–0.21%	$0.87	435	312
305	★★	CDA Emerging Markets Fund	Emerg		B	D	72%	12/95	–1.12%	$1.45	N/A	N/A
306	★★★★★	CDA European Fund	Europe		N/A	N/A	33%	12/95	0.12%	$1.45	N/A	N/A
307	★★★★★	CDA Int'l Equity Fund	InEq		N/A	N/A	33%	12/95	0.14%	$1.45	N/A	N/A
308	★★★½	CDA Money Market Fund	Money		N/A	N/A	65%	05/94	3.70%	$0.55	527	498
309	★★★★★	CDA Pacific Basin Fund	Asia		N/A	N/A	39%	05/96	0.20%	$1.45	N/A	N/A
310	★★	Century DJ Fund	USEq		D	D	54%	07/88	–0.29%	$1.80	459	993
311	★★★	Chou Associates Fund	USEq		B	C	45%	10/90	–0.17%	$2.04	751	310
312	★★½	Chou RRSP Fund	CdnEq		D	D	53%	10/90	–0.16%	$0.74	335	883
313	★★½	CIBC Balanced Income & Growth	Balan		D	D	50%	01/95	–9.74%	$2.25	268	393
314	★★★	CIBC Canadian Bond Fund	Bond		D	D	45%	01/95	–0.12%	$1.50	1124	389
315	★	CIBC Canadian Equity Fund	CdnEq		D	D	54%	01/95	–0.14%	$2.05	1138	312
316	★★½	CIBC Canadian Income Fund	Bond		B	B	55%	01/95	–0.04%	$1.35	N/A	N/A
317	★	CIBC Canadian Resource Fund	OilGas		N/A	N/A	40%	N/A	N/A	$2.30	N/A	N/A
318	★	CIBC Canadian T-Bill Fund	Money		N/A	N/A	88%	04/94	2.99%	$1.20	328	498
319	★★	CIBC Capital Appreciation Fund	CdnSm		D	C	38%	01/95	–0.19%	$2.40	283	897
320	★	CIBC Emerging Economies Fund	Emerg		N/A	N/A	43%	N/A	N/A	$2.50	N/A	N/A
321	★★½	CIBC Equity Income Fund	Div		D	D	45%	01/95	–0.14%	$2.10	989	1183
322	★★	CIBC European Equity Fund	Europe		N/A	N/A	14%	N/A	N/A	$2.25	N/A	N/A
323	★★★	CIBC Far East Prosperity Fund	Asia		A	A	58%	01/95	–0.19%	$2.85	N/A	N/A
324	★★★	CIBC Global Bond Fund	InBond		B	C	37%	06/96	2.20%	$1.80	N/A	N/A
325	★★	CIBC Global Equity Fund	InEq		C	A	53%	09/90	–0.11%	$2.35	908	254

				CONSISTENCY	RISK					EFFICIENCY	FIT	
Fund #	Rating	Fund name	Type	Up mkt	Down mkt	GICs better	Worst 12-mo. end	Worst 12-mo. chnge		MER	FundMate # sim.	FundMate # comp.
326	★★★★★	CIBC Global Technology Fund	Sector	N/A	N/A	14%	N/A	N/A		$2.25	N/A	N/A
327	★★★★★	CIBC Japanese Equity Fund	Japan	N/A	N/A	50%	N/A	N/A		$2.60	N/A	N/A
328	★	CIBC Money Market Fund	Money	N/A	N/A	67%	04/94	3.11%		$1.20	318	498
329	★★★	CIBC Mortgage Investment Fund	Mrtge	N/A	N/A	55%	12/78	–2.19%		$1.60	1088	708
330	★★★	CIBC Premium T-Bill Fund	Money	N/A	N/A	88%	04/94	3.58%		$0.58	328	498
331	★	CIBC US Dollar Money Market ($US)	InMon	N/A	N/A	100%	01/94	2.11%		$1.20	N/A	1224
332	★★★	CIBC US Equity Fund	USEq	N/A	N/A	41%	11/94	1.59%		$2.25	369	310
333	★★★	CIBC US Opportunities Fund	USEq	N/A	N/A	29%	N/A	N/A		$2.25	N/A	N/A
334	★★★	Clean Environment Balanced Fund	Balan	D	A	40%	01/95	–0.12%		$2.99	424	393
335	★★★	Clean Environment Equity Fund	CdnEq	B	D	38%	01/95	–0.18%		$2.99	1080	288
336	★★	Clean Environment Income Fund	Bond	C	A	67%	09/95	1.86%		$2.49	N/A	N/A
337	★★	Clean Environment Int'l Equity Fund	InEq	N/A	N/A	58%	01/95	–9.63%		$3.23	N/A	N/A
338	★★★	Co-operators Balanced Fund	Balan	A	B	43%	01/95	–6.99%		$2.07	569	393
339	★★½	Co-operators Canadian Equity Fund	CdnEq	C	A	44%	01/95	–7.04%		$2.07	705	N/A
340	★★★	Co-operators Fixed Income Fund	Bond	B	D	50%	01/95	–8.21%		$2.07	852	389
341	★★★★★	Co-operators US Equity Fund	USEq	N/A	N/A	50%	06/96	0.24%		$2.07	N/A	N/A
342	★★	Colonia Bond Fund	Bond	B	A	42%	01/95	–5.91%		$1.60	590	389
343	★	Colonia Equity Fund	CdnEq	D	D	50%	01/95	–0.15%		$2.14	415	N/A
344	★★	Colonia Money Market Fund	Money	N/A	N/A	81%	08/94	3.12%		$1.07	1001	578
345	★★½	Colonia Mortgage Fund	Mrtge	N/A	N/A	46%	12/94	–1.16%		$1.87	605	528
346	★★★★★	Colonia Special Growth Fund	CdnSm	A	B	37%	01/95	–9.36%		$2.14	634	754
347	★★★★★	Colonia Strategic Balanced Fund	Bond	N/A	N/A	50%	N/A	N/A		$0.25	N/A	N/A
348	★★★	Common Sense Asset Builder 1	Balan	N/A	N/A	43%	02/95	5.40%		$2.25	N/A	N/A
349	★★★	Common Sense Asset Builder 2	Balan	N/A	N/A	43%	02/95	5.08%		$2.26	N/A	N/A
350	★★★	Common Sense Asset Builder 3	Balan	N/A	N/A	43%	02/95	4.46%		$2.25	N/A	N/A

Fund #	Rating	Fund name	Type	CONSISTENCY: Performance trend 82 83 84 85 86 87 88 89 90 91 92 93 94 95 June 96	RISK: Up mkt	Down mkt	GICs better	Worst 12-mo. end	Worst 12-mo. chnge	EFFICIENCY: MER	FIT: FundMate # sim.	FundMate # comp.
351	★★★	Common Sense Asset Builder 4	Balan		N/A	N/A	46%	02/95	0.05%	$2.25	N/A	N/A
352	★★★	Common Sense Asset Builder 5	Balan		N/A	N/A	46%	02/95	3.07%	$2.26	N/A	N/A
353	★★★★½	Concorde Balanced Fund	Balan		N/A	N/A	42%	06/96	0.13%	$2.00	N/A	N/A
354	★★★	Concorde Croissance	CdnEq		A	B	44%	01/95	–7.45%	$2.14	1205	N/A
355	★★★★★	Concorde Dividend Fund	Div		N/A	N/A	6%	03/96	0.17%	$1.85	N/A	N/A
356	★½	Concorde Hypothèques	Mrtge		N/A	N/A	55%	01/95	–3.35%	$1.87	469	345
357	★★★	Concorde International Fund	InEq		N/A	N/A	33%	06/96	0.15%	$2.28	N/A	N/A
358	★½	Concorde Monétaire	Money		N/A	N/A	94%	05/94	4.06%	$1.25	1209	578
359	★★	Concorde Revenu	Bond		C	B	46%	01/95	–0.08%	$1.96	1204	389
360	★★½	Confed Equity Fund	CdnEq		C	B	49%	06/82	–0.33%	$2.00	362	312
361	★★★	Confed Fixed Income	Bond		C	B	44%	01/95	–7.25%	$2.00	363	389
362	★★★	Confed Life B	CdnEq		B	B	49%	06/82	–0.32%	$0.96	360	312
363	★★★	Confed Life C	Bond		C	B	43%	01/95	–7.07%	$1.44	361	389
364	★★★	Cornerstone Balanced Fund	Balan		A	D	44%	06/82	–0.32%	$2.39	912	393
365	★★★	Cornerstone Bond Fund	Bond		B	C	48%	01/95	–6.99%	$1.25	852	389
366	★★★	Cornerstone Cdn Growth	CdnEq		A	D	45%	09/90	–0.20%	$2.06	913	N/A
367	★★★	Cornerstone Global Fund	InEq		B	B	48%	08/88	–0.31%	$2.53	495	978
368	★★	Cornerstone Gov Money	Money		N/A	N/A	79%	05/94	3.70%	$1.03	468	498
369	★★½	Cornerstone US Fund	USEq		C	A	47%	08/88	–0.31%	$2.30	854	310
370	★★★	Cote 100 Amérique	USEq		N/A	N/A	40%	01/95	–0.18%	$1.40	371	310
371	★★★	Cote 100 Amérique REÉR	USEq		N/A	N/A	42%	01/95	–0.19%	$1.40	370	310
372	★★★★★	Cote 100 EXP	CdnEq		N/A	N/A	30%	03/95	5.50%	$2.00	N/A	N/A
373	★	Cote 100 REA - Action	CdnEq	N/A	N/A	N/A	43%	N/A	N/A	$2.00	N/A	N/A
374	★★★½	Cundill Value Fund	InEq		B	C	44%	12/90	–9.35%	$2.06	1173	254
375	★★★½	DGC Entertainment Ventures Corp.	Labor		N/A	N/A	63%	04/96	–2.87%	$6.30	N/A	N/A

				CONSISTENCY		RISK				EFFICIENCY	FIT	
Fund #	Rating	Fund name	Type	Performance trend 82 83 84 85 86 87 88 89 90 91 92 93 94 95 June 96	Up mkt	Down mkt	GICs better	Worst 12-mo. end	Worst 12-mo. chnge	MER	FundMate # sim.	FundMate # comp.
376	★★★	Dolphin Growth Fund	CdnEq		N/A	B	44%	06/82	–0.31%	$2.00	N/A	N/A
377	★★	Dominion Equity Resource Fund Inc.	OilGas		D	D	100%	06/86	–1.00%	$2.00	1029	505
378	★★★	Dynamic Americas Fund	USEq		C	B	46%	07/82	–0.16%	$2.59	1203	310
379	★★½	Dynamic Canadian Growth Fund	CdnEq		C	D	50%	05/88	–0.32%	$2.55	384	N/A
380	★★★½	Dynamic Dividend Fund	Div		C	B	45%	01/95	–6.51%	$1.61	381	1183
381	★★★	Dynamic Dividend Growth Fund	Div		A	A	49%	11/90	–0.11%	$1.81	321	1183
382	★★★★	Dynamic Europe Fund	Europe		B	A	53%	06/91	–0.17%	$2.70	1030	1012
383	★★★	Dynamic Far East Fund	Asia		C	A	52%	05/95	–8.65%	$3.50	N/A	N/A
384	★★★	Dynamic Fund of Canada	CdnEq		D	D	45%	06/82	–0.31%	$2.51	379	N/A
385	★★★½	Dynamic Global Bond Fund	InBond		B	A	50%	10/91	–2.09%	$1.94	1061	455
386	★★	Dynamic Global Millennia Fund	InEq		D	A	52%	01/95	–0.24%	$3.12	391	978
387	★★★	Dynamic Global Partners Fund	InBal		N/A	N/A	52%	08/95	1.22%	$2.68	N/A	N/A
388	★★★★★	Dynamic Global Resources Fund	OilGas		N/A	N/A	31%	06/96	0.57%	$3.42	N/A	N/A
389	★★½	Dynamic Government Income Fund	Bond		A	D	56%	01/94	–1.01%	$0.83	1177	1166
390	★★★	Dynamic Income Fund	Bond		A	A	48%	09/81	–7.35%	$1.68	1182	389
391	★★	Dynamic International Fund	InEq		C	A	49%	09/88	–0.38%	$2.79	282	755
392	★★	Dynamic Money Market Fund	Money		N/A	N/A	81%	04/94	3.57%	$0.59	318	498
393	★★★★	Dynamic Partners Fund	Balan		D	A	43%	06/96	–1.00%	$2.45	707	396
394	★★★	Dynamic Precious Metals Fund	Gold		D	D	46%	09/88	–0.27%	$2.57	554	1029
395	★★★★★	Dynamic Real Estate Equity Fund	Sector		N/A	N/A	8%	05/96	0.42%	$3.70	N/A	N/A
396	★★★	Dynamic Team Fund	Balan		D	B	49%	01/95	–9.41%	$0.98	784	393
397	★★½	Elliott & Page American Growth Fund	USEq		D	A	46%	08/88	–0.29%	$1.41	1047	310
398	★★★	Elliott & Page Asian Growth Fund	Asia		B	C	61%	10/95	–2.09%	$1.69	N/A	N/A
399	★★★	Elliott & Page Balanced Fund	Balan		B	C	47%	01/95	–8.35%	$1.93	364	393
400	★	Elliott & Page Bond Fund	Bond		D	D	51%	01/95	–9.45%	$1.68	987	389

				CONSISTENCY	RISK					EFFICIENCY	FIT	
Fund #	Rating	Fund name	Type	Up mkt	Down mkt	GICs better	Worst 12-mo. end	Worst 12-mo. chnge	MER	FundMate # sim.	FundMate # comp.
401	★★	Elliott & Page Emerging Markets	Emerg	D	C	65%	10/95	–0.20%	$1.80	N/A	N/A
402	★★★½	Elliott & Page Equity Fund	CdnEq	A	C	45%	10/90	–0.17%	$1.89	366	N/A
403	★★★	Elliott & Page Global Balanced Fund	InBal	N/A	N/A	43%	08/95	5.59%	$2.34	N/A	N/A
404	★★★	Elliott & Page Global Bond Fund	InBond	B	D	52%	05/96	–7.27%	$1.67	N/A	N/A
405	★★★	Elliott & Page Global Equity Fund	InEq	N/A	N/A	35%	08/95	1.85%	$1.60	N/A	N/A
406	★	Elliott & Page T-Bill Fund	Money	N/A	N/A	100%	06/96	4.04%	$2.12	N/A	N/A
407	★	Empire Asset Allocation Fund	Balan	N/A	N/A	52%	05/95	5.34%	$2.57	N/A	N/A
408	★★★	Empire Balanced Fund	Balan	C	B	49%	01/95	–7.38%	$2.57	924	393
409	★★½	Empire Bond Fund	Bond	C	C	50%	01/95	–6.84%	$2.18	1151	389
410	★★★	Empire Elite Equity Fund 5	CdnEq	C	B	44%	07/82	–0.28%	$2.57	415	N/A
411	★★★½	Empire Equity Growth Fund 3	CdnEq	C	D	44%	06/82	–0.22%	$2.57	415	N/A
412	★	Empire Foreign Curr. Cdn Bond Fund	InBond	D	D	57%	09/95	–3.89%	$2.18	N/A	N/A
413	★★★	Empire International Fund	InEq	B	B	49%	01/95	–0.11%	$2.57	1173	755
414	★	Empire Money Market Fund	Money	N/A	N/A	75%	06/94	3.17%	$1.54	392	498
415	★★★	Empire Premier Equity Fund 1	CdnEq	C	A	46%	06/82	–0.26%	$1.54	410	N/A
416	★★½	Equitable Life Asset Allocation	Balan	N/A	N/A	55%	06/96	7.58%	$2.25	N/A	N/A
417	★	Equitable Life Canadian Bond Fund	Bond	C	C	51%	01/95	–7.87%	$2.00	423	389
418	★★½	Equitable Life Canadian Stock Fund	CdnEq	B	A	45%	01/95	–5.70%	$2.25	422	N/A
419	★★★	Equitable Life International Fund	InEq	N/A	N/A	40%	10/95	–5.14%	$2.75	N/A	N/A
420	★	Equitable Life Money Market Fund	Money	N/A	N/A	95%	10/95	4.14%	$1.75	N/A	N/A
421	★	Equitable Life Mortgage Fund	Mrtge	N/A	N/A	55%	06/96	4.82%	$2.25	N/A	N/A
422	★★½	Equitable Life Seg. Common Stock	CdnEq	A	A	48%	08/88	–0.22%	$1.04	988	N/A
423	★★★½	Equitable Life Segregated Accum Inc	Bond	A	B	43%	01/95	–6.59%	$0.50	417	389
424	★★½	Ethical Balanced Fund	Balan	B	B	48%	01/95	–9.13%	$2.21	338	393
425	★★	Ethical Global Bond Fund	InBond	C	B	29%	05/96	4.19%	$1.97	N/A	N/A

Fund #	Rating	Fund name	Type	CONSISTENCY: Performance trend 82–June 96	RISK: Up mkt	RISK: Down mkt	RISK: GICs better	RISK: Worst 12-mo. end	RISK: Worst 12-mo. chnge	EFFICIENCY: MER	FIT: FundMate # sim.	FIT: FundMate # comp.
426	★★★	Ethical Growth Fund	CdnEq		A	D	54%	01/95	–7.82%	$2.24	1080	1185
427	★★★	Ethical Income Fund	Bond		A	B	48%	01/95	–9.12%	$1.66	700	389
428	★★★★½	Ethical Money Market Fund	Money		N/A	N/A	72%	06/94	3.63%	$1.30	592	498
429	★★½	Ethical North American Equity Fund	USEq		C	A	100%	06/82	–0.25%	$2.55	1212	310
430	★★★	Ethical Pacific Rim Fund	Asia		N/A	N/A	53%	06/96	0.10%	$2.60	N/A	N/A
431	★★	Ethical Special Equity Fund	CdnSm		N/A	N/A	29%	01/96	0.14%	$2.68	N/A	N/A
432	★½	Ferique American Fund	USEq	N/A	N/A	N/A	40%	N/A	N/A	$2.37	N/A	N/A
433	★★★	Ferique Balanced Fund	Balan		B	D	47%	06/82	–0.15%	$0.47	522	393
434	★★★	Ferique Bond Fund	Bond		A	A	50%	03/80	–0.14%	$0.65	861	389
435	★★★	Ferique Equity Fund	CdnEq		B	C	45%	06/82	–0.38%	$0.67	524	N/A
436	★	Ferique Growth Fund	CdnSm	N/A	N/A	N/A	25%	N/A	N/A	$0.00	N/A	N/A
437	★★½	Ferique International Fund	InEq		N/A	N/A	53%	08/95	–7.72%	$1.14	N/A	N/A
438	★★★★★	Ferique Short Term Income Fund	Money		N/A	N/A	61%	07/78	–5.03%	$0.49	867	578
439	★	FESA Enterprise Venture Capital	Labor	N/A	N/A	N/A	94%	02/96	–8.00%	$6.20	N/A	N/A
440	★★★	Fidelity Asset Manager Fund	InBal		B	C	37%	01/95	–0.07%	$2.86	1222	642
441	★★★★★	Fidelity Canadian Asset Allocation	Balan		N/A	N/A	39%	06/96	0.13%	$2.59	N/A	N/A
442	★★	Fidelity Canadian Bond Fund	Bond		D	D	50%	01/95	–0.12%	$1.97	898	389
443	★★★★	Fidelity Canadian Growth Company	CdnSm		N/A	N/A	22%	06/96	0.20%	$2.63	N/A	N/A
444	★	Fidelity Canadian Income Fund	Bond		N/A	N/A	35%	05/96	8.30%	$1.25	N/A	N/A
445	★★★	Fidelity Capital Builder Fund	CdnEq		D	C	46%	01/95	–0.16%	$2.57	1057	1185
446	★	Fidelity Cdn. Short Term Asset Fund	Money		N/A	N/A	91%	04/94	3.13%	$1.25	1087	578
447	★★★★★	Fidelity Emerging Markets Bond Fund	InBond		A	A	43%	02/95	–0.15%	$2.33	N/A	N/A
448	★★★★★	Fidelity Emerging Markets Portfolio	Emerg		A	A	33%	12/95	0.20%	$3.44	N/A	N/A
449	★★★★½	Fidelity European Growth Fund	Europe		N/A	N/A	42%	01/95	2.28%	$2.82	731	1012
450	★★★★½	Fidelity Far East Fund	Asia		A	A	42%	01/95	–0.22%	$2.82	744	1015

				CONSISTENCY	RISK					EFFICIENCY	FIT	
Fund #	Rating	Fund name	Type	Performance trend 82 83 84 85 86 87 88 89 90 91 92 93 94 95 June 96	Up mkt	Down mkt	GICs better	Worst 12-mo. end	Worst 12-mo. chnge	MER	FundMate # sim.	FundMate # comp.
451	★★★★★	Fidelity Growth America Fund	USEq		N/A	N/A	38%	09/94	–1.17%	$2.40	679	310
452	★★★	Fidelity International Portfolio	InEq		B	B	44%	09/90	–0.14%	$2.75	519	958
453	★★★½	Fidelity Japanese Growth Fund	Japan		C	B	49%	06/95	–0.24%	$3.01	739	1032
454	★★★	Fidelity Latin American Growth Fund	Latin		B	A	48%	02/95	–0.44%	$3.39	N/A	N/A
455	★★★½	Fidelity North American Income Fund	InBond		C	A	44%	01/95	–0.15%	$1.75	249	385
456	★★	Fidelity RSP Global Bond Fund	InBond		C	D	58%	12/94	–7.25%	$2.31	N/A	N/A
457	★★½	Fidelity Small Cap America Fund	USEq		N/A	N/A	50%	04/95	3.43%	$2.68	N/A	N/A
458	★	Fidelity US Money Market (SUS)	InMon		N/A	N/A	100%	06/96	4.41%	$1.25	N/A	N/A
459	★	First American (Guardian Timing)	USEq		N/A	N/A	57%	08/94	–8.46%	$2.80	371	1004
460	★★½	First Canadian Bond Fund	Bond		B	C	48%	01/95	–8.74%	$1.53	987	389
461	★★★	First Canadian Dividend Income Fund	Div		N/A	N/A	35%	10/95	9.56%	$1.81	N/A	N/A
462	★★	First Canadian Emerging Mkts Fund	Emerg		C	B	60%	11/95	–0.21%	$2.11	N/A	N/A
463	★★	First Canadian Equity Index	CdnEq		B	C	51%	10/90	–0.19%	$1.52	591	N/A
464	★	First Canadian European Growth Fund	Europe		N/A	N/A	40%	10/95	0.05%	$2.12	N/A	N/A
465	★★★★★	First Canadian Far East Growth Fund	Asia		N/A	N/A	45%	10/95	–3.98%	$2.05	N/A	N/A
466	★★½	First Canadian International Growth	InEq		N/A	N/A	43%	06/95	–5.66%	$1.99	796	958
467	★★★	First Canadian Japanese Growth Fund	Japan		D	B	55%	10/95	–0.13%	$2.02	N/A	N/A
468	★	First Canadian Money Market	Money		N/A	N/A	74%	06/94	3.63%	$1.11	592	498
469	★★½	First Canadian Mortgage Fund	Mrtge		N/A	N/A	54%	01/95	–2.13%	$1.18	494	708
470	★	First Canadian NAFTA Advantage Fund	USEq		N/A	N/A	40%	10/95	–2.39%	$2.11	N/A	N/A
471	★★	First Cdn. Asset Allocation	Balan		C	D	52%	01/95	–0.11%	$1.99	924	393
472	★★½	First Cdn. Growth Fund	CdnEq		B	D	50%	01/95	–0.12%	$2.30	N/A	N/A
473	★★★	First Cdn. International Bond Fund	InBond		B	C	47%	09/94	–1.43%	$2.00	N/A	N/A
474	★★½	First Cdn. Resource Fund	OilGas		C	B	47%	01/95	–0.19%	$2.30	N/A	N/A
475	★	First Cdn. Special Growth Fund	CdnSm		B	D	53%	01/95	–0.24%	$2.29	N/A	N/A

				CONSISTENCY		RISK				EFFICIENCY	FIT	
Fund #	Rating	Fund name	Type	Performance trend 82 83 84 85 86 87 88 89 90 91 92 93 94 95 June 96	Up mkt	Down mkt	GICs better	Worst 12-mo. end	Worst 12-mo. chnge	MER	FundMate # sim.	FundMate # comp.
476	★	First Cdn. T-Bill Fund	Money		N/A	N/A	94%	08/94	3.71%	$1.12	N/A	N/A
477	★★	First Cdn. US Growth Fund	USEq		N/A	N/A	41%	09/94	–1.67%	$2.26	N/A	N/A
478	★★½	First Heritage Fund	OilGas		C	B	50%	07/88	–0.24%	$4.24	182	505
479	★★★★★	First Ontario LSIF Ltd.	Labor		N/A	N/A	100%	06/96	1.73%	$1.96	N/A	N/A
480	★★★	Fonds de Professionnels Balanced	Balan		B	B	42%	01/95	–3.46%	$0.75	1135	393
481	★★★	Fonds de Professionnels Bond	Bond		B	A	45%	01/95	–3.81%	$0.75	671	389
482	★★½	Fonds de Professionnels Cdn. Equity	CdnEq		C	C	49%	09/90	–0.16%	$0.75	879	1185
483	★★★	Fonds de Professionnels Growth & Inc	Balan		N/A	N/A	33%	10/95	0.08%	$0.75	N/A	N/A
484	★★★	Fonds de Professionnels Intl Equity	InEq		N/A	N/A	42%	02/95	2.20%	$0.75	N/A	N/A
485	★★★★★	Fonds de Professionnels Short Term	Money		N/A	N/A	47%	06/94	3.93%	$0.40	1146	498
486	★★	Fonds Desjardins Actions	CdnEq		C	D	52%	08/88	–0.19%	$1.93	492	1185
487	★★	Fonds Desjardins Croissance	CdnEq		B	D	48%	01/95	–0.10%	$1.80	N/A	N/A
488	★	Fonds Desjardins Divers. Audacieux	Balan		N/A	N/A	47%	06/96	0.10%	$1.75	N/A	N/A
489	★	Fonds Desjardins Divers. Modéré	Balan		N/A	N/A	35%	06/96	9.09%	$1.65	N/A	N/A
490	★	Fonds Desjardins Divers. Secure	Balan		N/A	N/A	47%	06/96	7.14%	$1.55	N/A	N/A
491	★★★	Fonds Desjardins Dividendes	Div		B	D	45%	01/95	–0.07%	$1.80	N/A	N/A
492	★★	Fonds Desjardins Environnement	CdnEq		C	C	50%	01/95	–0.11%	$2.14	486	1185
493	★★	Fonds Desjardins Équilibre	Balan		B	D	49%	01/95	–7.94%	$1.96	586	393
494	★½	Fonds Desjardins Hypothèques	Mrtge		N/A	N/A	59%	01/95	–7.31%	$1.63	469	708
495	★★★	Fonds Desjardins International	InEq		B	B	47%	08/88	–0.26%	$2.37	1237	978
496	★	Fonds Desjardins Marché américain	USEq	N/A	N/A	N/A	60%	N/A	N/A	$1.80	N/A	N/A
497	★	Fonds Desjardins Mondial Équilibre	Balan	N/A	N/A	N/A	60%	N/A	N/A	$1.65	N/A	N/A
498	★★★★★	Fonds Desjardins Monétaire	Money		N/A	N/A	67%	08/94	3.66%	$1.12	502	578
499	★	Fonds Desjardins Obligations	Bond		B	A	47%	01/95	–8.82%	$1.62	503	389
500	★	Fonds Ficadre Actions	CdnEq		A	D	55%	05/88	–0.30%	$2.14	1205	1185

Fund #	Rating	Fund name	Type	Up mkt	Down mkt	GICs better	Worst 12-mo. end	Worst 12-mo. chnge	MER	FundMate # sim.	FundMate # comp.
501	★★★	Fonds Ficadre Équilibre	Balan	A	D	48%	08/88	–0.15%	$2.20	1210	393
502	★★★★½	Fonds Ficadre Money Market	Money	N/A	N/A	72%	08/94	2.98%	$1.14	498	973
503	★½	Fonds Ficadre Obligations	Bond	B	B	45%	01/95	–7.96%	$1.67	499	628
504	★★★	Friedberg Currency Fund	Sector	N/A	N/A	50%	04/96	–8.69%	$4.20	N/A	N/A
505	★½	Friedberg Double Gold Plus Fund	Gold	D	D	73%	04/91	–0.28%	$0.00	394	1029
506	★★½	G.T. Global America Growth Class	USEq	N/A	N/A	40%	06/96	2.83%	$2.95	N/A	N/A
507	★★★★★	G.T. Global Canada Growth Class	CdnEq	N/A	N/A	33%	12/95	0.13%	$2.95	N/A	N/A
508	★★★	G.T. Global Growth & Income Fund	InBal	N/A	N/A	55%	10/95	6.14%	$2.95	N/A	N/A
509	★★★	G.T. Global Infrastructure Class	Sector	N/A	N/A	50%	10/95	8.37%	$2.95	N/A	N/A
510	★★★★★	G.T. Global Latin America Class	Latin	B	A	45%	10/95	–0.11%	$2.95	N/A	N/A
511	★★★	G.T. Global Natural Resources Class	OilGas	N/A	N/A	40%	10/95	–2.38%	$2.95	N/A	N/A
512	★★★★★	G.T. Global Pacific Growth Class	Asia	N/A	N/A	60%	10/95	–9.38%	$2.95	N/A	N/A
513	★★★	G.T. Global Short-term Income 'A'	InBond	N/A	N/A	86%	N/A	N/A	$1.75	N/A	N/A
514	★★★	G.T. Global Short-term Income 'B'	InBond	N/A	N/A	86%	N/A	N/A	$2.25	N/A	N/A
515	★★★★★	G.T. Global Telecommunication Class	Sector	N/A	N/A	25%	10/95	0.25%	$2.95	N/A	N/A
516	★★½	G.T. Global World Bond Fund	InBond	A	B	65%	10/95	3.61%	$2.45	N/A	N/A
517	★★★	GBC Canadian Bond Fund	Bond	A	D	47%	01/95	–7.59%	$1.19	852	628
518	★★★★★	GBC Canadian Growth Fund	CdnSm	B	C	41%	01/95	–0.15%	$1.89	1028	897
519	★	GBC International Growth Fund	InEq	D	A	48%	02/95	–0.18%	$1.88	452	958
520	★★★★½	GBC Money Market Fund	Money	N/A	N/A	71%	05/94	3.90%	$0.75	701	498
521	★★★½	GBC North American Growth Fund Inc.	USEq	A	C	40%	10/90	–0.29%	$1.86	1232	310
522	★★	General Trust of Canada Balanced	Balan	D	C	53%	09/90	–0.10%	$2.12	683	393
523	★★★	General Trust of Canada Bond Fund	Bond	D	A	48%	01/95	–8.98%	$1.59	434	628
524	★★	General Trust of Canada Cdn Equity	CdnEq	D	C	48%	06/82	–0.36%	$1.84	435	1185
525	★★★	General Trust of Canada Growth Fund	CdnSm	D	C	47%	10/90	–0.23%	$2.16	1028	897

Fund #	Rating	Fund name	Type	Up mkt	Down mkt	GICs better	Worst 12-mo. end	Worst 12-mo. chnge	MER	FundMate # sim.	FundMate # comp.
526	★★½	General Trust of Canada Intl.	InEq	D	B	57%	09/90	–0.12%	$2.13	466	755
527	★★★	General Trust of Canada Money Mkt	Money	N/A	N/A	66%	05/94	3.42%	$1.12	438	578
528	★★★½	General Trust of Canada Mortgage	Mrtge	N/A	N/A	46%	03/80	–1.93%	$1.57	722	579
529	★★★	General Trust of Canada US Equity	USEq	B	D	42%	08/88	–0.28%	$2.15	521	310
530	★★★	GFM Emerging Markets Country(SUS)	Emerg	N/A	N/A	50%	06/96	9.40%	$1.50	N/A	N/A
531	★★½	Global Strategy Asia Fund	Asia	A	B	52%	01/95	–0.24%	$2.95	N/A	N/A
532	★★★	Global Strategy Bond Fund	Bond	N/A	N/A	57%	02/95	2.05%	$1.50	N/A	N/A
533	★★½	Global Strategy Canada Growth Fund	CdnEq	D	D	38%	01/95	–0.12%	$2.65	926	883
534	★★	Global Strategy Cdn Small Cap	CdnSm	N/A	N/A	39%	06/96	0.11%	$2.65	N/A	N/A
535	★★½	Global Strategy Div Foreign Bond	InBond	A	C	43%	05/96	4.93%	$2.29	N/A	N/A
536	★★★½	Global Strategy Div. Japan Plus	Japan	C	D	65%	06/95	–0.19%	$2.62	N/A	N/A
537	★	Global Strategy Divers. World Eqt.	InEq	N/A	N/A	44%	12/95	4.80%	$2.50	N/A	N/A
538	★½	Global Strategy Diversified Asia	Asia	C	B	61%	10/95	–0.16%	$2.70	N/A	N/A
539	★★★	Global Strategy Diversified Bond	InBond	A	A	46%	12/94	–7.85%	$2.29	550	1017
540	★	Global Strategy Diversified Europe	Europe	N/A	N/A	43%	01/95	–8.06%	$2.68	1246	1012
541	★½	Global Strategy Diversified Latin	Latin	D	D	58%	10/95	–0.34%	$2.70	N/A	N/A
542	★★★	Global Strategy Europe Plus	Europe	N/A	N/A	17%	12/95	0.12%	$2.95	N/A	N/A
543	★★★★★	Global Strategy Gold Plus Fund	Gold	B	D	33%	01/95	–0.07%	$2.95	N/A	N/A
544	★★★	Global Strategy Income Plus Fund	Balan	C	D	34%	01/95	–4.92%	$2.64	680	393
545	★★½	Global Strategy Japan Fund	Japan	D	B	56%	12/95	–0.10%	$2.62	N/A	N/A
546	★★★★½	Global Strategy Latin America Fund	Latin	D	B	54%	10/95	–0.25%	$2.95	N/A	N/A
547	★★	Global Strategy Money Market Fund	Money	N/A	N/A	77%	03/94	3.93%	$0.85	1049	498
548	★★★½	Global Strategy US Equity	USEq	N/A	N/A	17%	06/96	0.24%	$2.95	N/A	N/A
549	★★½	Global Strategy World Balanced	InBal	N/A	N/A	33%	03/96	7.77%	$2.58	N/A	N/A
550	★★★½	Global Strategy World Bond Fund	InBond	A	A	49%	12/94	–8.78%	$2.26	539	1017

Fund #	Rating	Fund name	Type	CONSISTENCY: Performance trend 82 83 84 85 86 87 88 89 90 91 92 93 94 95 June 96	Up mkt	RISK: Down mkt	GICs better	Worst 12-mo. end	Worst 12-mo. chnge	EFFICIENCY: MER	FIT: FundMate # sim.	FundMate # comp.
551	★★★★★	Global Strategy World Emerging Co.	InEq		N/A	N/A	17%	06/96	0.40%	$2.95	N/A	N/A
552	★★★★½	Global Strategy World Equity	InEq		N/A	N/A	33%	12/95	0.11%	$2.95	N/A	N/A
553	★★	GlobeInvest Emerg. Markets Country	Money		N/A	N/A	64%	N/A	N/A	$2.50	N/A	N/A
554	★★★	Goldfund Ltd. (CSA Mgnt)	OilGas		D	B	53%	09/88	–0.40%	$2.96	555	377
555	★★★	Goldtrust (CSA Mgnt)	Gold		D	D	52%	11/81	–0.43%	$2.42	554	1029
556	★	Great-West Cdn. Resource Fund (A)	OilGas	N/A	N/A	N/A	20%	N/A	N/A	$3.24	N/A	N/A
557	★	Great-West Life Balanced Fund (B)	Balan	N/A	N/A	N/A	60%	N/A	N/A	$2.76	N/A	N/A
558	★	Great-West Life Balanced Fund (M)	Balan	N/A	N/A	N/A	40%	N/A	N/A	$2.82	N/A	N/A
559	★★★	Great-West Life Balanced Fund (S)	Balan	N/A	N/A	N/A	60%	N/A	N/A	$2.76	N/A	N/A
560	★	Great-West Life Bond Fund (B)	Bond	N/A	N/A	N/A	60%	N/A	N/A	$2.28	N/A	N/A
561	★	Great-West Life Bond Fund (M)	Bond	N/A	N/A	N/A	60%	N/A	N/A	$2.31	N/A	N/A
562	★	Great-West Life Bond Fund (S)	Bond	N/A	N/A	N/A	60%	N/A	N/A	$2.28	N/A	N/A
563	★★	Great-West Life Canadian Bond Fund	Bond		D	C	50%	01/95	–8.79%	$2.16	517	628
564	★★★	Great-West Life Canadian Equity	CdnEq		C	C	46%	07/88	–0.17%	$2.64	1050	1185
565	★★	Great-West Life Diversified RS Fund	Balan		D	B	53%	01/95	–8.81%	$2.64	899	393
566	★★	Great-West Life Equity Fund (M)	CdnEq	N/A	N/A	N/A	40%	N/A	N/A	$2.82	N/A	N/A
567	★★★	Great-West Life Equity Fund (S)	CdnEq	N/A	N/A	N/A	60%	N/A	N/A	$2.76	N/A	N/A
568	★★	Great-West Life Equity Index Fund	CdnEq		C	C	52%	10/90	–0.20%	$2.64	591	883
569	★★★	Great-West Life Equity/Bond Fund	Balan		D	C	45%	01/95	–0.11%	$2.64	565	393
570	★	Great-West Life Government Bond	Bond		N/A	N/A	47%	05/96	0.06%	$2.16	N/A	N/A
571	★★★★★	Great-West Life Growth & Income (A)	Bond	N/A	N/A	N/A	20%	N/A	N/A	$2.76	N/A	N/A
572	★★★★★	Great-West Life Growth & Income (M)	Bond	N/A	N/A	N/A	40%	N/A	N/A	$2.82	N/A	N/A
573	★	Great-West Life Growth Equity (A)	CdnSm	N/A	N/A	N/A	20%	N/A	N/A	$3.18	N/A	N/A
574	★½	Great-West Life Income Fund	Balan		N/A	N/A	37%	05/96	8.62%	$2.16	N/A	N/A
575	★★★	Great-West Life International Bond	InBond		B	C	47%	05/96	4.17%	$2.52	N/A	N/A

				CONSISTENCY	RISK					EFFICIENCY	FIT	
Fund #	Rating	Fund name	Type	Performance trend 82 83 84 85 86 87 88 89 90 91 92 93 94 95 June 96	Up mkt	Down mkt	GICs better	Worst 12-mo. end	Worst 12-mo. chnge	MER	FundMate # sim.	FundMate # comp.
576	★★★	Great-West Life Int'l Equity	InEq		N/A	N/A	32%	11/95	5.87%	$3.00	N/A	N/A
577	★	Great-West Life Larger Co. Fund (M)	CdnEq	N/A	N/A	N/A	60%	N/A	N/A	$2.82	N/A	N/A
578	★	Great-West Life Money Market Fund	Money		N/A	N/A	72%	04/94	3.01%	$1.74	914	498
579	★★★	Great-West Life Mortgage Fund	Mrtge		N/A	N/A	53%	07/81	–5.21%	$2.40	738	528
580	★	Great-West Life N. A. Equity (B)	InEq	N/A	N/A	N/A	60%	N/A	N/A	$2.76	N/A	N/A
581	★	Great-West Life Smaller Company (M)	CdnSm	N/A	N/A	N/A	20%	N/A	N/A	$2.82	N/A	N/A
582	★	Great-West Life Strategic Inc. (A)	Bond	N/A	N/A	N/A	100%	N/A	N/A	$2.70	N/A	N/A
583	★½	Great-West Life US Equity Fund	USEq		N/A	N/A	26%	06/96	0.14%	$2.82	N/A	N/A
584	★★★	Green Line Asian Growth Fund	Asia		A	A	60%	01/95	–0.19%	$2.63	N/A	N/A
585	★★	Green Line Balanced Growth	Balan		A	C	48%	01/95	–0.09%	$2.26	850	393
586	★★	Green Line Balanced Income Fund	Balan		C	D	49%	09/90	–9.91%	$2.24	493	433
587	★★½	Green Line Blue Chip Equity Fund	CdnEq		C	D	49%	10/90	–0.14%	$2.25	903	1185
588	★★★	Green Line Canadian Bond Fund	Bond		A	C	46%	01/95	–7.95%	$0.97	734	628
589	★★½	Green Line Canadian Equity Fund	CdnEq		D	D	51%	10/90	–0.20%	$2.10	1138	1185
590	★★	Green Line Canadian Govt. Bond Fund	Bond		B	C	51%	01/95	–7.24%	$0.97	898	628
591	★★½	Green Line Canadian Index Fund	CdnEq		B	C	49%	10/90	–0.19%	$1.11	463	1185
592	★★★★★	Green Line Canadian Money Mkt	Money		N/A	N/A	67%	06/94	4.22%	$0.77	594	498
593	★★½	Green Line Canadian Mortgage	Mrtge		N/A	N/A	56%	01/95	–2.04%	$1.66	1088	708
594	★★★	Green Line Canadian T-Bill Fund	Money		N/A	N/A	93%	01/93	–1.00%	$0.76	592	498
595	★★★	Green Line Dividend Fund	Div		D	A	48%	09/90	–0.09%	$1.99	321	1183
596	★★★½	Green Line Emerging Markets	Emerg		B	A	48%	10/95	–0.24%	$2.68	242	1168
597	★½	Green Line Energy Fund	OilGas		N/A	N/A	47%	11/95	–5.90%	$2.33	N/A	N/A
598	★★★★★	Green Line European Growth Fund	Europe		N/A	N/A	16%	11/95	0.18%	$2.68	N/A	N/A
599	★★★	Green Line Global Government Bond	InBond		C	D	50%	09/94	–9.94%	$2.08	1053	455
600	★★★½	Green Line Global RSP Bond Fund	InBond		C	D	47%	05/96	1.75%	$2.03	N/A	N/A

Fund #	Rating	Fund name	Type	CONSISTENCY: Performance trend 82–June 96	RISK: Up mkt	RISK: Down mkt	RISK: GICs better	RISK: Worst 12-mo. end	RISK: Worst 12-mo. chnge	EFFICIENCY: MER	FIT: FundMate # sim.	FIT: FundMate # comp.
601	★★★★★	Green Line Global Select Fund	InEq		N/A	N/A	40%	02/95	4.90%	$2.47	N/A	N/A
602	★★★	Green Line International Equity	InEq		N/A	N/A	40%	08/95	–0.07%	$2.32	1237	755
603	★★★★½	Green Line Japanese Growth Fund	Japan		A	C	53%	11/95	–7.04%	$2.68	N/A	N/A
604	★★½	Green Line Latin Amer. Growth Fund	Latin		C	B	42%	11/95	–0.34%	$2.62	N/A	N/A
605	★★½	Green Line Mortgage-Backed Fund	Mrtge		N/A	N/A	56%	01/95	–1.76%	$1.65	738	1207
606	★★★★★	Green Line North Amer. Growth 'A'	InEq		N/A	N/A	33%	01/95	1.25%	$2.37	N/A	N/A
607	★★★★★	Green Line Precious Metals Fund	Gold		B	B	32%	12/95	0.24%	$2.33	N/A	N/A
608	★	Green Line Real Return Bond Fund	Bond		N/A	N/A	53%	04/96	–2.87%	$1.81	N/A	N/A
609	★★★	Green Line Resource Fund	OilGas		B	A	40%	01/95	–0.15%	$2.22	N/A	N/A
610	★★★★★	Green Line Science & Tech. Fund	Sector		N/A	N/A	40%	01/95	0.21%	$2.64	N/A	N/A
611	★★	Green Line Short Term Income Fund	Bond		B	A	43%	01/95	–1.28%	$1.25	970	628
612	★★½	Green Line US Money Mkt ($US)	InMon		N/A	N/A	100%	01/94	2.16%	$1.27	1063	1224
613	★★★½	Green Line US Index Fund ($US)	USEq		C	C	37%	08/88	–0.19%	$0.78	271	310
614	★★★	Green Line Value Fund	CdnEq		B	B	47%	01/95	–0.14%	$2.15	N/A	N/A
615	★★★	Greystone Managed Global Fund	InEq		N/A	N/A	38%	04/95	–0.03%	$2.45	N/A	N/A
616	★	Greystone Managed Wealth Fund	Balan		N/A	N/A	59%	03/95	–6.02%	$2.85	N/A	N/A
617	★	Growsafe Balanced Fund	Balan		D	B	50%	01/95	–3.59%	$2.00	N/A	N/A
618	★★	Growsafe Canadian Equity Fund	CdnEq		C	B	47%	01/95	–0.03%	$2.25	N/A	N/A
619	★	Growsafe Canadian Money Market	Money		N/A	N/A	100%	12/94	1.60%	$0.90	N/A	N/A
620	★★½	Growsafe International Balanced	InBal		C	B	57%	12/94	8.00%	$2.45	N/A	N/A
621	★★½	Growsafe US Equity Fund	USEq		N/A	N/A	50%	N/A	N/A	$1.35	N/A	N/A
622	★★★	Guardian American Equity Fund 'A'	USEq		B	D	45%	08/88	–0.20%	$2.30	1064	310
623	★	Guardian American Equity Fund 'B'	USEq		N/A	N/A	33%	N/A	N/A	$2.95	N/A	N/A
624	★★★★★	Guardian Asia Pacific Fund 'A'	Asia		N/A	N/A	59%	10/95	1.97%	$1.90	N/A	N/A
625	★★★★½	Guardian Asia Pacific Fund 'B'	Asia	96: N/A	N/A	N/A	67%	N/A	N/A	$2.99	N/A	N/A

				CONSISTENCY		RISK				EFFICIENCY	FIT	
Fund #	Rating	Fund name	Type	Performance trend 82 83 84 85 86 87 88 89 90 91 92 93 94 95 June 96	Up mkt	Down mkt	GICs better	Worst 12-mo. end	Worst 12-mo. chnge	MER	FundMate # sim.	FundMate # comp.
626	★★★	Guardian Canadian Balanced Fund 'A'	Balan		C	A	100%	09/84	–1.00%	$1.61	1112	433
627	★	Guardian Canadian Balanced Fund 'B'	Balan		N/A	N/A	50%	N/A	N/A	$2.53	N/A	N/A
628	★½	Guardian Canadian Income Fund 'A'	Bond		D	A	60%	05/95	–1.02%	$1.24	834	1242
629	★★★	Guardian Canadian Income Fund 'B'	Bond		N/A	N/A	67%	N/A	N/A	$1.85	N/A	N/A
630	★★★★	Guardian Canadian Money Market 'A'	Money		N/A	N/A	65%	04/94	3.70%	$0.89	N/A	498
631	★	Guardian Canadian Money Market 'B'	Money		N/A	N/A	100%	N/A	N/A	$1.50	N/A	N/A
632	★★★★★	Guardian Emerging Markets Fund 'A'	Emerg		A	D	68%	11/95	–1.94%	$1.53	N/A	N/A
633	★★★★★	Guardian Emerging Markets Fund 'B'	Emerg		N/A	N/A	50%	N/A	N/A	$2.98	N/A	N/A
634	★★★½	Guardian Enterprise Fund 'A'	CdnSm		A	C	47%	06/82	–0.25%	$2.14	1028	979
635	★★★★★	Guardian Enterprise Fund 'B'	CdnSm		N/A	N/A	17%	N/A	N/A	$2.95	N/A	N/A
636	★★★	Guardian Foreign Income Fund 'A'	InBond		A	B	36%	05/96	7.44%	$1.96	N/A	N/A
637	★★★★½	Guardian Foreign Income Fund 'B'	InBond		N/A	N/A	50%	N/A	N/A	$2.66	N/A	N/A
638	★★★★★	Guardian Global Equity Fund 'A'	InEq		C	C	43%	09/90	–0.27%	$2.21	796	755
639	★★★	Guardian Global Equity Fund 'B'	InEq		N/A	N/A	33%	N/A	N/A	$2.93	N/A	N/A
640	★★★★	Guardian Growth Equity Fund 'A'	CdnEq		D	C	45%	01/95	–0.12%	$2.15	587	1185
641	★★	Guardian Growth Equity Fund 'B'	CdnSm		N/A	N/A	17%	N/A	N/A	$2.91	N/A	N/A
642	★★★	Guardian International Balanced 'A'	InBal		B	D	64%	06/94	–0.98%	$2.40	192	1155
643	★★★½	Guardian International Balanced 'B'	InBal		N/A	N/A	50%	N/A	N/A	$2.99	N/A	N/A
644	★★★½	Guardian International Income 'A'	InBond		A	B	57%	12/94	–6.30%	$1.96	1170	455
645	★★★½	Guardian International Income 'B'	InBond		N/A	N/A	50%	N/A	N/A	$2.66	N/A	N/A
646	★★★	Guardian Monthly Dividend Fund 'A'	Div		D	C	53%	01/95	–5.02%	$1.25	380	1183
647	★	Guardian Monthly Dividend Fund 'B'	Div		N/A	N/A	33%	N/A	N/A	$1.87	N/A	N/A
648	★★★★★	Guardian US Money Market ($US) 'A'	InMon		N/A	N/A	98%	12/93	2.47%	$0.89	N/A	1224
649	★	Guardian US Money Market ($US) 'B'	InMon		N/A	N/A	100%	N/A	N/A	$1.53	N/A	N/A
650	★	Hansberger Asian Fund	Asia		C	B	58%	01/95	–0.22%	$3.01	N/A	N/A

Fund #	Rating	Fund name	Type	Up mkt	Down mkt	GICs better	Worst 12-mo. end	Worst 12-mo. chnge	MER	FundMate # sim.	FundMate # comp.
651	★½	Hansberger European Fund	Europe	C	C	47%	01/95	–9.34%	$2.62	243	1012
652	★★★	Hercules Emerging Markets Debt Fund	InBond	A	B	47%	05/96	9.21%	$2.13	N/A	N/A
653	★★★	Hercules European Value Fund	Europe	N/A	N/A	40%	04/95	2.38%	$2.80	N/A	N/A
654	★★★	Hercules Global Short-Term Fund	InBond	A	B	67%	12/94	1.52%	$1.54	N/A	N/A
655	★★★	Hercules Latin American Value Fund	Latin	A	D	57%	02/95	–0.44%	$2.88	N/A	N/A
656	★★★	Hercules Pacific Basin Value Fund	Asia	D	D	53%	06/95	–0.17%	$2.84	N/A	N/A
657	★★★	Hercules World Bond Fund	InBond	A	A	43%	12/94	–4.25%	$2.11	N/A	N/A
658	★★★	Hongkong Bank Americas Fund	InEq	N/A	N/A	37%	11/95	7.81%	$2.84	N/A	N/A
659	★★★	Hongkong Bank Asian Growth Fund	Asia	A	A	52%	01/95	–0.13%	$2.46	N/A	N/A
660	★★★	Hongkong Bank Balanced Fund	Balan	C	B	54%	01/95	–0.10%	$2.08	789	433
661	★★★	Hongkong Bank Canadian Bond Fund	Bond	N/A	N/A	28%	05/96	8.12%	$1.69	N/A	N/A
662	★★★½	Hongkong Bank Dividend Income Fund	Div	N/A	N/A	39%	12/95	0.13%	$2.73	N/A	N/A
663	★	Hongkong Bank Emerging Markets Fund	Emerg	D	C	53%	11/95	–0.23%	$3.11	N/A	N/A
664	★★★	Hongkong Bank Equity Fund	CdnEq	D	B	45%	10/90	–0.16%	$2.15	1057	1185
665	★★★	Hongkong Bank European Growth Fund	Europe	N/A	N/A	21%	11/95	0.14%	$2.71	N/A	N/A
666	★★½	Hongkong Bank Global Bond Fund	InBond	C	B	42%	06/96	2.80%	$2.37	N/A	N/A
667	★	Hongkong Bank Money Market Fund	Money	N/A	N/A	79%	05/94	3.49%	$0.97	725	498
668	★★★★★	Hongkong Bank Mortgage Fund	Mrtge	N/A	N/A	40%	01/95	1.07%	$1.76	1062	708
669	★	Hongkong Bank Small Cap Growth Fund	CdnSm	N/A	N/A	44%	12/95	6.07%	$3.08	N/A	N/A
670	★★★	HRL Balanced Fund	Balan	D	A	47%	01/95	–0.11%	$1.75	1044	433
671	★★½	HRL Bond Fund	Bond	C	C	53%	01/95	–0.08%	$1.50	1151	628
672	★½	HRL Canadian Fund	CdnEq	D	D	54%	01/95	–0.20%	$1.75	761	1185
673	★★★★★	HRL Instant $$ Fund	Money	N/A	N/A	64%	04/94	4.17%	$0.50	725	498
674	★★½	HRL Overseas Growth Fund	InEq	N/A	N/A	46%	02/95	–8.94%	$1.75	1237	958
675	★★★	Hyperion Asian Fund	Asia	B	B	47%	01/95	–0.21%	$3.26	238	1015

Fund #	Rating	Fund name	Type	Up mkt	Down mkt	GICs better	Worst 12-mo. end	Worst 12-mo. chnge	MER	FundMate # sim.	FundMate # comp.
676	★★★	Hyperion Aurora Fund	CdnSm	N/A	N/A	41%	01/95	–0.20%	$2.54	N/A	N/A
677	★★★½	Hyperion European Fund	Europe	C	B	49%	07/91	–0.14%	$3.03	731	1012
678	★★★	Hyperion Fixed Income Fund	Bond	D	D	47%	01/95	–0.12%	$2.10	700	628
679	★★★★	Hyperion Value Line Equity Fund	USEq	N/A	N/A	40%	09/94	–6.78%	$3.01	451	310
680	★★★	ICM Balanced Fund	Balan	B	B	49%	10/90	–9.62%	$1.83	565	433
681	★★★★★	ICM Short Term Investment Fund	Money	N/A	N/A	67%	07/94	5.15%	$1.00	592	498
682	★★★	Imperial Growth Canadian Equity	CdnEq	C	C	44%	06/82	–0.27%	$1.95	1181	1185
683	★★	Imperial Growth Diversified Fund	Balan	C	B	49%	01/95	–4.75%	$2.00	859	433
684	★	Imperial Growth Money Market Fund	Money	N/A	N/A	84%	05/94	2.90%	$1.50	1209	578
685	★★★	Imperial Growth North American Eqt.	USEq	D	C	45%	06/82	–0.29%	$1.62	763	310
686	★★★	Industrial Alliance Bond Fund	Bond	B	C	43%	01/95	–7.32%	$1.61	689	628
687	★★★	Industrial Alliance Diversified Fund	Balan	N/A	C	50%	01/88	–4.75%	$1.61	N/A	N/A
688	★★★½	Industrial Alliance Ecoflex Fund A	CdnEq	A	C	44%	01/95	–5.16%	$2.14	697	883
689	★½	Industrial Alliance Ecoflex Fund B	Bond	C	C	46%	01/95	–7.82%	$2.14	686	628
690	★★★	Industrial Alliance Ecoflex Fund D	Balan	B	C	34%	01/95	–5.37%	$2.14	699	756
691	★	Industrial Alliance Ecoflex Fund H	Mrtge	N/A	N/A	49%	01/95	–1.24%	$2.14	696	708
692	★★★½	Industrial Alliance Ecoflex Fund I	InEq	N/A	N/A	33%	N/A	N/A	$2.14	N/A	N/A
693	★	Industrial Alliance Ecoflex Fund M	Money	N/A	N/A	89%	05/94	2.67%	$1.61	695	498
694	★★★★	Industrial Alliance Int'l Fund	InEq	N/A	N/A	33%	N/A	N/A	$1.61	N/A	N/A
695	★	Industrial Alliance Money Mkt. Fund	Money	N/A	N/A	88%	06/94	2.75%	$1.61	693	502
696	★★★½	Industrial Alliance Mortgage Fund	Mrtge	N/A	N/A	39%	01/95	–7.16%	$1.61	691	708
697	★★★	Industrial Alliance Stocks Fund	CdnEq	A	C	49%	08/88	–0.14%	$1.61	688	883
698	★★★	Industrial American Fund	USEq	D	D	45%	09/90	–0.17%	$2.39	369	310
699	★★½	Industrial Balanced Fund	Balan	D	C	46%	01/95	–8.49%	$2.39	1035	756
700	★★★	Industrial Bond Fund	Bond	D	D	47%	01/95	–0.12%	$2.14	1120	628

				CONSISTENCY	RISK					EFFICIENCY	FIT	
Fund #	Rating	Fund name	Type	Up mkt	Down mkt	GICs better	Worst 12-mo. end	Worst 12-mo. chnge	MER	FundMate # sim.	FundMate # comp.
701	★★★★★	Industrial Cash Management	Money	N/A	N/A	72%	05/94	0.04%	$0.50	710	578
702	★★★½	Industrial Dividend Fund Ltd.	Div	B	A	51%	10/90	–0.22%	$2.41	381	646
703	★★★	Industrial Equity Fund Ltd.	CdnSm	D	C	47%	01/91	–0.29%	$2.42	1027	979
704	★★★	Industrial Future Fund	CdnEq	A	B	48%	10/90	–0.17%	$2.41	564	1185
705	★★★	Industrial Growth Fund	CdnEq	C	B	49%	06/82	–0.17%	$2.39	706	1185
706	★★½	Industrial Horizon Fund	CdnEq	C	A	55%	10/90	–0.15%	$2.39	1201	1185
707	★★★	Industrial Income Fund	Balan	C	D	46%	03/80	–0.15%	$1.89	975	756
708	★★★½	Industrial Mortgage Securities	Mrtge	N/A	N/A	51%	01/95	–9.95%	$1.88	738	1207
709	★★½	Industrial Pension Fund	CdnEq	B	B	49%	10/90	–0.23%	$2.47	706	1185
710	★	Industrial Short-Term Fund	Money	N/A	N/A	97%	04/94	2.98%	$1.39	701	578
711	★	Integrated Growth Fund	Labor	N/A	N/A	89%	08/95	–0.22%	$6.52	N/A	N/A
712	★	InvesNat Blue Chip Amer Equity ($US)	USEq	N/A	N/A	47%	01/95	–0.10%	$2.30	1232	310
713	★	InvesNat Canadian Bond Fund	Bond	C	A	50%	01/95	–0.06%	$1.52	1136	628
714	★★★	InvesNat Canadian Equity Fund	CdnEq	B	B	54%	10/90	–0.10%	$2.13	1157	1185
715	★★★★★	InvesNat Corporate Cash Mgmt Fund	Money	N/A	N/A	71%	06/96	5.72%	$0.58	N/A	N/A
716	★★	InvesNat Dividend Fund	Div	C	B	41%	01/95	–3.28%	$1.78	1116	1183
717	★★★	InvesNat European Equity Fund	Europe	N/A	N/A	40%	07/93	–0.07%	$2.24	677	1012
718	★★★★★	InvesNat Far East Equity Fund	Asia	N/A	N/A	50%	08/95	–4.55%	$2.47	N/A	N/A
719	★½	InvesNat International RSP Bond	InBond	B	A	65%	03/96	5.76%	$2.22	N/A	N/A
720	★★★½	InvesNat Japanese Equity Fund	Japan	A	D	50%	08/95	–0.16%	$2.51	N/A	N/A
721	★★½	InvesNat Money Market Fund	Money	N/A	N/A	91%	05/94	3.72%	$1.13	725	578
722	★★★★½	InvesNat Mortgage Fund	Mrtge	N/A	N/A	28%	01/95	5.05%	$1.53	1088	708
723	★½	InvesNat Retirement Balanced Fund	Balan	C	B	55%	09/90	–6.05%	$2.11	765	1065
724	★★	InvesNat Short Term Government Bond	Bond	B	A	51%	01/95	–2.64%	$1.43	713	628
725	★★★★	InvesNat Treasury Bill Fund	Money	N/A	N/A	89%	05/94	3.78%	$0.82	721	578

Fund #	Rating	Fund name	Type	Up mkt	Down mkt	GICs better	Worst 12-mo. end	Worst 12-mo. chnge	MER	FundMate # sim.	FundMate # comp.
726	★	InvesNat US Money Market Fund (SUS)	InMon	N/A	N/A	100%	12/93	1.90%	$1.11	N/A	1224
727	★★★	Investors Asset Allocation Fund	Balan	B	D	48%	01/95	–7.64%	$2.65	N/A	N/A
728	★★★	Investors Canadian Equity Fund	CdnEq	C	A	49%	03/88	–0.14%	$2.40	747	1185
729	★★½	Investors Corporate Bond Fund	Bond	N/A	N/A	52%	07/95	7.33%	$1.90	N/A	N/A
730	★★★½	Investors Dividend Fund	Div	C	D	48%	06/82	–0.15%	$2.33	1116	1183
731	★★★	Investors European Growth Fund	Europe	A	B	43%	02/93	–4.34%	$2.24	677	1012
732	★★½	Investors Global Bond Fund	InBond	C	D	51%	09/94	–2.90%	$2.18	1128	455
733	★★★	Investors Global Fund	InEq	B	A	47%	08/88	–0.23%	$2.43	495	978
734	★★½	Investors Government Bond Fund	Bond	B	B	48%	07/81	–7.74%	$1.89	987	628
735	★★★½	Investors Growth Plus Portfolio	InBal	A	A	51%	09/90	–8.47%	$0.18	771	642
736	★★★	Investors Growth Portfolio Fund	InEq	B	B	44%	09/90	–0.16%	$0.18	733	978
737	★★	Investors Income Plus Portfolio	Balan	C	C	40%	01/95	–5.52%	$0.17	707	1065
738	★★★	Investors Income Portfolio Fund	Mrtge	N/A	N/A	39%	01/95	–5.41%	$0.17	965	1207
739	★★★★★	Investors Japanese Growth Fund	Japan	D	C	47%	09/90	–0.35%	$2.42	1032	453
740	★★	Investors Money Market Fund	Money	N/A	N/A	77%	05/94	3.53%	$1.07	775	578
741	★★★	Investors Mortgage Fund	Mrtge	N/A	N/A	52%	01/95	–3.06%	$1.89	1054	1207
742	★★★	Investors Mutual of Canada	Balan	D	A	48%	06/82	–0.21%	$2.35	748	756
743	★★★	Investors North American Growth	InEq	A	C	47%	06/82	–0.24%	$2.38	749	978
744	★★★★½	Investors Pacific International	Asia	B	A	45%	01/95	–0.13%	$2.53	238	1015
745	★★★★	Investors Real Property Fund	Sector	N/A	N/A	77%	09/93	–3.37%	$2.36	868	28
746	★★★	Investors Retirement Gth. Portfolio	CdnEq	B	A	51%	09/90	–0.13%	$0.20	747	1185
747	★★½	Investors Retirement Mutual Fund	CdnEq	B	A	47%	06/82	–0.27%	$2.38	728	1185
748	★★	Investors Retirement Plus Portfolio	Balan	C	A	52%	09/90	–5.53%	$0.18	742	756
749	★★★	Investors Special Fund	InEq	A	C	47%	05/82	–0.32%	$2.38	743	978
750	★★★	Investors Summa Fund	CdnEq	C	C	47%	10/90	–0.23%	$2.44	640	883

Fund #	Rating	Fund name	Type	Up mkt (CONSISTENCY)	Down mkt (RISK)	GICs better (RISK)	Worst 12-mo. end (RISK)	Worst 12-mo. chnge (RISK)	MER (EFFICIENCY)	FundMate # sim. (FIT)	FundMate # comp. (FIT)
751	★★★	Investors US Growth Fund	USEq	A	B	45%	08/88	–0.20%	$2.37	311	310
752	★★★	Investors World Growth Portfolio	InEq	N/A	N/A	37%	01/95	–1.21%	$0.19	774	978
753	★★½	Ivy Canadian Fund	CdnEq	A	A	40%	01/95	9.07%	$2.42	747	1185
754	★★★	Ivy Enterprise Fund	CdnSm	C	A	47%	06/82	–0.27%	$2.39	1226	897
755	★★½	Ivy Foreign Equity Fund	InEq	N/A	N/A	40%	09/94	6.80%	$2.50	963	978
756	★★★	Ivy Growth & Income Fund	Balan	A	C	40%	01/95	–1.64%	$2.59	723	1065
757	★★★	Ivy Mortgage Fund	Mrtge	N/A	N/A	52%	01/95	–2.25%	$1.90	N/A	N/A
758	★★½	Jones Heward American Fund	USEq	D	C	48%	08/88	–0.26%	$2.50	622	310
759	★★½	Jones Heward Bond Fund	Bond	D	C	48%	01/95	–9.59%	$1.75	898	628
760	★★½	Jones Heward Canadian Balanced Fund	Balan	D	B	49%	01/95	–0.11%	$2.40	565	756
761	★★★	Jones Heward Fund Ltd.	CdnEq	D	D	45%	06/82	–0.35%	$2.50	704	1185
762	★★★	Jones Heward Money Market Fund	Money	N/A	N/A	81%	06/96	5.35%	$1.00	N/A	N/A
763	★★★	Laurentian American Equity Fund Ltd	USEq	D	B	41%	07/82	–0.20%	$2.65	685	459
764	★★★	Laurentian Asia Pacific Fund	Asia	N/A	N/A	50%	05/96	4.97%	$2.70	N/A	N/A
765	★	Laurentian Canadian Balanced Fund	Balan	C	C	50%	01/95	–6.31%	$2.65	924	756
766	★★½	Laurentian Canadian Equity Fund Ltd	CdnEq	D	C	47%	06/82	–0.27%	$2.66	591	1185
767	★★★	Laurentian Commonwealth Fund Ltd.	InEq	D	A	44%	07/82	–0.11%	$2.70	774	978
768	★★★	Laurentian Dividend Fund Ltd.	Div	C	D	48%	06/82	–0.14%	$2.65	989	1183
769	★★★	Laurentian Emerging Markets Fund	Emerg	C	C	61%	12/95	9.34%	$2.95	N/A	N/A
770	★	Laurentian Europe Fund	Europe	N/A	N/A	28%	03/96	0.10%	$2.70	N/A	N/A
771	★★★	Laurentian Global Balanced Fund	InBal	B	B	53%	12/90	–2.82%	$2.70	735	642
772	★½	Laurentian Government Bond Fund	Bond	C	A	46%	01/95	–2.31%	$2.14	1081	628
773	★★★	Laurentian Income Fund	Bond	C	B	49%	03/80	–0.11%	$2.14	734	628
774	★★★	Laurentian International Fund Ltd	InEq	C	A	42%	07/82	–0.19%	$2.70	767	978
775	★★★	Laurentian Money Market Fund	Money	N/A	N/A	78%	06/94	3.46%	$1.10	701	578

				CONSISTENCY		RISK				EFFICIENCY	FIT	
Fund #	Rating	Fund name	Type	Performance trend 82 83 84 85 86 87 88 89 90 91 92 93 94 95 June 96	Up mkt	Down mkt	GICs better	Worst 12-mo. end	Worst 12-mo. chnge	MER	FundMate # sim.	FundMate # comp.
776	★★★	Laurentian Special Equity Fund	CdnSm		D	A	49%	01/95	–0.12%	$2.65	907	979
777	★★★	Leith Wheeler Balanced Fund	Balan		C	C	49%	09/90	–0.06%	$1.18	855	756
778	★★	Leith Wheeler Canadian Equity Fund	CdnEq		N/A	N/A	44%	09/95	7.98%	$1.50	N/A	N/A
779	★★★½	Leith Wheeler Fixed Income Fund	Bond		N/A	N/A	40%	06/96	8.96%	$0.80	N/A	N/A
780	★★★★★	Leith Wheeler Money Market Fund	Money		N/A	N/A	88%	06/96	5.43%	$0.64	N/A	N/A
781	★★★	Leith Wheeler US Equity Fund	USEq		N/A	N/A	40%	10/95	0.11%	$1.34	N/A	N/A
782	★★★	London Life Bond	Bond		C	D	48%	01/95	–9.25%	$2.00	1151	628
783	★★★	London Life Canadian Equity	CdnEq		C	A	46%	09/90	–0.23%	$2.00	900	1185
784	★★★	London Life Diversified	Balan		D	A	45%	10/90	–9.08%	$2.00	569	975
785	★★	London Life International Equity	InEq		N/A	N/A	50%	06/96	0.10%	$2.50	N/A	N/A
786	★★★½	London Life Money Market	Money		N/A	N/A	63%	04/94	2.99%	$1.30	1146	1040
787	★★★	London Life Mortgage	Mrtge		N/A	N/A	46%	04/80	–0.11%	$2.00	741	909
788	★★	London Life US Equity	USEq		D	D	49%	09/90	–0.29%	$2.00	1212	459
789	★★★	Lotus (MKW) Balanced Fund	Balan		D	D	46%	01/95	–0.13%	$2.14	660	756
790	★★★½	Lotus (MKW) Bond Fund	Bond		N/A	N/A	50%	02/95	6.05%	$0.98	N/A	N/A
791	★★★	Lotus (MKW) Canadian Equity Fund	CdnSm		B	B	47%	01/95	–0.23%	$2.16	N/A	N/A
792	★★★★★	Lotus (MKW) Income Fund	Money		N/A	N/A	63%	07/94	4.16%	$0.80	959	1184
793	★★★	Lotus (MKW) International Bond Fund	InBond		D	A	56%	05/96	–2.46%	$1.10	N/A	N/A
794	★	Lotus (MKW) Int'l Equity Fund	InEq		N/A	N/A	54%	05/96	5.64%	$2.21	N/A	N/A
795	★★★	Mackenzie Sentinel Canada Equity	CdnEq		C	A	54%	11/90	–0.22%	$2.15	706	1185
796	★★	Mackenzie Sentinel Global Fund	InEq		D	C	51%	08/88	–0.30%	$0.82	1237	755
797	★★★★★	Manulife Cabot Blue Chip Fund	CdnEq		N/A	N/A	43%	02/95	4.33%	$25.00	N/A	N/A
798	★★★★★	Manulife Cabot Canadian Equity Fund	CdnEq		N/A	N/A	43%	02/95	4.96%	$2.50	N/A	N/A
799	★★	Manulife Cabot Canadian Growth Fund	CdnSm		N/A	N/A	54%	02/95	–0.21%	$2.00	N/A	N/A
800	★	Manulife Cabot Diversified Bond	Bond		N/A	N/A	57%	02/95	–2.34%	$2.00	N/A	N/A

Fund #	Rating	Fund name	Type	Up mkt	Down mkt	GICs better	Worst 12-mo. end	Worst 12-mo. chnge	MER	FundMate # sim.	FundMate # comp.
801	★★	Manulife Cabot Emerging Growth Fund	CdnSm	N/A	N/A	54%	02/95	–0.18%	$2.50	N/A	N/A
802	★★★	Manulife Cabot Global Equity Fund	InEq	N/A	N/A	54%	02/95	–4.70%	$2.50	N/A	N/A
803	★★★	Manulife Cabot Money Market Fund	Money	N/A	N/A	86%	06/96	5.00%	$1.25	N/A	N/A
804	★★★	Manulife Vistafund 1 Amer. Stock	USEq	N/A	N/A	33%	06/96	0.18%	$1.63	N/A	N/A
805	★★★	Manulife Vistafund 1 Bond Fund	Bond	D	D	48%	01/95	–0.11%	$1.63	813	628
806	★★★	Manulife Vistafund 1 Cap. Gains Gth	CdnEq	B	B	46%	08/88	–0.16%	$1.63	814	1185
807	★★★	Manulife Vistafund 1 Diversified	Balan	C	B	49%	01/95	–8.24%	$1.63	815	756
808	★★★	Manulife Vistafund 1 Equity Fund	CdnEq	B	A	48%	06/82	–0.19%	$1.63	816	1185
809	★★★	Manulife Vistafund 1 Global Bond	InBond	C	A	56%	05/96	3.80%	$1.63	N/A	N/A
810	★★	Manulife Vistafund 1 Global Equity	InEq	N/A	N/A	56%	12/95	8.12%	$1.63	N/A	N/A
811	★★★	Manulife Vistafund 1 Short Term Sec	Money	N/A	N/A	69%	05/94	3.12%	$1.63	819	1040
812	★★★	Manulife Vistafund 2 Amer. Stock	USEq	N/A	N/A	33%	06/96	0.17%	$2.38	N/A	N/A
813	★★	Manulife Vistafund 2 Bond Fund	Bond	D	D	49%	01/95	–0.12%	$2.38	805	628
814	★★½	Manulife Vistafund 2 Cap. Gains Gth	CdnEq	B	C	47%	08/88	–0.17%	$2.38	806	1185
815	★★	Manulife Vistafund 2 Diversified	Balan	D	B	50%	01/95	–8.93%	$2.38	807	756
816	★★	Manulife Vistafund 2 Equity Fund	CdnEq	C	A	49%	06/82	–0.20%	$2.38	808	1185
817	★★	Manulife Vistafund 2 Global Bond	InBond	B	A	56%	05/96	3.95%	$2.38	N/A	N/A
818	★	Manulife Vistafund 2 Global Equity	InEq	N/A	N/A	56%	12/95	7.32%	$2.38	N/A	N/A
819	★	Manulife Vistafund 2 Short Term Sec	Money	N/A	N/A	76%	05/94	2.34%	$2.38	811	1040
820	★★★★	Marathon Equity Fund	CdnSm	A	A	46%	03/88	–0.40%	$2.50	776	979
821	★★★	Margin of Safety Fund (Hillery Inv)	USEq	C	C	51%	10/90	–0.18%	$2.04	751	1178
822	★★½	Maritime Life American Growth & Inc	USEq	N/A	N/A	25%	08/95	7.63%	$2.30	N/A	N/A
823	★★½	Maritime Life Balanced Fund	Balan	B	B	47%	01/95	–5.52%	$1.97	924	756
824	★★½	Maritime Life Bond Fund	Bond	C	C	49%	01/95	–8.43%	$1.99	987	628
825	★★★	Maritime Life Canadian Equity Fund	CdnEq	N/A	N/A	36%	06/96	0.14%	$2.05	N/A	N/A

				CONSISTENCY	RISK					EFFICIENCY	FIT	
Fund #	Rating	Fund name	Type	Performance trend 82–June 96	Up mkt	Down mkt	GICs better	Worst 12-mo. end	Worst 12-mo. chnge	MER	FundMate # sim.	FundMate # comp.
826	★	Maritime Life Dividend Income Fund	Div		N/A	N/A	39%	06/96	8.93%	$2.05	N/A	N/A
827	★	Maritime Life Global Equity Fund	InEq		N/A	N/A	50%	12/95	4.47%	$2.30	N/A	N/A
828	★★½	Maritime Life Growth Fund	CdnEq		C	D	47%	06/82	–0.31%	$1.97	1080	1185
829	★	Maritime Life Money Market Fund	Money		N/A	N/A	80%	07/94	2.94%	$1.75	962	1184
830	★★★	Maritime Life Pacific Basin Fund	Asia		C	D	54%	10/95	–0.13%	$2.30	N/A	N/A
831	★★★★★	Maritime Life S&P500 Fund	USEq		N/A	N/A	17%	06/96	0.24%	$1.90	N/A	N/A
832	★★★	Mawer Canadian Bond Fund	Bond		B	C	44%	01/95	–7.77%	$0.87	861	628
833	★½	Mawer Canadian Equity Fund	CdnEq		D	B	44%	01/95	–0.11%	$1.34	879	1185
834	★★★½	Mawer Canadian Income Fund	Bond		B	B	48%	01/95	–6.51%	$0.92	832	628
835	★★½	Mawer Canadian Money Market Fund	Money		N/A	N/A	69%	05/94	3.68%	$0.67	1087	1040
836	★★★	Mawer Cdn. Bal. Retirement Savings	Balan		B	C	45%	01/95	–0.06%	$0.87	837	756
837	★★★	Mawer Cdn. Diversified Investment	Balan		B	D	44%	01/95	–6.30%	$1.27	836	756
838	★	Mawer High Yield Bond Fund	Bond	N/A	N/A	N/A	0%	N/A	N/A	$1.17	N/A	N/A
839	★★★½	Mawer New Canada Fund	CdnSm		B	A	44%	01/95	–0.10%	$1.28	1028	897
840	★★★	Mawer US Equity Fund	USEq		N/A	N/A	38%	09/94	1.27%	$1.75	1212	459
841	★★★	Mawer World Investment Fund	InEq		C	A	48%	02/95	–3.93%	$1.75	1173	755
842	★	McDonald Asia Plus	Asia		N/A	N/A	63%	N/A	N/A	$2.80	N/A	N/A
843	★★	McDonald Canada Plus	Balan		N/A	N/A	50%	06/96	8.47%	$2.71	N/A	N/A
844	★★	McDonald Emerging Economies	InEq		N/A	N/A	50%	N/A	N/A	$3.66	N/A	N/A
845	★★½	McDonald Enhanced Bond	Bond		N/A	N/A	75%	N/A	N/A	$2.50	N/A	N/A
846	★	McDonald Euro Plus	Europe		N/A	N/A	38%	N/A	N/A	$2.50	N/A	N/A
847	★★	McDonald New America	USEq		N/A	N/A	25%	N/A	N/A	$2.50	N/A	N/A
848	★★★	McDonald New Japan	Japan		N/A	N/A	25%	N/A	N/A	$2.50	N/A	N/A
849	★★★½	McLean Budden American Growth Fund	USEq		B	A	40%	09/90	–1.99%	$1.75	854	370
850	★★★	McLean Budden Balanced Fund	Balan		A	D	48%	01/95	–8.81%	$1.00	855	756

				CONSISTENCY	RISK					EFFICIENCY	FIT	
Fund #	Rating	Fund name	Type	Performance trend 82 83 84 85 86 87 88 89 90 91 92 93 94 95 June 96	Up mkt	Down mkt	GICs better	Worst 12-mo. end	Worst 12-mo. chnge	MER	FundMate # sim.	FundMate # comp.
851	★★★	McLean Budden Equity Growth Fund	CdnEq		A	C	47%	10/90	–0.18%	$0.75	856	1185
852	★★★½	McLean Budden Fixed Income Fund	Bond		B	D	43%	01/95	–8.30%	$1.00	857	628
853	★★★	McLean Budden Money Market Fund	Money		N/A	N/A	67%	04/94	3.77%	$0.75	673	1040
854	★★★★½	McLean Budden Pooled American Eqt.	USEq		A	B	43%	08/88	–0.29%	$0.50	849	1004
855	★★★★★	McLean Budden Pooled Balanced Fund	Balan		A	C	66%	01/95	–7.46%	$0.50	850	756
856	★★★½	McLean Budden Pooled Canadian Eqt.	CdnEq		A	C	50%	06/82	–0.23%	$0.50	828	1185
857	★★★★½	McLean Budden Pooled Fixed Income	Bond		A	B	45%	01/95	–6.98%	$1.00	852	628
858	★★½	McLean Budden Pooled Offshore Eqt.	InEq		D	B	47%	12/90	–0.18%	$0.50	1237	755
859	★★★	MD Balanced Fund	Balan		B	C	36%	01/95	–6.38%	$1.04	683	756
860	★½	MD Bond and Mortgage Fund	Bond		N/A	N/A	56%	N/A	N/A	$1.17	N/A	N/A
861	★★★★	MD Bond Fund	Bond		A	B	42%	01/95	–7.80%	$1.03	1179	628
862	★★★	MD Dividend Fund	Div		B	B	38%	01/95	–4.68%	$1.09	768	1183
863	★★★½	MD Emerging Markets Fund	Emerg		B	B	63%	11/95	–6.80%	$2.52	N/A	N/A
864	★★★	MD Equity Fund	CdnEq		D	A	45%	10/90	–0.13%	$1.02	705	1185
865	★★	MD Global Bond Fund	InBond		C	D	58%	05/96	–9.58%	$1.13	N/A	N/A
866	★★★★½	MD Growth Fund	InEq		A	D	43%	09/90	–0.18%	$1.04	1173	755
867	★★★	MD Money Fund	Money		N/A	N/A	66%	05/94	3.92%	$0.53	835	1040
868	★★★★★	MD Realty Fund A Units	Sector		N/A	N/A	80%	02/94	–0.29%	$1.50	869	1227
869	★★★★	MD Realty Fund B Units	Sector		N/A	N/A	80%	02/94	–0.31%	$1.50	868	1227
870	★★½	MD Select Fund	CdnEq		C	C	42%	01/95	–9.61%	$1.08	N/A	N/A
871	★★★½	MD US Equity Fund	USEq		N/A	N/A	31%	09/94	–7.56%	$1.06	429	459
872	★	Merrill Lynch Canadian Equity Fund	CdnEq	N/A	N/A	N/A	60%	N/A	N/A	$2.25	N/A	N/A
873	★	Merrill Lynch Capital Asset Fund	Balan	N/A	N/A	N/A	80%	N/A	N/A	$2.25	N/A	N/A
874	★	Merrill Lynch Emerging Markets Fund	Emerg	N/A	N/A	N/A	40%	N/A	N/A	$2.25	N/A	N/A
875	★	Merrill Lynch World Allocation Fund	InBal	N/A	N/A	N/A	80%	N/A	N/A	$2.25	N/A	N/A

Fund #	Rating	Fund name	Type	CONSISTENCY: Performance trend 82 83 84 85 86 87 88 89 90 91 92 93 94 95 June 96	Up mkt	RISK: Down mkt	GICs better	Worst 12-mo. end	Worst 12-mo. chnge	EFFICIENCY: MER	FIT: FundMate # sim.	FundMate # comp.
876	★★★★★	Merrill Lynch World Bond Fund	InBond	N/A	N/A	N/A	60%	N/A	N/A	$1.90	N/A	N/A
877	★★	Metlife MVP Balanced Fund	Balan		D	C	50%	01/95	–0.10%	$2.00	836	1065
878	★★	Metlife MVP Bond Fund	Bond		D	D	53%	01/95	–8.34%	$2.00	1071	628
879	★½	Metlife MVP Equity Fund	CdnEq		D	C	50%	08/88	–0.21%	$2.00	1050	1185
880	★★½	Metlife MVP Growth Fund	CdnSm		C	B	34%	01/95	–0.14%	$2.00	518	897
881	★	Metlife MVP Money Market Fund	Money		N/A	N/A	100%	06/94	3.12%	$1.50	922	1040
882	★★★	Metlife MVP US Equity Fund	USEq		N/A	N/A	41%	01/95	–4.05%	$2.00	1212	459
883	★★	Middlefield Growth Fund	CdnEq		D	A	52%	01/95	–0.15%	$2.83	864	1185
884	★	Millennia III American Equity 1	USEq	N/A	N/A	N/A	43%	N/A	N/A	$2.80	N/A	N/A
885	★	Millennia III American Equity 2	USEq		N/A	N/A	43%	N/A	N/A	$2.98	N/A	N/A
886	★	Millennia III Canadian Balanced 1	Balan		N/A	N/A	43%	N/A	N/A	$2.74	N/A	N/A
887	★	Millennia III Canadian Equity 1	CdnEq		N/A	N/A	29%	N/A	N/A	$2.75	N/A	N/A
888	★	Millennia III Canadian Equity 2	CdnEq		N/A	N/A	29%	N/A	N/A	$2.93	N/A	N/A
889	★★★★★	Millennia III Income Fund 1	Bond	N/A	N/A	N/A	43%	N/A	N/A	$2.23	N/A	N/A
890	★★★½	Millennia III Income Fund 2	Bond	N/A	N/A	N/A	43%	N/A	N/A	$2.41	N/A	N/A
891	★	Millennia III Int'l Equity 1	InEq	N/A	N/A	N/A	71%	N/A	N/A	$2.90	N/A	N/A
892	★	Millennia III Int'l Equity 2	InEq		N/A	N/A	71%	N/A	N/A	$3.08	N/A	N/A
893	★	Millennia III Money Market Fund 1	Money		N/A	N/A	100%	N/A	N/A	$1.45	N/A	N/A
894	★	Millennia III Money Market Fund 2	Money		N/A	N/A	100%	N/A	N/A	$1.63	N/A	N/A
895	★★½	Millennium Diversified Fund	Balan		C	B	48%	01/95	–9.25%	$2.00	N/A	N/A
896	★★★★★	Millennium Next Generation Fund	CdnSm		N/A	N/A	42%	01/95	–8.00%	$2.00	N/A	N/A
897	★★★	Multiple Opportunities Fund	CdnSm		A	B	43%	09/88	–0.51%	$3.48	820	754
898	★	Mutual Bond Fund	Bond		D	C	46%	01/95	–8.67%	$1.85	904	628
899	★★½	Mutual Diversifund 40	Balan		A	C	47%	10/90	–0.11%	$1.78	924	756
900	★★½	Mutual Equifund	CdnEq		A	B	47%	10/90	–0.24%	$1.80	903	1185

				CONSISTENCY	RISK					EFFICIENCY	FIT	
Fund #	Rating	Fund name	Type	Up mkt	Down mkt	GICs better	Worst 12-mo. end	Worst 12-mo. chnge		MER	FundMate # sim.	FundMate # comp.
901	★	Mutual Money Market	Money	N/A	N/A	79%	04/94	3.68%		$1.02	N/A	1040
902	★★½	Mutual Premier American Fund	USEq	N/A	N/A	33%	09/94	–1.32%		$2.42	1064	459
903	★★	Mutual Premier Blue Chip Fund	CdnEq	A	B	42%	01/95	–8.61%		$2.30	900	1185
904	★½	Mutual Premier Bond Fund	Bond	C	B	49%	01/95	–8.70%		$1.90	898	1008
905	★★★★	Mutual Premier Diversified Fund	Balan	N/A	N/A	33%	08/95	0.08%		$2.36	N/A	N/A
906	★★	Mutual Premier Emerging Markets	Money	N/A	N/A	56%	N/A	N/A		$3.83	N/A	N/A
907	★★★	Mutual Premier Growth Fund	CdnSm	B	A	33%	01/95	–8.31%		$2.29	518	897
908	★★★	Mutual Premier International Fund	InEq	N/A	N/A	36%	01/95	–6.24%		$2.37	1237	958
909	★★★	Mutual Premier Mortgage Fund	Mrtge	N/A	N/A	50%	01/95	–1.13%		$1.58	1088	1207
910	★★★★★	NAL-Balanced Growth Fund	Balan	N/A	N/A	38%	09/95	0.11%		$2.00	N/A	N/A
911	★★★	NAL-Canadian Bond Fund	Bond	B	A	47%	01/95	–6.38%		$1.75	1136	1008
912	★★★	NAL-Canadian Diversified Fund	Balan	A	C	47%	01/95	–7.73%		$1.75	815	756
913	★★★	NAL-Canadian Equity Fund	CdnEq	A	D	48%	08/88	–0.16%		$1.75	1050	1185
914	★	NAL-Canadian Money Market Fund	Money	N/A	N/A	69%	07/94	3.19%		$1.25	853	1184
915	★★★	NAL-Equity Growth Fund	CdnEq	N/A	N/A	43%	10/95	0.06%		$2.00	N/A	N/A
916	★★★	NAL-Global Equity Fund	InEq	N/A	N/A	52%	02/93	–6.43%		$2.50	1237	958
917	★★½	NAL-US Equity Fund	USEq	N/A	N/A	43%	01/95	7.92%		$2.25	N/A	N/A
918	★★★★	National Life Balanced Fund	Balan	A	C	46%	01/95	–7.18%		$0.75	899	756
919	★★★½	National Life Equities Fund	CdnEq	A	B	45%	08/88	–0.12%		$0.75	1205	1185
920	★★★★★	National Life Fixed Income Fund	Bond	A	B	40%	01/95	–6.66%		$0.75	904	1008
921	★★★★½	National Life Global Equities Fund	InEq	N/A	N/A	38%	02/95	–4.27%		$2.40	N/A	N/A
922	★★★★★	National Life Money Market Fund	Money	N/A	N/A	75%	04/94	4.53%		$0.75	901	1040
923	★★	National Trust American Equity Fund	USEq	N/A	N/A	51%	01/95	–7.36%		$2.81	451	459
924	★★★	National Trust Balanced Fund	Balan	B	D	45%	01/95	–9.33%		$1.83	899	756
925	★★★	National Trust Canadian Bond Fund	Bond	A	D	50%	07/81	–0.11%		$1.34	773	1008

				CONSISTENCY	RISK					EFFICIENCY	FIT	
Fund #	Rating	Fund name	Type	Performance trend 82 83 84 85 86 87 88 89 90 91 92 93 94 95 June 96	Up mkt	Down mkt	GICs better	Worst 12-mo. end	Worst 12-mo. chnge	MER	FundMate # sim.	FundMate # comp.
926	★★★	National Trust Canadian Equity Fund	CdnEq		D	D	46%	06/82	–0.21%	$1.60	828	883
927	★★	National Trust Dividend Fund	Div		D	B	38%	01/95	–8.78%	$1.87	768	1183
928	★	National Trust Emerging Markets	Emerg		C	C	74%	08/95	–0.34%	$3.10	N/A	N/A
929	★★	National Trust Int'l Equity Fund	InEq		N/A	N/A	48%	08/95	–4.63%	$2.79	N/A	N/A
930	★★★½	National Trust Int'l RSP Bond Fund	InBond		B	A	35%	05/96	7.53%	$2.10	N/A	N/A
931	★	National Trust Money Market Fund	Money		N/A	N/A	85%	06/94	3.52%	$1.17	725	1040
932	★★★	National Trust Mortgage Fund	Mrtge		N/A	N/A	38%	01/95	–1.46%	$1.53	1054	1207
933	★	National Trust Special Equity Fund	CdnSm		C	D	43%	01/95	–0.23%	$2.46	518	897
934	★★	Navigator American Value Inv.	USEq		N/A	N/A	57%	04/96	0.16%	$2.72	N/A	N/A
935	★★	Navigator Asia Pacific Fund	Asia		N/A	N/A	64%	04/96	9.16%	$2.99	N/A	N/A
936	★★★★	Navigator Canadian Income Fund	Bond		N/A	N/A	29%	08/95	9.37%	$2.45	N/A	N/A
937	★★★★	Navigator Latin America Fund	Latin		N/A	N/A	42%	06/96	0.21%	$2.88	N/A	N/A
938	★★★★★	Navigator Value Inv. Retirement	CdnEq		A	A	34%	01/95	–0.12%	$2.77	1057	1185
939	★★½	NN Balanced Fund	Balan		B	D	52%	01/95	–7.78%	$2.25	924	756
940	★★★	NN Can-Am Fund	USEq		N/A	N/A	32%	01/95	–5.20%	$2.25	613	529
941	★★★	NN Can-Asian Fund	Asia		A	D	41%	01/95	–0.23%	$2.25	N/A	N/A
942	★★★★	NN Can-Euro Fund	InEq		N/A	N/A	42%	06/96	0.20%	$2.25	N/A	N/A
943	★★	NN Canadian 35 Index	CdnEq		A	B	53%	10/90	–0.16%	$2.00	766	883
944	★★★★½	NN Dividend Fund	Div		N/A	N/A	28%	05/95	9.41%	$2.00	N/A	N/A
945	★★	NN Elite Fund	InBal		N/A	N/A	58%	10/95	9.00%	$2.75	N/A	N/A
946	★★★★★	NN Money Market Fund	Money		N/A	N/A	74%	06/94	4.04%	$0.75	1175	1040
947	★	NN T-Bill Fund	Money		N/A	N/A	83%	05/94	3.09%	$1.75	946	1040
948	★★★	O'Donnell American Sector Growth	USEq		N/A	N/A	50%	N/A	N/A	$2.65	N/A	N/A
949	★★★★★	O'Donnell Canadian Emerging Growth	CdnSm		N/A	N/A	17%	N/A	N/A	$2.55	N/A	N/A
950	★★★★★	O'Donnell Growth Fund	CdnSm		N/A	N/A	17%	N/A	N/A	$2.55	N/A	N/A

				CONSISTENCY																RISK				EFFICIENCY	FIT	
Fund #	Rating	Fund name	Type	Performance trend 82	83	84	85	86	87	88	89	90	91	92	93	94	95	June 96	Up mkt	Down mkt	GICs better	Worst 12-mo. end	Worst 12-mo. chnge	MER	FundMate # sim.	FundMate # comp.
951	★★★	O'Donnell High Income Fund	Bond																N/A	N/A	67%	N/A	N/A	$2.00	N/A	N/A
952	★	O'Donnell Money Market Fund	Money																N/A	N/A	83%	N/A	N/A	$1.00	N/A	N/A
953	★	O'Donnell Short Term Fund	Money																N/A	N/A	83%	N/A	N/A	$1.35	N/A	N/A
954	★	O'Donnell US Mid-Cap Fund	USEq															N/A	N/A	N/A	33%	N/A	N/A	$2.65	N/A	N/A
955	★★★	OHA Balanced Fund	Balan																B	A	38%	01/95	–5.44%	$0.86	912	975
956	★★★½	OHA Bond Fund	Bond																A	C	48%	01/95	–7.67%	$0.67	773	1008
957	★★★	OHA Canadian Equity Fund	CdnEq																C	B	41%	01/95	–0.16%	$0.73	1205	938
958	★★½	OHA Foreign Equity Fund	InEq																N/A	N/A	38%	06/96	7.20%	$0.87	1202	978
959	★★★★★	OHA Short Term Fund	Money																N/A	N/A	91%	07/94	4.19%	$0.69	1058	1040
960	★★★	Ontario Teachers Group Balanced	Balan																C	B	49%	01/95	–0.07%	$1.00	1026	975
961	★★½	Ontario Teachers Group Diversified	CdnEq																C	B	48%	06/82	–0.27%	$1.00	1050	1185
962	★★★★	Ontario Teachers Group Fixed Value	Money																N/A	N/A	71%	05/94	4.24%	$0.50	867	1040
963	★	Ontario Teachers Group Global	InEq																N/A	N/A	53%	01/95	–3.68%	$1.00	1172	978
964	★★★	Ontario Teachers Group Growth	CdnSm																D	B	49%	06/82	–0.29%	$1.00	1028	897
965	★★★	Ontario Teachers Group Mortgage Inc	Mrtge																N/A	N/A	55%	01/95	1.67%	$0.75	1218	1207
966	★★★	Optima Strategy Canadian Equity	CdnEq																A	C	100%	07/93	–0.96%	$0.42	828	883
967	★★	Optima Strategy Canadian Fixed Income	Bond																A	D	100%	04/93	–1.01%	$0.41	773	1008
968	★★★½	Optima Strategy Global Fixed Income	InBond																B	D	48%	03/96	1.82%	$0.49	N/A	N/A
969	★★★★★	Optima Strategy Int'l Equity	InEq																N/A	N/A	48%	06/95	1.02%	$0.48	N/A	N/A
970	★½	Optima Strategy Short Term Income	Bond																C	A	45%	01/95	–4.15%	$0.34	1081	1008
971	★★★★	Optima Strategy US Equity	USEq																N/A	N/A	32%	05/95	0.11%	$0.43	N/A	N/A
972	★	Optimum Fonds d'Actions	CdnEq																D	D	48%	01/95	–0.14%	$1.61	N/A	N/A
973	★★★★½	Optimum Fonds d'Épargne	Money																N/A	N/A	68%	05/94	3.78%	$0.80	819	1040
974	★★★½	Optimum Fonds d'Obligations	Bond																A	C	47%	01/95	–7.03%	$1.38	734	1008
975	★★½	Optimum Fonds Équilibre	Balan																B	D	49%	01/95	–0.07%	$1.38	707	1065

				CONSISTENCY	RISK					EFFICIENCY	FIT	
Fund #	Rating	Fund name	Type	Performance trend 82 83 84 85 86 87 88 89 90 91 92 93 94 95 June 96	Up mkt	Down mkt	GICs better	Worst 12-mo. end	Worst 12-mo. chnge	MER	FundMate # sim.	FundMate # comp.
976	★★★	Optimum Fonds Internationales	InEq		N/A	N/A	38%	06/96	9.95%	$1.97	N/A	N/A
977	★★★★★	Orbit North American Equity Fund	InEq	N/A	N/A	N/A	40%	N/A	N/A	$2.50	N/A	N/A
978	★½	Orbit World Fund	InEq		D	A	49%	12/95	–0.12%	$2.50	602	755
979	★★★★★	Pacific Special Equity Fund	CdnSm		A	D	33%	01/95	–0.12%	$2.82	1216	820
980	★★★★★	Phillips Hager & North SUS Money Market	InMon		N/A	N/A	100%	01/94	2.63%	$0.53	1063	1224
981	★★★★★	Phillips Hager & North Cdn Money Market	Money		N/A	N/A	69%	05/94	0.04%	$0.51	1058	1040
982	★	Phillips Hager & North Int'l Equity Fund	InEq		N/A	N/A	46%	08/95	–2.12%	$1.49	N/A	N/A
983	★★★	Phillips Hager & North N.A. Equity Fund	InEq		N/A	N/A	43%	02/95	–0.20%	$1.12	1225	755
984	★★★★★	PH&N Short Term Bond & Mortgage	Mrtge		N/A	N/A	52%	01/95	–2.02%	$0.67	N/A	N/A
985	★★★★★	Phillips Hager & North Bal Pens Tr	Balan		A	A	43%	10/90	–0.06%	$0.92	986	1065
986	★★★½	Phillips Hager & North Balanced	Balan		A	B	42%	01/95	–4.38%	$0.92	985	1065
987	★★★★	Phillips Hager & North Bond Fund	Bond		A	B	48%	09/81	–0.12%	$0.60	898	1008
988	★★★	Phillips Hager & North Cdn. Equity	CdnEq		A	A	44%	06/82	–0.41%	$1.13	990	1185
989	★★★★½	Phillips Hager & North Div. Income	Div		B	B	46%	03/82	–0.14%	$1.19	768	1183
990	★★★	Phillips Hager & North RSP/RIF Eqt	CdnEq		A	B	42%	06/82	–0.39%	$1.21	988	1185
991	★★★½	Phillips Hager & North US Equity	USEq		A	B	40%	08/88	–0.22%	$1.12	1162	459
992	★★★★★	Phillips Hager & North Vintage	CdnEq		A	C	37%	08/88	–0.18%	$1.75	990	1185
993	★	Prosperity American Performance	USEq		N/A	N/A	54%	01/95	–8.60%	$6.14	622	459
994	★★★½	Protected American Fund	InBal		D	C	59%	02/89	–4.88%	$2.30	251	642
995	★★★★★	Prudential American Equity Fund	USEq		N/A	N/A	29%	06/96	0.31%	$2.26	N/A	N/A
996	★★★	Prudential Diversified Invest Fund	Balan		D	D	47%	01/95	–0.14%	$1.50	899	756
997	★★★★★	Prudential Dividend Fund of Canada	Div		A	A	44%	09/90	–0.18%	$1.50	989	1183
998	★★★★★	Prudential Global Equity Fund	InEq		N/A	N/A	35%	06/96	0.13%	$2.51	N/A	N/A
999	★★★	Prudential Growth Fund of Canada	CdnEq		A	C	44%	06/82	–0.36%	$1.75	814	1185
1000	★★★	Prudential Income Fund of Canada	Bond		C	B	48%	01/95	–9.51%	$1.50	1120	1008

Fund #	Rating	Fund name	Type	Performance trend June 96	Up mkt	Down mkt	GICs better	Worst 12-mo. end	Worst 12-mo. chnge	MER	FundMate # sim.	FundMate # comp.
1001	★★★★★	Prudential Money Market Fd of Can.	Money		N/A	N/A	69%	05/94	4.34%	$0.65	1108	1040
1002	★★★★★	Prudential Natural Res. of Canada	OilGas		A	A	42%	01/91	–0.14%	$1.75	1003	505
1003	★★★½	Prudential Precious Metals of Can.	Gold		A	C	50%	01/91	–0.30%	$1.75	394	1029
1004	★	Pursuit American Fund	USEq		D	B	100%	02/91	–1.00%	$2.00	758	459
1005	★	Pursuit Canadian Equity Fund	CdnEq		B	D	62%	09/88	–1.00%	$2.00	1181	1185
1006	★★★	Pursuit Global Bond Fund	InBond		N/A	N/A	55%	N/A	N/A	$2.00	N/A	N/A
1007	★★★★★	Pursuit Global Equity Fund	InEq		N/A	N/A	27%	N/A	N/A	$2.50	N/A	N/A
1008	★½	Pursuit Income Fund	Bond		D	A	54%	09/88	–1.00%	$1.00	1048	1158
1009	★★★★★	Pursuit Money Market Fund	Money		N/A	N/A	55%	07/94	4.36%	$0.50	786	1184
1010	★★★	Quebec Growth Fund	CdnSm		N/A	N/A	42%	06/96	0.19%	$1.90	N/A	N/A
1011	★½	Regent Dragon 888 Fund	Asia		D	D	65%	08/95	–0.16%	$3.21	N/A	N/A
1012	★	Regent Europa Performance Fund	Europe		N/A	N/A	60%	01/95	–4.98%	$3.01	731	382
1013	★★	Regent International Fund	InEq		C	D	53%	09/90	–0.19%	$2.62	858	755
1014	★★	Regent Korea Fund	Asia		D	A	54%	12/95	–0.24%	$3.67	1016	1015
1015	★★	Regent Nippon Fund	Asia		C	D	49%	06/95	–0.27%	$3.26	1016	1014
1016	★★★	Regent Tiger Fund	Asia		D	D	49%	12/95	–0.19%	$3.35	1014	1015
1017	★★★	Regent World Income Fund	InBond		A	B	51%	03/95	1.28%	$2.16	249	455
1018	★★★½	Resolute Growth Fund	CdnSm		N/A	N/A	37%	01/95	–0.11%	$2.00	N/A	N/A
1019	★★	Retrocom Growth Fund Inc.	Labor		N/A	N/A	100%	06/96	–3.00%	$6.16	N/A	N/A
1020	★★½	Rothschild Select American Equity	USEq	N/A	N/A	N/A	67%	N/A	N/A	$3.25	N/A	N/A
1021	★★★★★	Rothschild Select Canadian Balanced	Balan	N/A	N/A	N/A	33%	N/A	N/A	$2.99	N/A	N/A
1022	★★★★★	Rothschild Select Canadian Equity	CdnEq	N/A	N/A	N/A	33%	N/A	N/A	$2.90	N/A	N/A
1023	★★	Rothschild Select Int'l Bond	InBond	N/A	N/A	N/A	100%	N/A	N/A	$2.70	N/A	N/A
1024	★★★★★	Rothschild Select Int'l Equity	InEq	N/A	N/A	N/A	33%	N/A	N/A	$3.25	N/A	N/A
1025	★★★	Royal Asian Growth Fund	Asia		A	B	47%	01/95	–0.19%	$2.64	N/A	N/A

				CONSISTENCY			RISK				EFFICIENCY	FIT	
Fund #	Rating	Fund name	Type	Performance trend 82 83 84 85 86 87 88 89 90 91 92 93 94 95 June 96	Up mkt	Down mkt	GICs better	Worst 12-mo. end	Worst 12-mo. chnge	MER	FundMate # sim.	FundMate # comp.
1026	★★★	Royal Balanced Fund	Balan		C	A	44%	01/95	–7.74%	$2.31	1044	756
1027	★★	Royal Canadian Growth Fund	CdnSm		C	C	41%	01/95	–0.17%	$2.31	1028	897
1028	★★	Royal Canadian Small Cap Fund	CdnSm		C	C	43%	01/95	–0.19%	$2.20	1027	979
1029	★★★½	Royal Energy Fund	OilGas		D	C	51%	06/82	–0.42%	$2.11	478	505
1030	★★★★★	Royal European Growth Fund	Europe		A	C	50%	08/88	–0.24%	$2.68	677	1012
1031	★★★	Royal International Equity Fund	InEq		N/A	N/A	44%	01/95	–3.72%	$2.50	796	978
1032	★★★★★	Royal Japanese Stock Fund	Japan		D	A	50%	09/90	–0.34%	$2.64	739	453
1033	★★	Royal Latin American Fund	Latin		N/A	N/A	36%	N/A	N/A	$3.86	N/A	N/A
1034	★★★★★	Royal Lepage Commercial Real Estate	Sector		N/A	N/A	78%	02/94	–5.72%	$3.40	1227	868
1035	★★	Royal Life Balanced Fund	Balan		C	D	43%	01/95	–9.20%	$2.34	924	756
1036	★★★½	Royal Life Canadian Growth Fund	CdnSm		N/A	N/A	21%	12/95	0.21%	$2.35	N/A	N/A
1037	★★★	Royal Life Equity Fund	CdnEq		B	A	53%	01/91	–9.29%	$2.37	828	1185
1038	★★	Royal Life Income Fund	Bond		C	C	47%	01/95	–0.09%	$1.88	1151	1008
1039	★★½	Royal Life Int'l Equity Fund	InEq		N/A	N/A	47%	11/95	6.17%	$2.60	N/A	N/A
1040	★★★★★	Royal Life Money Market Fund	Money		N/A	N/A	73%	08/94	4.38%	$1.00	914	1184
1041	★★★★★	Royal Life Science & Technology	Sector		N/A	N/A	27%	N/A	N/A	$2.53	N/A	N/A
1042	★★★★★	Royal Life US Equity Fund	USEq		N/A	N/A	25%	N/A	N/A	$2.25	N/A	N/A
1043	★★★½	Royal Precious Metals Fund	Gold		A	A	47%	09/91	–0.17%	$2.21	1003	1029
1044	★★★	Royal Trust Advantage Balanced Fund	Balan		C	A	46%	01/95	–7.12%	$1.83	1026	756
1045	★★★	Royal Trust Advantage Growth Fund	Balan		C	A	47%	08/88	–0.11%	$1.99	1044	975
1046	★★★	Royal Trust Advantage Income Fund	Balan		C	B	46%	01/95	–5.98%	$1.69	1044	1065
1047	★★½	Royal Trust American Stock Fund	USEq		C	B	48%	08/88	–0.24%	$2.15	1064	1004
1048	★★★	Royal Trust Bond Fund	Bond		C	B	50%	01/95	–8.84%	$1.39	1056	1008
1049	★	Royal Trust Canadian Money Market Fund	Money		N/A	N/A	77%	04/94	3.32%	$1.29	1058	1040
1050	★★½	Royal Trust Canadian Stock Fund	CdnEq		B	B	47%	06/82	–0.34%	$1.90	1057	1185

Fund #	Rating	Fund name	Type	Up mkt	Down mkt	GICs better	Worst 12-mo. end	Worst 12-mo. chnge	MER	FundMate # sim.	FundMate # comp.
1051	★	Royal Trust Canadian T-Bill Fund	Money	N/A	N/A	98%	05/94	2.63%	$1.07	1059	1040
1052	★★	Royal Trust Growth & Income Fund	Div	B	D	54%	01/95	–8.12%	$2.22	1060	1183
1053	★★★★	Royal Trust International Bond Fund	InBond	C	C	45%	09/94	–4.07%	$1.86	1128	455
1054	★★★★	Royal Trust Mortgage Fund	Mrtge	N/A	N/A	43%	01/95	–1.62%	$1.74	932	1207
1055	★	Royal Trust US Money Market ($US)	InMon	N/A	N/A	100%	11/93	2.01%	$1.83	1063	1224
1056	★★½	RoyFund Bond Fund	Bond	B	A	52%	01/95	–7.41%	$1.52	1048	1008
1057	★★★	RoyFund Canadian Equity Fund	CdnEq	B	A	45%	06/82	–0.39%	$2.09	1050	1185
1058	★	RoyFund Canadian Money Market Fund	Money	N/A	N/A	75%	04/94	3.40%	$1.28	1049	1040
1059	★★½	RoyFund Canadian T-Bill Fund	Money	N/A	N/A	92%	04/94	3.65%	$0.91	1058	1040
1060	★★★	RoyFund Dividend Fund	Div	B	C	37%	01/95	–6.90%	$1.86	768	1183
1061	★★★	RoyFund International Income Fund	InBond	C	C	54%	09/94	–1.52%	$1.97	1128	455
1062	★★★★	RoyFund Mortgage Fund	Mrtge	N/A	N/A	36%	01/95	–7.33%	$1.81	1088	1207
1063	★	RoyFund US Dollar Money ($US)	InMon	N/A	N/A	100%	09/93	2.03%	$1.22	1055	1224
1064	★★★	RoyFund US Equity Fund	USEq	N/A	N/A	44%	01/95	3.31%	$2.09	1047	1004
1065	★★	Saxon Balanced Fund	Balan	A	D	49%	03/88	–0.19%	$1.87	996	975
1066	★★½	Saxon Small Cap (Howson Tattersall)	CdnSm	C	B	50%	10/90	–0.26%	$1.87	933	897
1067	★★½	Saxon Stock Fund	CdnEq	A	D	52%	03/88	–0.19%	$1.87	1205	1185
1068	★★★½	Saxon World Growth	InEq	A	D	43%	09/90	–0.27%	$1.87	1172	978
1069	★★★	Sceptre Asian Growth Fund	Asia	B	D	50%	01/95	–0.20%	$2.40	238	1015
1070	★★★½	Sceptre Balanced Fund	Balan	A	A	46%	01/95	–8.75%	$1.57	1026	1065
1071	★★★	Sceptre Bond Fund	Bond	B	C	42%	01/95	–6.24%	$1.25	925	1008
1072	★★★★★	Sceptre Equity Fund	CdnSm	A	A	43%	10/90	–0.13%	$1.68	1028	897
1073	★★★★½	Sceptre International Fund	InEq	A	C	40%	08/88	–0.14%	$2.10	858	755
1074	★★★★★	Sceptre Money Market Fund	Money	N/A	N/A	69%	05/94	3.83%	$0.75	1108	1040
1075	★★★½	Scotia CanAm Growth Fund	USEq	N/A	N/A	28%	01/95	–1.85%	$1.34	N/A	N/A

				CONSISTENCY	RISK					EFFICIENCY	FIT	
Fund #	Rating	Fund name	Type	Performance trend 82 83 84 85 86 87 88 89 90 91 92 93 94 95 June 96	Up mkt	Down mkt	GICs better	Worst 12-mo. end	Worst 12-mo. chnge	MER	FundMate # sim.	FundMate # comp.
1076	★★★	Scotia CanAm Income Fund	InBond		C	B	46%	09/94	–4.05%	$1.60	1154	455
1077	★★	Scotia Excelsior Amer Equity Growth	USEq		C	A	49%	08/88	–0.34%	$2.19	1047	821
1078	★★★	Scotia Excelsior Balanced Fund	Balan		B	A	48%	01/95	–7.93%	$2.01	1026	756
1079	★★	Scotia Excelsior Cdn. Blue Chip	CdnEq		D	D	52%	08/88	–0.20%	$2.11	903	1185
1080	★★★	Scotia Excelsior Cdn. Growth Fund	CdnEq		A	B	46%	06/82	–0.30%	$2.11	814	1185
1081	★★	Scotia Excelsior Defensive Income	Bond		B	A	53%	01/95	–3.60%	$1.37	970	1008
1082	★★★	Scotia Excelsior Dividend Fund	Div		C	C	44%	01/95	–0.06%	$1.07	716	1183
1083	★★	Scotia Excelsior Global Bond Fund	InBond		D	D	50%	06/96	–4.48%	$1.82	N/A	N/A
1084	★★★	Scotia Excelsior Income Fund	Bond		A	B	50%	01/95	–6.77%	$1.37	925	1008
1085	★★★	Scotia Excelsior Int'l Fund	InEq		B	D	45%	08/88	–0.23%	$2.24	1132	978
1086	★★★★★	Scotia Excelsior Latin American	Latin		A	C	40%	10/95	–5.00%	$2.11	N/A	N/A
1087	★	Scotia Excelsior Money Market Fund	Money		N/A	N/A	86%	04/94	3.61%	$1.00	1091	1040
1088	★★★★½	Scotia Excelsior Mortgage Fund	Mrtge		N/A	N/A	30%	01/95	–2.34%	$1.56	1062	1207
1089	★★★★★	Scotia Excelsior Pacific Rim Fund	Asia		N/A	N/A	45%	10/95	8.28%	$2.12	N/A	N/A
1090	★★★	Scotia Excelsior Prec. Metals Fund	Gold		C	C	41%	01/95	–0.18%	$2.19	N/A	N/A
1091	★★★★★	Scotia Excelsior Premium T-Bill	Money		N/A	N/A	91%	04/94	4.00%	$0.52	1087	1040
1092	★	Scotia Excelsior T-Bill Fund	Money		N/A	N/A	96%	04/94	3.74%	$1.00	1087	1040
1093	★★★½	Scotia Excelsior Total Return Fund	Balan		D	C	44%	01/95	–0.11%	$2.32	1078	756
1094	★★	Scudder Canadian Equity Fund	CdnEq		N/A	N/A	38%	N/A	N/A	$1.25	N/A	N/A
1095	★★★	Scudder Canadian Short Term Bond	Bond		N/A	N/A	25%	N/A	N/A	$0.50	N/A	N/A
1096	★★★★★	Scudder Emerging Markets Fund	Emerg		N/A	N/A	13%	N/A	N/A	$2.00	N/A	N/A
1097	★★★½	Scudder Global Fund	InEq		N/A	N/A	13%	N/A	N/A	$1.75	N/A	N/A
1098	★★★	Scudder Greater Europe Fund	Europe		N/A	N/A	0%	N/A	N/A	$1.75	N/A	N/A
1099	★★½	Scudder Pacific Fund	Asia		N/A	N/A	50%	N/A	N/A	$1.75	N/A	N/A
1100	★★½	Special Opportunities Fund	OilGas		B	C	55%	01/95	–0.22%	$2.13	1043	505

				CONSISTENCY	RISK					EFFICIENCY	FIT	
Fund #	Rating	Fund name	Type	Performance trend 82 83 84 85 86 87 88 89 90 91 92 93 94 95 June 96	Up mkt	Down mkt	GICs better	Worst 12-mo. end	Worst 12-mo. chnge	MER	FundMate # sim.	FundMate # comp.
1101	★★½	Spectrum Canadian Equity Fund 'A'	CdnEq		N/A	N/A	33%	06/96	9.76%	$2.08	N/A	N/A
1102	★★	Spectrum Canadian Equity Fund 'B'	CdnEq		N/A	N/A	39%	06/96	9.44%	$2.32	N/A	N/A
1103	★★	Spectrum Canadian Equity Fund 'C'	CdnEq		N/A	N/A	33%	06/96	9.15%	$2.57	N/A	N/A
1104	★★	Spectrum Canadian Equity Fund 'D'	CdnEq		D	A	54%	10/90	–0.17%	$2.28	1050	1185
1105	★	Spectrum Cash Reserve Fund 'A'	Money		N/A	N/A	89%	06/96	5.10%	$1.12	N/A	N/A
1106	★	Spectrum Cash Reserve Fund 'B'	Money		N/A	N/A	89%	06/96	5.10%	$1.12	N/A	N/A
1107	★	Spectrum Cash Reserve Fund 'C'	Money		N/A	N/A	89%	06/96	5.10%	$1.12	N/A	N/A
1108	★★	Spectrum Cash Reserve Fund 'D'	Money		N/A	N/A	72%	05/94	3.61%	$1.11	1133	1040
1109	★★★	Spectrum Diversified Fund 'A'	Balan		N/A	N/A	39%	06/96	0.10%	$1.82	N/A	N/A
1110	★★½	Spectrum Diversified Fund 'B'	Balan		N/A	N/A	39%	06/96	9.26%	$2.08	N/A	N/A
1111	★★	Spectrum Diversified Fund 'C'	Balan		N/A	N/A	39%	06/96	8.92%	$2.33	N/A	N/A
1112	★★	Spectrum Diversified Fund 'D'	Balan		D	C	50%	01/95	–0.10%	$2.28	924	1065
1113	★★½	Spectrum Dividend Fund 'A'	Div		N/A	N/A	22%	06/96	0.10%	$1.46	N/A	N/A
1114	★★	Spectrum Dividend Fund 'B'	Div		N/A	N/A	28%	06/96	0.10%	$1.71	N/A	N/A
1115	★	Spectrum Dividend Fund 'C'	Div		N/A	N/A	28%	06/96	9.80%	$1.96	N/A	N/A
1116	★★★	Spectrum Dividend Fund 'D'	Div		D	C	49%	01/95	–8.92%	$1.61	989	1183
1117	★★★½	Spectrum Government Bond Fund 'A'	Bond		N/A	N/A	39%	05/96	7.11%	$1.50	N/A	N/A
1118	★★★	Spectrum Government Bond Fund 'B'	Bond		N/A	N/A	39%	05/96	6.79%	$1.76	N/A	N/A
1119	★★★	Spectrum Government Bond Fund 'C'	Bond		N/A	N/A	39%	05/96	0.07%	$2.01	N/A	N/A
1120	★★★	Spectrum Government Bond Fund 'D'	Bond		D	D	45%	01/95	–0.13%	$1.76	1214	1008
1121	★★½	Spectrum Interest Fund 'A'	Bond		N/A	N/A	33%	05/96	7.41%	$1.44	N/A	N/A
1122	★★½	Spectrum Interest Fund 'B'	Bond		N/A	N/A	33%	05/96	7.39%	$1.69	N/A	N/A
1123	★★	Spectrum Interest Fund 'C'	Bond		N/A	N/A	33%	05/96	7.11%	$1.94	N/A	N/A
1124	★★½	Spectrum Interest Fund 'D'	Bond		D	D	48%	01/95	–0.11%	$1.59	1151	1008
1125	★★	Spectrum Int'l Bond Fund 'A'	InBond		D	C	50%	06/96	–7.71%	$1.97	N/A	N/A

Fund #	Rating	Fund name	Type	CONSISTENCY: Performance trend 82 83 84 85 86 87 88 89 90 91 92 93 94 95 June 96	RISK: Up mkt	RISK: Down mkt	RISK: GICs better	RISK: Worst 12-mo. end	RISK: Worst 12-mo. chnge	EFFICIENCY: MER	FIT: FundMate # sim.	FIT: FundMate # comp.
1126	★★½	Spectrum Int'l Bond Fund 'B'	InBond		D	C	44%	06/96	–1.31%	$1.79	N/A	N/A
1127	★★	Spectrum Int'l Bond Fund 'C'	InBond		D	C	50%	06/96	–4.60%	$2.03	N/A	N/A
1128	★★★	Spectrum Int'l Bond Fund 'D'	InBond		C	C	44%	09/94	–3.06%	$2.28	1053	455
1129	★★	Spectrum Int'l Equity Fund 'A'	InEq		N/A	N/A	50%	12/95	5.97%	$2.28	N/A	N/A
1130	★½	Spectrum Int'l Equity Fund 'B'	InEq		N/A	N/A	50%	12/95	5.63%	$2.32	N/A	N/A
1131	★	Spectrum Int'l Equity Fund 'C'	InEq		N/A	N/A	50%	12/95	5.47%	$2.57	N/A	N/A
1132	★★½	Spectrum Int'l Equity Fund 'D'	InEq		C	B	56%	08/88	–0.22%	$2.83	1085	978
1133	★★★	Spectrum Savings Fund	Money		N/A	N/A	71%	05/94	3.74%	$0.99	1108	1040
1134	★★★	Sportfund Inc.	Labor		N/A	N/A	88%	06/96	7.50%	$6.74	N/A	N/A
1135	★★★	Standard Life Balanced Mutual Fund	Balan		B	C	41%	01/95	–0.07%	$2.00	1140	1065
1136	★★★	Standard Life Bond Mutual Fund	Bond		B	C	48%	01/95	–7.23%	$1.50	911	1008
1137	★★★★★	Standard Life Canadian Dividend	Div		N/A	N/A	30%	10/95	0.13%	$1.50	N/A	N/A
1138	★★★	Standard Life Equity Mutual Fund	CdnEq		A	B	45%	01/95	–6.44%	$2.00	988	1185
1139	★★	Standard Life Growth Equity Fund	CdnSm		N/A	N/A	30%	10/95	2.71%	$2.00	N/A	N/A
1140	★★★	Standard Life Ideal Balanced Fund	Balan		A	B	46%	03/88	–4.99%	$2.00	1135	1065
1141	★★★	Standard Life Ideal Bond Fund	Bond		C	C	46%	01/95	–8.25%	$1.50	857	1008
1142	★★★	Standard Life Ideal Equity Fund	CdnEq		A	A	47%	08/88	–0.18%	$2.00	1050	1185
1143	★★★★★	Standard Life Ideal Money Market	Money		N/A	N/A	78%	10/94	4.22%	$0.90	N/A	N/A
1144	★★★	Standard Life International Bond	InBond		D	B	35%	05/96	5.52%	$2.00	N/A	N/A
1145	★★★	Standard Life International Equity	InEq		N/A	N/A	50%	10/95	1.95%	$2.00	N/A	N/A
1146	★★★½	Standard Life Money Market Fund	Money		N/A	N/A	89%	04/94	3.33%	$0.90	901	1040
1147	★★★	Standard Life Natural Resources	OilGas		N/A	N/A	35%	10/95	–3.43%	$2.00	N/A	N/A
1148	★★½	Standard Life US Equity Fund	USEq		N/A	N/A	30%	10/95	0.15%	$2.00	N/A	N/A
1149	★	Stone & Co. Flagship Stock Fund	CdnEq		N/A	N/A	38%	N/A	N/A	$2.85	N/A	N/A
1150	★★★	Strategic Value Fund	InEq	N/A	N/A	N/A	50%	N/A	N/A	$2.25	N/A	N/A

Fund #	Rating	Fund name	Type	Up mkt	Down mkt	GICs better	Worst 12-mo. end	Worst 12-mo. chnge	MER	FundMate # sim.	FundMate # comp.
1151	★★★½	Talvest Bond Fund	Bond	C	C	46%	01/95	–7.98%	$1.99	987	1008
1152	★★	Talvest Diversified Fund	Balan	C	A	51%	01/95	–0.04%	$2.42	855	975
1153	★★★	Talvest Dividend Fund	Div	N/A	N/A	33%	N/A	N/A	$1.99	N/A	N/A
1154	★★★	Talvest Foreign Pay Canadian Bond	InBond	B	D	50%	09/94	–4.73%	$2.15	732	455
1155	★★★½	Talvest Global Diversified Fund	InBal	C	B	51%	07/91	–8.71%	$2.75	440	642
1156	★½	Talvest Global RRSP Fund Inc.	InEq	N/A	N/A	50%	02/95	–0.11%	$2.50	1132	978
1157	★★½	Talvest Growth Fund Inc.	CdnEq	B	C	52%	06/82	–0.30%	$2.40	1138	1185
1158	★★★	Talvest Income Fund	Bond	A	B	47%	01/95	–3.85%	$1.50	970	1008
1159	★★★★★	Talvest Money Fund	Money	N/A	N/A	68%	06/87	2.66%	$0.85	1175	1040
1160	★★	Talvest New Economy	CdnEq	A	D	52%	11/94	–0.10%	$2.50	N/A	N/A
1161	★★★★	Talvest US Diversified Fund	InBal	A	C	55%	06/91	–0.99%	$2.27	440	642
1162	★★★	Talvest US Growth Fund Ltd.	USEq	B	B	46%	08/88	–0.26%	$2.25	854	1004
1163	★★★★★	Teachers' RSP - Equity Section	CdnEq	N/A	N/A	25%	06/96	0.21%	$1.00	N/A	N/A
1164	★★½	Templeton Balanced Fund	Balan	B	C	55%	08/91	–1.07%	$2.45	1044	955
1165	★½	Templeton Canadian Asset Allocation	Balan	N/A	N/A	50%	10/95	7.00%	$2.15	N/A	N/A
1166	★	Templeton Canadian Bond Fund	Bond	D	A	53%	01/95	–5.56%	$1.65	898	1008
1167	★★	Templeton Canadian Stock Fund	CdnEq	C	B	57%	09/90	–0.16%	$2.44	1138	883
1168	★★★★★	Templeton Emerging Markets Fund	Emerg	B	B	48%	02/95	–0.16%	$3.28	596	242
1169	★★★½	Templeton Global Balanced Fund	InBal	N/A	N/A	40%	10/95	6.60%	$2.55	N/A	N/A
1170	★★★½	Templeton Global Bond Fund	InBond	A	B	51%	01/95	–3.56%	$2.25	1154	455
1171	★★★	Templeton Global Smaller Companies	InEq	A	D	47%	09/90	–0.21%	$2.62	1172	978
1172	★★★½	Templeton Growth Fund Ltd.	InEq	A	D	42%	07/82	–0.18%	$2.00	1173	978
1173	★★★½	Templeton International Stock Fund	InEq	A	C	49%	09/90	–0.14%	$2.55	1172	755
1174	★★★	Templeton Int'l Balanced Fund	InBal	N/A	N/A	40%	10/95	3.20%	$2.55	N/A	N/A
1175	★★★	Templeton Treasury Bill Fund	Money	N/A	N/A	71%	05/94	3.89%	$0.75	1058	1040

CONSISTENCY					RISK					EFFICIENCY	FIT	
Fund #	Rating	Fund name	Type	Performance trend 82 83 84 85 86 87 88 89 90 91 92 93 94 95 June 96	Up mkt	Down mkt	GICs better	Worst 12-mo. end	Worst 12-mo. chnge	MER	FundMate # sim.	FundMate # comp.
1176	★	Top Fifty Equity Fund	CdnEq		D	D	54%	09/90	–0.16%	$2.92	1138	1185
1177	★	Top Fifty T-Bill/Bond Fund	Bond		D	D	61%	01/95	–0.10%	$2.62	1071	1008
1178	★★	Top Fifty US Equity Fund	USEq		N/A	N/A	43%	01/95	–7.86%	$3.18	923	821
1179	★	Tradex Bond Fund	Bond		D	D	48%	01/95	–10.00%	$1.59	861	1008
1180	★★★	Tradex Emerging Mkts Country Fund	Emerg		B	A	53%	05/96	8.71%	$3.58	N/A	N/A
1181	★★★½	Tradex Equity Fund Ltd.	CdnEq		A	B	44%	06/82	–0.25%	$1.39	992	1185
1182	★	Trans-Canada Bond Fund (Sagit)	Bond		C	A	55%	01/95	–3.61%	$2.49	1084	1008
1183	★★★	Trans-Canada Dividend Fund (Sagit)	Div		A	B	50%	09/90	–0.12%	$3.00	989	1082
1184	★★★½	Trans-Canada Money Market (Sagit)	Money		N/A	N/A	71%	03/94	4.32%	$0.56	1198	1040
1185	★★	Trans-Canada Pension Fund (Sagit)	CdnEq		D	A	61%	01/93	–0.21%	$3.00	957	999
1186	★★	Trans-Canada Value Fund (Sagit)	CdnEq		D	C	49%	06/82	–0.26%	$3.00	1205	1185
1187	★★½	Triax Growth Fund Inc.	Labor	N/A	N/A	N/A	60%	N/A	N/A	$1.85	N/A	N/A
1188	★	Trillium Growth Capital Inc.	Labor		N/A	N/A	81%	02/96	–10.00%	$8.50	N/A	N/A
1189	★★★	Trimark - The Americas Fund	InEq		N/A	N/A	44%	02/95	–0.12%	$2.52	1225	755
1190	★★★★★	Trimark Advantage Bond Fund	Bond		N/A	N/A	37%	06/96	0.11%	$1.25	N/A	N/A
1191	★★★★★	Trimark Canadian Bond Fund	Bond		N/A	N/A	42%	05/96	9.70%	$1.25	N/A	N/A
1192	★★★★	Trimark Canadian Fund	CdnEq		B	A	47%	10/90	–0.16%	$1.54	1199	1185
1193	★	Trimark Discovery Fund	Sector	N/A	N/A	N/A	100%	N/A	N/A	$0.00	N/A	N/A
1194	★★★★	Trimark Fund	InEq		A	D	40%	09/90	–0.22%	$1.53	1202	978
1195	★★★	Trimark Government Income Fund	Bond		A	A	55%	01/95	–6.71%	$1.25	N/A	N/A
1196	★★★★½	Trimark Income Growth Fund	Balan		A	B	38%	09/90	–0.11%	$1.73	1200	975
1197	★★★★★	Trimark Indo-Pacific Fund	Asia		N/A	N/A	67%	10/95	6.00%	$2.74	N/A	N/A
1198	★★★★½	Trimark Interest Fund	Money		N/A	N/A	74%	04/94	3.68%	$0.75	1049	1040
1199	★★★	Trimark RSP Equity Fund	CdnEq		B	B	46%	09/90	–0.15%	$2.00	1192	1185
1200	★★★½	Trimark Select Balanced Fund	Balan		A	B	42%	01/95	–4.99%	$2.21	1196	1065

				CONSISTENCY	RISK					EFFICIENCY	FIT	
Fund #	Rating	Fund name	Type	Performance trend 82 83 84 85 86 87 88 89 90 91 92 93 94 95 June 96	Up mkt	Down mkt	GICs better	Worst 12-mo. end	Worst 12-mo. chnge	MER	FundMate # sim.	FundMate # comp.
1201	★★★½	Trimark Select Canadian Growth Fund	CdnEq		B	A	40%	01/95	–4.83%	$2.30	1199	1185
1202	★★★	Trimark Select Growth Fund	InEq		A	D	42%	09/90	–0.18%	$2.25	1194	978
1203	★★½	Trust Prêt & Revenu American Fund	USEq		A	B	100%	08/88	–0.29%	$2.15	902	1004
1204	★★★	Trust Prêt & Revenu Bond Fund	Bond		B	C	46%	01/95	–7.95%	$1.50	987	1008
1205	★★	Trust Prêt & Revenu Canadian Fund	CdnEq		A	C	100%	06/82	–0.36%	$1.77	1050	1185
1206	★★★★★	Trust Prêt & Revenu Dividend Fund	Div		N/A	N/A	6%	03/96	0.18%	$1.62	N/A	N/A
1207	★★	Trust Prêt & Revenu H Fund	Mrtge		N/A	N/A	60%	01/95	–3.17%	$1.65	1218	1062
1208	★★½	Trust Prêt & Revenu International	InEq		N/A	N/A	29%	03/96	0.13%	$2.06	N/A	N/A
1209	★★	Trust Prêt & Revenu Money Market	Money		N/A	N/A	77%	04/94	0.04%	$1.17	1091	1040
1210	★★★	Trust Prêt & Revenu Retirement Fund	Balan		A	C	100%	09/81	–0.10%	$1.81	899	975
1211	★	Trust Prêt & Revenu World Bond Fund	InBond		D	A	59%	04/96	6.12%	$1.93	N/A	N/A
1212	★★★	United American Equity Fund	USEq		B	C	39%	07/82	–0.19%	$2.45	882	1004
1213	★★★½	United American Growth Fund Ltd.	USEq		A	D	43%	10/90	–0.23%	$2.23	923	751
1214	★★★	United Canadian Bond Fund	Bond		D	D	51%	01/95	–0.12%	$1.92	1120	1008
1215	★★★	United Canadian Equity Fund	CdnEq		C	C	45%	06/82	–0.29%	$2.34	926	1185
1216	★★★★	United Canadian Growth Fund	CdnSm		B	A	43%	06/82	–0.41%	$2.46	907	897
1217	★★★★★	United Canadian Interest Fund	Money		N/A	N/A	57%	12/94	4.20%	$1.39	959	1184
1218	★★★	United Canadian Mortgage Fund	Mrtge		N/A	N/A	62%	01/95	–4.28%	$1.88	932	1207
1219	★★★	United Canadian Portfolio of Funds	Balan		B	C	46%	01/95	–0.08%	$1.17	924	1065
1220	★★	United Global Equity Fund	InEq		N/A	N/A	51%	02/95	–0.11%	$2.74	796	978
1221	★★★	United Global Growth Fund	InEq		C	D	46%	10/90	–0.34%	$2.53	858	978
1222	★★★★	United Global Portfolio of Funds	InBal		A	D	45%	01/95	–8.57%	$0.78	440	642
1223	★★★	United Global Telecommunications	Sector		N/A	N/A	38%	04/95	8.80%	$2.80	N/A	N/A
1224	★★★★	United US Dollar Money Market	InMon		N/A	N/A	99%	10/92	2.11%	$0.77	726	612
1225	★★★	Universal Americas Fund	InEq		C	D	47%	02/95	–0.19%	$2.45	N/A	755

Fund #	Rating	Fund name	Type	Up mkt	Down mkt	GICs better	Worst 12-mo. end	Worst 12-mo. chnge	MER	FundMate # sim.	FundMate # comp.
1226	★★★	Universal Canadian Growth Fund Ltd	CdnSm	D	B	48%	10/90	–0.20%	$2.43	703	897
1227	★★★★★	Universal Canadian Resource Fund	Sector	N/A	N/A	48%	06/82	–0.39%	$2.43	1034	868
1228	★★★★★	Universal European Opportunities	Europe	N/A	N/A	24%	09/95	0.25%	$2.58	N/A	N/A
1229	★★½	Universal Far East Fund	Asia	B	B	55%	01/95	–0.17%	$2.56	N/A	N/A
1230	★½	Universal Growth Fund	InEq	N/A	N/A	43%	06/96	9.76%	$2.35	N/A	N/A
1231	★★½	Universal Japan Fund	Japan	C	A	58%	06/95	–0.24%	$2.58	N/A	N/A
1232	★★★★★	Universal US Emerging Growth Fund	USEq	N/A	N/A	36%	06/94	3.58%	$2.46	712	751
1233	★	Universal US Money Market (SUS)	InMon	N/A	N/A	100%	06/96	0.04%	$1.25	N/A	N/A
1234	★★★	Universal World Asset Allocation	InBal	D	A	58%	02/95	–4.45%	$2.45	N/A	N/A
1235	★★★½	Universal World Balanced RRSP	InBal	N/A	N/A	46%	02/95	–5.76%	$2.43	N/A	N/A
1236	★★★½	Universal World Emerging Growth	Emerg	A	D	45%	02/95	–0.20%	$2.55	N/A	N/A
1237	★★½	Universal World Equity Fund	InEq	D	C	48%	09/90	–0.14%	$2.46	796	958
1238	★★★	Universal World Growth RRSP Fund	InEq	N/A	N/A	48%	10/95	3.42%	$2.46	N/A	N/A
1239	★★½	Universal World Income RRSP Fund	Bond	D	D	52%	09/81	–0.16%	$2.21	1124	1008
1240	★★★	Universal World Prec. Metals Fund	Gold	C	B	48%	02/95	–8.42%	$2.56	N/A	N/A
1241	★★½	Universal World Tactical Bond Fund	InBond	C	B	58%	05/96	4.23%	$2.48	N/A	N/A
1242	★★★	University Avenue Bond Fund	Bond	A	B	46%	01/95	–3.09%	$1.96	967	1008
1243	★★★★★	University Avenue Canadian Fund	CdnEq	B	C	36%	01/95	–0.19%	$2.54	992	1185
1244	★★	University Avenue Growth Fund	USEq	D	D	56%	08/88	–0.29%	$2.90	763	1004
1245	★★★½	Vengrowth Investment Fund Inc.	Labor	N/A	N/A	88%	03/96	2.90%	$5.21	N/A	N/A
1246	★★★	Vision Europe Fund	Europe	B	A	44%	06/93	–2.15%	$3.15	731	1012
1247	★★★★★	Working Opportunity Fund	Labor	N/A	N/A	80%	02/95	5.79%	$4.00	1248	1248
1248	★★★★★	Working Ventures Canadian Fund Inc.	Labor	N/A	N/A	76%	01/95	2.47%	$2.69	1247	1247
1249	★★	Zweig Global Managed Assets	InBal	N/A	N/A	55%	N/A	N/A	$3.40	N/A	N/A
1250	★★★	Zweig Strategic Growth	USEq	N/A	N/A	43%	09/94	–1.65%	$2.62	622	940

THE TOP FUNDS HALL OF FAME

Inductees to the *Top Funds Hall of Fame* are easy to pick — they are, quite simply, the best in the business. Here they are, listed in alphabetical order:

WARREN BUFFETT

He lives and works in Omaha, Nebraska. He doesn't sit glued to his computer; in fact, he doesn't even have one. And he doesn't seem to care about what happens in the stock market. His name is Warren Buffett, and with a fortune estimated at $9.2 billion, he's currently the second-richest man in America, according to Forbes magazine. At last count, a $10,000 investment with Buffett in 1956 is now worth over $75 million.

Warren Buffett is Chairman of **Berkshire Hathaway,** a management firm that invests in various companies and is itself traded on the New York Stock Exchange. Its share price? About US$18,000 — making Berkshire Hathaway shares the most expensive in the world!

His basic approach is to search for large businesses with "enduring and mouth-watering economics that are run by able and shareholder-oriented management." What kind of businesses are these? "We try," Buffett says, "to stick to businesses that we understand... They must be relatively simple and stable... If there's a lot of technology, we won't understand it." He adds: "You should never invest in an idea you can't illustrate with a crayon."

Buffett takes what he describes as a "Rip Van Winkle" approach. "We don't think we can get long-term investment success by flitting from flower to flower, so we stay with them as long as they remain good businesses." He believes you should never sell a great business as long as it remains good, regardless of how high the stock price gets. "What would be the point?" he asks. "You might invest the money in something less great."

What about technical analysis, forecasting, business cycles, interest-rate trends and all the other things that are supposed to be important in the selection process? Buffett says that "we do not have, never have had, and never will have an opinion about where the stock market, interest rates, or business activity will be a year from now." The only value of stock forecasters, he adds, "is to make fortune tellers look good." If you buy and hold good businesses over the long term, the rest just doesn't matter!

ALEX CHRIST

Alex Christ is best known as the manager of the **Industrial Growth Fund**, which he introduced in 1967, and which still holds Canada's top 25-year performance record for RRSP-eligible funds. A $10,000 investment in Industrial Growth in 1967 had grown to over $400,000 by mid-1996.

Educated at Harvard, where he earned an MBA, Christ worked for several years in the investment business as a researcher before taking on Industrial Growth. He is a top-down manager — one who analyses macroeconomic trends and developments and then identifies undervalued stocks within attractive industry sectors. A shy and unpretentious man, Christ has seen his fund grow to the point where assets under management are now $1.3 billion. Despite some uncharacteristic weakness in the returns achieved by the fund during the recent recession, many industry watchers anticipate continued strong growth for the fund under Christ's leadership.

ROBERT KREMBIL

Robert Krembil is Chairman of the Board of **Trimark**, a company he founded in 1981 along with Arthur Labatt and Mike Axford. The company was almost called Allmark — an acronym formed from the founders' initials (AL, MA, RK). But another company in the industry had the same name, so it was changed to Trimark in recognition of the three founders. Today it is the second-largest mutual fund in the country, with about $17 billion under management for about 850,000 investors.

Krembil began his career as an analyst with Excelsior Life in 1964, and later managed pensions at Canada Permanent Trust Company. In 1971 he earned an MBA and became a Chartered Financial Analyst. The next year, he started his own company in partnership with Russ Morrison. In 1977, he joined Bolton Tremblay as an investment manager of the mutual fund division when they bought his company and he stayed there until 1981, when he and his partners founded Trimark Investment Management Company.

Well-known in the industry and respected by his peers, Krembil is a growth manager who has enjoyed (along with his investors) great success with the **Trimark Fund**, an international fund with substantial US holdings.

PETER LYNCH

Ten thousand dollars invested with Peter Lynch in the **Fidelity Magellan Fund** in 1977 grew to $280,000 by May 1990 when he retired as the fund manager. During much of that 13-year period, the fund was one of the top-rated general equity funds in the US.

Lynch was educated at Boston College and helped pay for his tuition by working as a caddy. Much of the discussion he heard on the golf course related to investing and stocks and he became intrigued by the subject.

In college, except for the required courses, he avoided science, math, and accounting and (like Frank Mersch of **Altamira**) was much more interested in history, political science, and the philosophy of the ancient Greeks. Looking back, Lynch says, "It's obvious that studying history and philosophy was much better preparation for the stock market than say, studying statistics. Investing in stocks is an art, not a science, and people who have been trained to rigidly quantify everything have a big disadvantage."

One of Lynch's first stock picks, purchased while he was in his second year at Boston College went from $7 to over $32 in less than two years. That, along with his caddying income, provided the funds necessary for him to attend the Wharton School of Finance at the University of Pennsylvania. While there, he applied for — and got — a summer job at Fidelity.

After completing his graduate degree, he served two years in the military and returned from Korea in 1969 to join Fidelity as a permanent employee and research analyst. In 1974, he was promoted from assistant director of research to director of research and in May of 1977, he took over the Fidelity Magellan fund. At that time, the fund had $20 million in assets and about 40 stocks. By the time he left, the fund owned over 1,400 stocks and had grown to $9 billion.

Lynch's approach is similar to Warren Buffett's, who Lynch describes as "the greatest investor of them all." Both men look for good companies with solid management — especially those which are undervalued or unappreciated — and hold them for the long term. Lynch, however, owned more stocks than Buffett would ever have considered.

Now retired from active money management, Lynch remains a member of the Fidelity Board of Trustees, writes a regular column for *Worth* magazine, and has written three bestselling financial books: *Beating the Street, One Up On Wall Street,* and *Learn to Earn*. He lives in Boston with his wife and daughters.

FRANK MERSCH

There's no doubt Frank Mersch has brought some excitement to the mutual fund industry in Canada. He's largely responsible for Altamira's extraordinary growth — driven by the eye-popping results he's delivered in the **Altamira Equity Fund**. He's also comparatively young, outspoken, and has a substantially greater public profile than his fellow hall-of-famers.

Mersch's father was a mechanic. He was raised in Toronto and attended the University of Toronto where his emphasis was, perhaps surprisingly, in history and philosophy. It's an academic background that shows, since he always views the business cycle from a historical context, and uses it as a framework from which to make informed decisions.

He started in the business in 1976 and quickly gained experience as a trader, analyst, portfolio manager, and pension fund administrator of both equities and fixed-income products, mostly in the Canadian market.

In October 1987, Mersch became a principal in Altamira Management Ltd., where he is currently responsible for equity investment policy and strategy, as well as equity research and senior portfolio management. He has been a consistently top-quartile manager with Altamira, he put Alberta on the map as a result of his investment presence there, and he has made a ton of money for Altamira investors. He is well respected within the Canadian investment community for his successful investment style (I characterize him as a sector rotator), based on his belief in themes and concepts to achieve growth for investors.

Mersch describes himself as a growth manager or perhaps a "sector overweighter" and adds that "we're top-down, bottom-up." His team develops a game plan and then concentrates on the geographic or economic areas (top-down) and the stocks (bottom-up) to complete the strategy.

Although he started managing virtually all of Altamira's new funds, he has now passed them on to a growing and very capable team including Susan Coleman, Ian Joseph and Cedric Rabin. He continues, however, to manage the Altamira Equity Fund, one of Canada's biggest.

With a 5-year average growth of over 23% Mersch has been so successful that he could coast through the next few years without taking any significant risks, and still be assured of a top spot in 10-year rankings. But he's still making bets with his flagship equity fund and is getting involved in new, more specialized funds — such as one that focuses on distressed companies. He'll be a major force in Canadian investing for years to come.

GEORGE SOROS

George Soros's **Quantum Fund** has been one of the most successful investment vehicles of all time — a $10,000 investment in 1969, with dividends reinvested, would be worth well over $20 million today! Of course, that's assuming you had the nerve to ride along with Soros and his managers (who are paid according to profits, not the amount of money managed). With virtually no restrictions on types of investment (including currencies), as well as the freedom to use leverage and short-selling, the fund has made fabulous profits at some times, and taken serious hits at others. In 1992, for example, the Quantum Fund saw an opportunity to go short on the British pound sterling. The result? A one billion dollar profit! That was followed by a position on the Japanese yen in 1994, which didn't work so well — the fund lost $600 million in February of that year — although this was completely recovered by year end.

Soros was born in Hungary in 1930 and survived the Nazi occupation of his country. When the Russians arrived after the war, his father encouraged him to go to England, where he ended up spending several unhappy years as a travelling salesman. Then, in 1953, he got a break with a London financial institution whose managing director was, like Soros, an expatriate Hungarian. It was there that he met a co-worker whose father owned a small brokerage company in New York. One thing led to another, and in September 1956, Soros arrived in the US, where almost immediately he began trading in international arbitrage (buying securities in one country and selling them in another).

For the next 12 years, Soros worked unspectacularly in the investment business while continuing to educate himself. Finally, in 1968-69, he convinced his firm to establish a few small investment funds using a model portfolio he had been developing. In 1973, he left his employer to establish his own hedge fund, the Soros Fund (later, the Quantum Fund), with about $12 million of capital.

His success has been phenomenal. The Quantum Fund has delivered a nearly 35% average annual return to shareholders over 26 years — and that's after management's participation in profits. Today, he runs Soros Fund Management, the principal investment advisor to Quantum Fund, a Curaçao-based investment firm. His fund trades at a steep premium of about 30% — and, sorry, but you'll need to go offshore to buy it.

SIR JOHN TEMPLETON

Widely regarded as one of the wisest investors in the world, Sir John Templeton is the father of global investing. His most famous success is the **Templeton Growth Fund**, which had its inception in Toronto in 1954. A $10,000 investment made at that time would have grown to $2 million by mid-1992 and $3.7 million by 1996.

Starting with selected investments in few countries in 1954, Templeton's reach now extends to about 30 nations — and is growing constantly. Today, the Franklin/Templeton group of funds manages about $50 billion worldwide for close to a million investors.

In addition to his reputation as the first truly global investor, Sir John is also known for his ability to find investment bargains — he is a classic "value investor." He is also a textbook contrarian: "Buy at the point of maximum pessimism" is a standard Templeton creed.

Born in Tennessee, Sir John earned a law degree and studied as a Rhodes scholar at Oxford before entering the investment business. In the late 1960s he moved to the Bahamas. He became a British subject and was knighted in 1986. In 1988, he handed over the day-to-day management of the Growth Fund to Mark Holowesko, although he still maintains an office next to Holowesko and still works as a consultant.

Sir John has been described by *Forbes* magazine as one of the handful of true investment greats in a field of crowded mediocrity and bloated reputations. I'm inclined to agree: there's no one more deserving of a place in the *Top Funds* Hall of Fame.

GLOSSARY

AMR (Average Monthly Rank). A rating system based on a fund's monthly performance relative to its peer-group. Monthly performance scores are averaged to provide a fund's ranking within its group.

Asset allocation. The relative proportions of equities, bonds, cash, real estate, and other asset types held in a portfolio at a given time. In a mutual fund, the portfolio manager often varies these proportions in order to maximize return when economic conditions change.

Automatic reinvestment. An option available to investors in a mutual fund or other investment whereby income (dividends, interest, or capital gains) distributions are used to purchase additional units of the fund.

Balanced portfolio. A balanced portfolio is the distribution of investments into several asset categories to help increase returns and reduce risk. The basic components of a balanced portfolio are cash, bonds, Canadian and international equities, real estate, oil, gas, and gold. The weighting of the different components varies depending on one's age and aggressiveness as an investor.

Bear market. A stock market whose index of representative stocks, such as the Toronto Stock Exchange 300 Composite Index, is declining in value. A "bearish" investor believes share prices will fall.

Blue-chip stocks. Stocks with good investment qualities. They are usually common shares of well-established companies with good earning records and regular dividend payments that are known nationally for the quality and wide acceptance of their products and services.

Bond. A debt instrument issued by governments and corporations. A bond is a promise by the issuer to pay the full amount of the debt on maturity, plus interest payments at regular intervals.

Bottom-up. A style of investing which places a priority on examining companies that may be appropriate for investment. Less emphasis is placed on macroeconomic considerations. See also *Top-down.*

Bull market. A stock market whose index has been rising in value. A "bullish" investor believes share prices will rise.

Canada Deposit Insurance Corporation (CDIC). An agency of the Government of Canada which insures the deposits of Canadians in banks and trust companies up to $60,000.

Capital Cost Allowance (CCA). A tax deduction available to reflect the depreciation of various types of assets. Applied to buildings (either commercial or residential), CCA can be used to shelter rental income from real estate investment trusts (REITs).

Capital gain (loss). A profit (or loss) made on the sale of an asset when the market price rises above or falls below the purchase price — usually in real estate, stocks, bonds, or other capital assets.

Closed-end fund. A mutual fund in which the total number of units is limited. If units are not purchased when the fund is initially offered, they can only be purchased from another owner. They often trade on stock exchanges.

Common share. A class of stock that represents ownership, or equity, in a company. Common shares entitle the holder to a share in the company's profits, usually as a dividend. They may also carry a voting privilege.

Consumer Price Index (CPI). A statistical measure of the cost of living for consumers. Often used to demonstrate general increases in the level of inflation over a period of time.

Current yield. As applied to money market funds, it refers to the actual rate of return over the past seven days, annualized.

Cyclical stock. A stock within a specific industry sector that is particularly sensitive to changes in economic conditions. The natural resources sector tends to be cyclical, as do particular stocks in the sector.

Deferred sales charge (DSC). An increasingly popular alternative to mutual funds that charge front-end acquisition fees. Here, a fee is paid when the investor sells units in the fund. This usually begins at 4.5% of the units' value in the first year and declines by 0.5% to 1% per year, eventually reaching 0% several years into the future. Sometimes called an Exit Fee.

Distribution fees. Fees levied by some mutual fund companies on the value of units purchased with a back-end load or deferred sales charge. While most funds have stopped charging these fees, a few hold-outs remain.

Distributions. The payments made by a mutual fund to its unitholders of the interest, dividends, and/or capital gains earned during the year. Shareholders may either take distributions in cash or reinvest them in additional shares of the fund.

Diversification. Spreading investment risk by investing in a variety of asset categories (stocks, bonds, gold) in different industries and/or countries.

Dividend tax credit. A special tax credit applied to reduce the effective rate of tax paid on Canadian dividend income.

Dividend. A portion of a company's profit paid out to common and preferred shareholders, the amount having been decided on by the company's board of directors. A dividend may be in the form of cash or additional stock. A preferred dividend is usually a fixed amount, while a common dividend may fluctuate with the earnings of the company.

Dollar-cost averaging. An investment program in which contributions are made at regular intervals with specific and equal dollar amounts. This often results in a lower average cost per unit because more units are purchased when the prices are depressed than when they are high.

Equity funds. Mutual funds that invest in common and preferred shares.

Ex-dividend. The date on which distributions that have been declared by a mutual fund are deducted from total net assets. The price of the fund's shares or units will be reduced by the amount of the distribution.

Fixed asset mix. For balanced funds, an approach which fixes the asset mix to be maintained in the fund: often 50–60% equity and 40–50% fixed income. Compare to an asset allocation fund, where there is no pre-set fixed asset mix.

Fixed-income funds. Mutual funds that invest in mortgages, bonds, or a combination of both. Mortgages and bonds are issued at a fixed rate of interest and are known as fixed-income securities.

Front-end commission charge. An acquisition fee based on the total value of mutual fund units purchased. The fees can range from 2%

to 9%, but average 4% to 5% on most purchases.

GIC (Guaranteed Investment Certificate). A deposit certificate usually issued by a bank or trust company. An interest-bearing investment that matures after a specified term, usually anywhere from 30 days to 5 years. The interest remains fixed during this period.

Growth investing. An approach to investing which places greater emphasis on a stock's future growth potential than on its current price. A growth manager may therefore be prepared to pay a higher price for a stock than a value manager would if he or she believes it has attractive future growth potential. It is seen as a more aggressive style of management than value investing.

Growth stock. Shares of a company whose earnings are expected to grow faster than average.

Hedging. The strategy of taking positions in more than one commodity, security, or asset category in an attempt to reduce investment risk. An investment in gold or oil/natural gas, for example, is often seen as a hedge or protection against inflation.

Income splitting. The process of diverting taxable income from an individual in a high tax bracket to one in a lower tax bracket.

Index fund. A mutual fund designed to match the performance of a recognized group of publicly traded stocks, such as those represented by the TSE 300 Index or the Standard & Poor's 500 Index in the US.

Index. For stocks, an indicator of broad market performance. The Dow Jones industrial average includes the shares of 30 large companies; the Toronto Stock Exchange's composite index includes 300 companies; the Standard & Poor's index contains 500 companies. Developed from statistics that measure the state of the economy, based on the performance of stocks or other key indicators such as the Consumer Price Index.

Investment fund. See *Mutual fund.*

Leverage. Using borrowed funds to maximize the rate of return on investment. A potentially dangerous strategy if the investment declines in value.

Limited partnership. See *Tax shelter.*

Liquidity. The ease with which an asset can be sold and converted into cash at its full value.

Management expense ratio (MER). The total of all management and other fees charged to the fund, shown as a percentage of the fund's total assets, or as a dollar amount per $100 of assets.

Management fee. The amount paid annually by a mutual fund to its managers. The average annual fee in Canada is between 1% and 2% of the value of the fund's assets.

Marginal tax rate. The rate at which tax is calculated on the next dollar of income earned. This rate increases at progressively higher income brackets.

Market timing. The process of shifting from one type of investment to another with the intention of maximizing the return as market conditions change.

MBS (Mortgage-backed securities). These provide higher yields than many other savings options by investing in first mortgages on residential properties.

Money market fund. Fixed-income mutual funds that invest in short-term securities (maturing within one year).

Mortgage. A legal instrument given by a borrower to the lender entitling the lender to take over pledged property if conditions of the loan are not met.

Mutual fund. A professionally managed pool of assets, representing the contributions of many investors, which is used to purchase a portfolio of securities that meets specific investment objectives. See *Open-end fund* and *Closed-end fund.*

Net asset value (NAV). The value of a fund's assets, less its liabilities. The NAV is used to calculate the buying or selling price of shares or units in a fund, usually expressed as the net asset value per share (NAVPS).

Net asset value per share (NAVPS). The total market value of all securities owned by a mutual fund, less its liabilities, divided by the number of units outstanding.

No-load fund. A mutual fund that does not charge a fee for buying or selling its units.

Open-end fund. A mutual fund whose units are offered for sale on a continuous basis; the fund will also buy back units at their current price (net asset value per share). Sometimes called an investment fund. The most common type of mutual fund.

Portfolio. A group of securities held or owned for investment purposes by an individual or institution. An investor's portfolio may contain common and preferred shares, bonds, options, and other types of securities.

Prospectus. A legal document describing a new issue of securities or a mutual fund that is to be sold to the public. The prospectus must be prepared in accordance with provincial securities commission regulations. It must contain information on any material facts that can have an impact on the value of the investment, such as the fund's investment objectives and policies, services offered, or fees charged. It must also identify any investment restrictions, as well as the officers of the company.

Real estate investment trust (REIT). A form of real estate mutual fund with the difference that the REIT trades on a stock exchange. As a result, it provides greater liquidity than is usually available through a traditional real estate mutual fund. The units generally trade at a discount from net asset value.

Real rate of return. The stated rate of return, less inflation and taxes.

Registered investment. A security held in a tax-sheltered plan — most often an RRSP or RRIF — which has been approved by Revenue Canada.

Risk tolerance. The ability of a person to tolerate risk. Risk tolerance is a function of the individual's personality and other factors, and is an important element in determining investment strategy.

Risk-free return. The return available from securities that have no risk of loss. Short-term securities issued by the government (such as Treasury bills) normally provide a risk-free return.

Risk. The possibility that some or all of the money put into an investment will be lost.

RRIF (Registered Retirement Income Fund). A non-annuity investment vehicle for maturing RRSPs. One of the options available to RRSP holders upon cashing in their retirement funds at age 69 or sooner. RRIFs generally provide for a series of payments that increase each year.

RRSP (Registered Retirement Savings Plan). A savings program approved by Revenue Canada that permits tax-deferred saving for retirement purposes. Contributions to an RRSP are tax-deductible. Earnings on contributions are sheltered from tax while they remain in the plan.

Sector rotation. A style of investing that identifies prospective investments (or the weighting of an investment portfolio) according to which sectors of the economy are poised to do well. Often associated with the "top-down" approach to investing.

Segregated funds. Funds sold and administered by life insurance companies.

Self-directed RRSP. An RRSP whose investments are controlled by the plan holder. A self-directed RRSP may include stocks, bonds, residential mortgages, or other types of investments approved by Revenue Canada.

Systematic withdrawal plan (SWP). A plan for withdrawing money from a mutual fund on a regular basis — monthly, quarterly, semi-annually, or annually. Used mostly by investors who require a steady stream of income from their investments.

Tax shelter. An investment that, by government regulation, can be made with untaxed or partly taxed dollars. The creation of tax losses in order to offset an individual's taxable income from other sources thereby reduces tax liability.

Taxable income. The amount of annual income that is used to calculate how much income tax must be paid: total earnings for the year, minus deductions.

Term deposit. Similar to a guaranteed investment certificate. An interest-bearing investment to which an investor commits funds for a specified term and rate of interest.

Top-down. A style of investing that considers the economic "big picture" to identify sectors of the economy that are expected to outperform. Less importance is attached to identifying individual companies which may do well. See also *Bottom-up*.

Total return. The amount of income earned from an investment, together with its capital appreciation, expressed as a percentage of the original amount invested. It indicates an investment's performance over a stated period.

Treasury bills. Short-term debt securities sold by governments, usually with maturities of three months to one year. They carry no stated interest rate, but trade at a discount to their face value. The discount represents the market's valuation of the future return at maturity.

Unit. In mutual funds, a unit represents a portion, or share, of the total value of the fund. Units are purchased by investors, and rise or fall proportionately with the net asset value of the fund.

Value investing. An approach to investing that attempts, through the use of various analytical models, to identify companies which are fundamentally strong but which may be out of favour in the marketplace and trading at prices which represent a good 'buy.' This conservative approach is often associated with Sir John Templeton and is one which many investment managers claim to use.

Volatility. A measure of a mutual fund's tendency to fluctuate in value. More volatile funds are traditionally considered to have a greater degree of risk, although the fluctuation in value may, in fact, be either up or down.

INDEX

TOP FUNDS 1997